TESTS OF SUPERPOWER

Timely Reports to Keep
Journalists, Scholars and the Public
Abreast of Developing Issues, Events and Trends

Editorial Research Reports
Published by Congressional Quarterly Inc.
1414 22nd Street, N.W.
Washington, D.C. 20037

About the Cover

The cover was designed by Richard Pottern

PRINTED IN THE UNITED STATES OF AMERICA

Editor, Hoyt Gimlin
Assistant, Susan Waterman
Production Manager, I. D. Fuller
Assistant Production Manager, Maceo Mayo

Library of Congress Cataloging-in-Publication Data

Tests of superpower.

   "Editorial research reports."
   Bibliography: p.
   Includes index.
   1. Nuclear disarmament — United States. 2. Nuclear disarmament — Soviet Union. 3. Detente. 4. United States — Foreign relations — Soviet Union. 5. Soviet Union — Foreign relations — United States. I. Congressional Quarterly Inc. II. Editorial Research Reports.
JX1974.7.T46   1987   327.1' 74   86-24103
ISBN 0-87187-426-1 (pbk.)

Contents

Foreword

For four decades the United States and the Soviet Union have engaged in tests of strength and will on issue after issue throughout the world. This superpower testing has been the one constant in U.S.-Soviet relations, whether in cold war or détente. And it continues into the present, at a time when attitudes are characterized by ambivalence. We invite your attention to the 10 reports in this book for a more complete understanding of how and where the two countries stand apart, and of how they sometimes find common ground to set aside their disagreements.

Above all else, nuclear arms issues are paramount. How far U.S. and Soviet negotiators are capable of moving toward agreement will likely determine when President Reagan and Soviet leader Mikhail S. Gorbachev meet again, after their inconclusive pre-summit in Iceland. Their first meeting in Geneva in November 1985 settled no outstanding disputes but nevertheless was a symbolic event indicating a desire to improve relations that had been badly strained by the Soviet invasion of Afghanistan in December 1979. No longer was Reagan speaking of the "evil empire," and Gorbachev, who had come to power only the previous February in the latest Kremlin succession, placed his personal stamp on arms control negotiations.

All the while, Washington and Moscow have been making offers and counteroffers, focusing on missile strength in Europe and Reagan's Strategic Defense Initiative — his "Star Wars" plan to intercept and destroy approaching enemy missiles while they are still airborne. This book also looks at non-nuclear, but often deadly, superpower testing that is surfacing in the western Pacific and is being carried on by surrogate forces in Africa, the Middle East and Central America. The 10 reports that make up *Tests of Superpower* carry the date of original issue by Editorial Research Reports. For new developments, see the "update" page at the beginning of most reports.

Hoyt Gimlin
Editor

Washington, D.C.
October 1986

U.S.-SOVIET SUMMITRY

by

Mary H. Cooper

Nov. 1
1985

Editor's Update: The first summit meeting, in Geneva, produced no breakthrough on arms control but the two principals, President Reagan and Soviet leader Mikhail S. Gorbachev, agreed to meet again. They did indeed meet in Iceland, Oct. 11-12, 1986, at a hastily convened "pre-summit"—so described in advance by Reagan administration officials as a prelude to still another meeting at which substantive topics would be discussed.

However, as it turned out, both sides bargained hard in Iceland over a broad range of arms control measures but reached an impasse over the president's refusal to yield to the Soviet demand that the United States scrap his Strategic Defense Initiative, or "Star Wars" program *(see Star Wars report, p. 67)*. Despite recriminations against each other, both sides expressed cautious hope that another meeting would follow, presumably in the United States, at which the issues could be addressed anew.

U.S.-SOVIET SUMMITRY

THE GLACIAL SILENCE that has characterized relations between the leaders of the world's two superpowers in the 1980s will be broken later this month when President Reagan and Soviet leader Mikhail S. Gorbachev meet in Geneva "at the summit." Rarely has the prospect of a summit meeting engendered such widespread attention and concern. Hardly a day has passed since Reagan issued his invitation to meet with the new Soviet leader that some new development has not led political figures, academics and commentators to speculate on the chances for success in Geneva.

The Nov. 19-20 encounter will be the first direct dialogue between the leaders of the superpowers since June 1979, when President Jimmy Carter met Soviet leader Leonid I. Brezhnev in Vienna to sign the SALT II treaty setting limits on both countries' strategic arsenals. The Geneva summit will last about 12 hours, eight of them dedicated to substantive dialogue (see box, p. 14). Despite Reagan's last-minute attempt to give high priority to regional conflicts in which the Soviet Union is involved, arms control will dominate the meeting.

The flurry of diplomatic activity that has preceded this summit reflects the importance attributed to it by both leaders, neither of whom has ever participated in such a high-level U.S.-Soviet meeting. Despite his efforts to play down the significance of the encounter — the White House still refers to the summit as a mere "meeting" — Reagan has made an about-face in going to Geneva. During his first term, he adopted a confrontational tone toward the Soviet Union and dismissed summitry, saying that the Soviets had used past meetings to extract arms control agreements that put the United States at a disadvantage. In any case, said Raymond Garthoff, a former ambassador to Bulgaria and an expert on the Soviet Union, "the Reagan administration's rhetorically confrontational stance has meant that much attention is focused on this summit, in addition to the fact that it is the first in six years." [1]

Reagan's decision to engage in superpower summitry is not free of risks. His grasp of the matter of arms control is far from

---

[1] Garthoff, of the Brookings Institution in Washington, D.C., is author of *Détente and Confrontation* (1985). Persons quoted in this report were interviewed by the author unless otherwise noted.

complete, as demonstrated by his recent incorrect assertion that the United States is "still well behind the Soviet Union in literally every kind of offensive weapon, both conventional and in the strategic weapons." [2] Reagan and his advisers evidently hope that his lack of expertise will be compensated by the conversational talents and flair for simplifying issues that have won the president the title of "great communicator."

Reagan's risks pale beside those Gorbachev assumes by going to Geneva only eight months after taking over the Kremlin leadership. While Reagan has just three years left to leave his imprint on American diplomacy, Gorbachev's first summit may well be only a beginning. At 54 years of age, he is by far the youngest of recent Soviet leaders and may reasonably hope to find himself in charge into the next century. To do so, however, he must avoid making the kind of foreign policy mistakes that led to the downfall of Nikita S. Khrushchev *(see p. 11)*.

Reagan first proposed the meeting in a letter to Gorbachev that Vice President George Bush delivered March 12 when he attended the funeral of Gorbachev's immediate predecessor, Konstantin U. Chernenko. Gorbachev finally accepted the invitation July 3, setting off the struggle between the two men to gain the high ground in world opinion before they meet.

Maneuvering in the Propaganda War

Both leaders and their respective bureaucracies have demonstrated ample skill in the business of public relations. Reagan and Gorbachev have tirelessly marketed themselves and their arms control proposals with an eye toward winning support at home, among their opponent's home audience and the citizens of Western Europe. On July 29 Gorbachev announced that, "wishing to set a good example," the Soviet Union would "stop unilaterally any nuclear explosions starting from Aug. 6 this year," not coincidentally the 40th anniversary of the day the United States dropped the first atomic bomb on Hirsoshima, Japan. Continuation of the moratorium past Jan. 1, 1986, Gorbachev said, would depend on whether the United States also stopped nuclear testing. Unwilling to hand the Soviets an easy victory in the intensifying diplomatic tennis match, the White House dismissed the moratorium as propaganda, saying that it would not slow Soviet weapons production because the country had accelerated its nuclear testing prior to the announcement and could easily resume tests in January.

The maneuvering heated up with a visit of a U.S. congressional

---

[2] Press conference, Sept. 17. While the Soviet Union possesses more intercontinental ballistic missiles, attack submarines, troops and tanks, the United States holds a numerical advantage in other weapons, including strategic nuclear warheads, air-launched cruise missiles and bombs, and aircraft carriers.

Mikhail S. Gorbachev talking to Soviet workers

delegation to Moscow and a surprise interview Gorbachev granted *Time* magazine.[3] On both occasions Gorbachev left the impression of a sharp, tough but reasonable and non-polemical leader and, most ominously for the White House, one well-versed in foreign affairs and defense issues. He appealed to American public opinion by telling *Time* editors he attached "tremendous importance" to the summit, in contrast to Reagan's cautions against raising "false hopes."

The Kremlin's public relations campaign seemed to catch the White House off guard as it reacted defensively to Gorbachev's assertions. To his appeal for a breakthrough in arms control the administration said that the Soviet Union had not offered any concrete proposals. Reagan dismissed Gorbachev's condemnation of the Strategic Defense Initiative (SDI), saying categorically that it would not become a "bargaining chip" in Geneva. SDI, Reagan's controversial program to develop a space-based defense against nuclear attack, was already emerging as the central issue on the summit agenda.

The next stage of the Kremlin's "charm offensive" was the visit of the new Soviet foreign minister, Eduard A. Shevardnadze, to the United States in late September when he addressed the United Nations General Assembly and met with Reagan and Secretary of State George P. Shultz. The trip coincided with the resumption in Geneva of arms control negotiations, which began with great fanfare in March but have not yet produced any concrete results.[4]

---

[3] *Time*, Sept. 9, 1985, pp. 16-33.
[4] The latest round is scheduled to adjourn Nov. 1. For background, see "Arms Control Negotiations," *E.R.R.*, 1985 Vol. I, pp. 145-168.

Like Gorbachev, Shevardnadze presented a striking contrast to the past. Unlike his dour predecessor, Andrei A. Gromyko, Shevardnadze had a relaxed and even friendly air about him as well as a flair for one-liners. In his speech to the General Assembly Sept. 24, he continued the verbal assault against SDI, calling for an international space research program of "Star Peace" in contrast to "Star Wars" as SDI is called by its detractors. Addressing the same forum the previous day, Shultz accused the Soviet Union of making "blatantly one-sided" accusations and inviting Moscow to "get down to real business, with the seriousness the subject deserves."

Gorbachev took up Shultz' challenge during a widely publicized visit to Paris in October, his first trip to the West since assuming the Kremlin leadership in March. He used the occasion to publicize the centerpiece of his pre-summit proposals, an arms reduction proposal Shevardnadze had reportedly presented to Reagan in Washington. If Reagan would give up SDI, Gorbachev said, the Soviet Union would agree to a 50 percent cut in both sides' nuclear weapons, an even deeper reduction in offensive weapons than the United States had previously sought.

It remained to be seen just how successful Gorbachev's Paris trip was to be. While saying the proposal deserved further study, the White House nonetheless reacted coolly. Gorbachev did not reignite the Western European peace movement of the early 1980s.[5] His welcome to the French capital was tepid at best, and President François Mitterrand, while highly critical of SDI, refused to join Gorbachev in denouncing the program. And he rebuffed Gorbachev's invitation to negotiate a separate arms control agreement, as did Great Britain, the other European nuclear power.

But Gorbachev's failure to win allies in Western Europe did not translate into unconditional support for Reagan. Shortly after his speech to the U.N. General Assembly Oct. 24 in which he called for a joint U.S.-Soviet initiative to resolve conflicts in five countries where insurgents are challenging Soviet-supported governments, Reagan met with the leaders of five industrialized democracies, who told him that arms control remained the most important item on the summit agenda.[6] British Prime Minister Margaret Thatcher urged Reagan to respond to Gorbachev's arms control proposal in a manner that would

---

[5] For background, see "West Germany's Missile Election," *E.R.R.*, 1983 Vol. I, pp. 149-68; and "Christian Peace Movement, *E.R.R.*, 1983 Vol. I, pp. 353-72.
[6] The leaders of Britain, West Germany, Japan, Italy and Canada attended the meeting with Reagan. The leaders were in New York to celebrate the 40th anniversary of the founding of the United Nations. For background, see "United Nations at Forty," *E.R.R.*, 1985 Vol. II, pp. 737-56. Mitterrand of France declined Reagan's invitation to the pre-summit meeting.

break the "deadlock in Geneva." Thatcher and West German Chancellor Helmut Kohl later told reporters that they were given to understand that Reagan would offer a counterproposal on arms control before the summit.

Reagan's Reversal on Value of Summit

Reagan came to office in 1981 denouncing the Soviet Union as an "evil empire" that had ignored arms control agreements reached through summitry in the 1970s. Maintaining that the Soviet Union had surpassed the United States in nuclear weaponry as a result, Reagan launched a campaign to close this "window of vulnerability" by modernizing the American nuclear arsenal through increased defense spending. In particular, he denounced the SALT II treaty Carter and Brezhnev signed at the 1979 summit. The Senate never ratified the treaty *(see p. 15)*, but the administration, in Reagan's words, "has not taken any actions which would undercut existing arms control agreements," including SALT.[7] Reagan also spurned suggestions for a summit, saying it was pointless unless it was based on a well-prepared agenda and had clear prospects for success.

On Nov. 18, 1981, Reagan offered his own arms control proposal, START — an acronym for strategic arms reduction talks — based on a one-third cut in strategic nuclear warheads for both sides. Negotiations on this proposal eventually bogged down. But while they were still under way, Reagan announced on March 23, 1983, that the United States would embark on a Strategic Defense Initiative to determine the feasibility of building in space a defensive "umbrella" composed of laser and particle-beam weapons able to protect the United States from incoming nuclear missiles. Critics have said Star Wars is technologically unfeasible and too expensive. The congressional Office of Technology Assessment has projected that the research program would cost $33 billion in its first six years alone.[8]

Just why Reagan decided to reverse course and on his own initiative invite Gorbachev to meet with him is a matter of some debate. Reagan spent most of his first term working to revamp the domestic economy. Now, some observers say, the president is seeking greater status as a statesman before leaving office in 1989. Reagan signaled a change in attitude even before his reelection. "We're ready for constructive negotiations with the Soviet Union," he told the General Assembly in September 1984. "We recognize that there is no sane alternative to negotiations on arms control and other issues between our two nations, which have the capacity to destroy civilization as we know it."

---

[7] Statement of June 10, 1985.
[8] Office of Technology Assessment, "Ballistic Missile Defense Technologies," September 1985.

7

But the invitation still came as a surprise. He told a news conference March 21 that he issued it "because ... it's our turn to be the host." Perhaps more to the point, Reagan had long stated the need to negotiate with the Soviets "from a position of strength," and administration spokesmen say this condition has been met. "In the past four years here in the United States, and more broadly in the West, we have experienced a political, economic and social renewal of historic proportion," said national security adviser Robert C. McFarlane, who reportedly has assumed a leading role in preparing the president for the summit. "America has regained its moorings, it is leading, and peace is more secure." Shultz said that Reagan's other condition for a summit had also been met: "There will be an extensive preparatory effort, so we won't have a situation where two people just get together and say 'hello,' with no preparation." [9]

Gorbachev's Rise, the Risks of Reforms

Another reason why Reagan has put off a summit may well have been the unprecedented turnover in the Soviet leadership. When Reagan took office, Brezhnev, who had presided over the Kremlin since the late 1960s and had met at the summit with three American presidents, was ailing. He died Nov. 10, 1982. His successor, former KGB head Yuri V. Andropov, died in February 1984, and was followed by Chernenko, a Brezhnev protégé. Chernenko's retirement from active leadership due to illness allowed younger party secretaries like Gorbachev to gain positions of power even before Chernenko's death March 10.

In some respects Gorbachev's political ascent represents a break in Soviet political tradition. He is the first Soviet leader to come to power as the youngest member of both the Politburo and the Secretariat of the Central Committee, whose combined membership of 21 makes up the top Kremlin leadership. Since his selection as party general secretary in March, Gorbachev has consolidated his power by replacing members of the Brezhnev generation with younger men known to share his views on economic and bureaucratic reform.

Gorbachev has called for greater devolution of responsibility for industrial and agricultural production from the central ministries to the local level, picking up a theme introduced by Andropov but largely ignored by Chernenko. The Soviet economy has performed poorly, especially in recent years, with frequent shortages of food and consumer goods. Proposals for reform have appeared with increasing frequency, and Gorbachev's choice of Nikolai Ryzhkov, an expert in industrial management, as chairman of the Council of Ministers, or pre-

---

[9] McFarlane addressed the Channel City Club and Women's Forum Aug. 19, Santa Barbara, Calif. Shultz spoke July 3 at a news conference.

mier of the Soviet Union, would suggest that he is eager for change. But reform itself poses considerable risks to the new leadership, which is now busy preparing a five-year plan for 1986-1990 to present to the 27th Communist Party Congress scheduled for next February.[10]

Western perceptions of the new Kremlin leadership have been colored by hopes that it will move the Soviet Union closer to the Western conception of democracy. Gorbachev's first trip to the West, a four-day visit to England in December 1984, before Chernenko's death, did much to fuel these expectations. "I like Mr. Gorbachev," Prime Minister Thatcher told an enthusiastic public. "We can do business together." Press reports focused on his friendly manner and on his stylish wife, Raisa, who accompanied him. After the aged and rigid figures who had dominated the Kremlin for so many years, few seemed eager to heed the warning of one British member of Parliament who said after meeting Gorbachev that "he is as tough as old boots — that's important to remember." [11]

Experienced Kremlin watchers also warn against expecting sweeping reform in the Soviet Union. "Gorbachev clearly has political as well as economic changes in mind," wrote Archie Brown of Oxford University. "But to attempt to foist upon him notions of pluralistic democracy would be wrong and misleading. Pluralism is simply not on the political agenda in the Soviet Union." [12]

Impact of Past Summits

S UMMITRY as a method of conducting diplomacy is by no means limited to U.S.-Soviet relations. Heads of state have long met to settle international issues considered too delicate for their diplomatic representatives to handle alone. Although the post-World War II U.S.-Soviet meetings have given new meaning to the term, many influential decisions of this century were made during summit meetings.

Woodrow Wilson was the first U.S. president to go abroad to negotiate with other leaders. His decision to attend the Paris Peace Conference of 1919 caused an uproar in the United

---

[10] See, for example, "The Novosibirsk Report," *Survey* (London), spring 1984, and Marshall I. Goldman, "Gorbachev and Economic Reform," *Foreign Affairs*, fall 1985. For background, see "Communist Economies," *E.R.R.*, 1984 Vol. II, pp. 957-976.

[11] Peter Temple-Morris, quoted in *Newsweek*, March 25, 1985, p. 10.

[12] Archie Brown, "Gorbachëv: New Man in the Kremlin," *Problems of Communism*, May-June 1985, p. 21.

States; it was the first time a sitting president had journeyed to Europe, and many people thought he should not leave the country.[13] The conference, called to negotiate an end to World War I, was hardly an unequivocal success. It produced the Versailles Treaty, which held Germany morally responsibile for the war and assessed reparations against the country. The treaty was later cited as the main reason for the disastrous rise to power of Adolf Hitler.

The United States and the Soviet Union engaged in summitry on several occasions during World War II. President Franklin D. Roosevelt and British Prime Minister Winston Churchill met in 1943 with Soviet leader Josef Stalin in Tehran where they invited him to join their alliance and to drive Hitler's troops out of Eastern Europe. The three men met again in Yalta in early 1945 to determine the boundaries of postwar Europe.[14] Roosevelt died shortly after the Yalta meeting, and President Truman attended the final trilateral summit of World War II, held later that year in Potsdam. As a result of that meeting, Stalin was able to consolidate his hold on Eastern Europe.

Truman, who took a more pessimistic view of the Kremlin's intentions than Roosevelt, drastically changed U.S. policy toward the Soviet Union, especially after 1949, the year the Soviet Union exploded its first nuclear bomb and Mao Tse-tung's communist forces came to power in China, presenting the threat of a Sino-Soviet alliance. Truman's goal was to "contain" the Soviet Union.

It was during the same period that the term "summit" became the acronym for diplomacy at the highest level. Winston Churchill, who had introduced the term "Iron Curtain" to define the closed boundaries dividing postwar Europe, spoke in 1950 of the need for a "parley at the summit" to ease intensifying Cold War tensions.

Khrushchev vs. Eisenhower, Kennedy

Churchill's call went unheeded until 1955, when President Dwight D. Eisenhower met in Geneva with Soviet Premier Nikolai A. Bulganin, British Prime Minister Anthony Eden and French Premier Edgar Faure. The Soviet Union, however, rebuffed Eisenhower's "open skies" proposal, which would have allowed aerial surveillance of both sides' military installations around the world, and the meeting produced no formal agreements. It did offer a moment of optimism, called the "spirit of Geneva," that East-West relations might be improved in future

---

[13] The other participants were French Premier Georges Clemenceau, British Prime Minister Lloyd George and Italian Premier Vittorio Orlando.
[14] For a recent assessment of Yalta's impact, see Adam Ulam, "Forty Years After Yalta," *The New Republic*, Feb. 11, 1985.

Winston Churchill, Franklin D. Roosevelt and Josef Stalin at Yalta

talks on nuclear energy. That optimism dissipated abruptly when the Soviet Union sent in troops to quell the Hungarian revolt of 1956.

While he did not abandon Truman's containment policy, Eisenhower continued to seek an agreement to control nuclear weapons. To this end he invited Nikita S. Khrushchev, who had risen to the top of a collective leadership after Stalin's death in 1953, for a tour of the United States in 1959. As in Geneva, the meeting — the first bilateral U.S.-Soviet summit — produced no formal agreements but another moment of optimism, called this time the "spirit of Camp David," after the presidential retreat in Maryland where the two conferred.

Khrushchev was a flamboyant figure capable of sudden shifts in policy, which Eisenhower was to discover in 1960. In May of that year the Soviets shot down an American U-2 spy plane over Sverdlovsk and captured its pilot, Francis Gary Powers, who confessed that he was a CIA agent. When Eisenhower refused to apologize for the overflight, Khrushchev abruptly canceled a summit that had been scheduled to take place in Paris, as well as his invitation to Eisenhower to visit the Soviet Union. It would have been the first time an American president had visited the country since Yalta.

It was after his encounter the following year with the newly elected John F. Kennedy that Khrushchev was to make the mistake that ultimately led to his downfall. Meeting in June 1961 in Vienna, the two leaders discussed the rising tension in Berlin, war in Laos and the feasibility of a nuclear test ban. Once again, summitry produced no formal agreements. Khrushchev apparently decided the young president was weak. Berlin was partitioned just two months after the summit and the

Soviets later began installing missiles in Cuba. In October 1962 Kennedy announced a naval blockade of Cuban ports and demanded that the Soviets withdraw the missiles. This crisis was to bring the two superpowers closer to the brink of conflict than at any other time to date. In the end, Khrushchev backed down and withdrew the missiles. He was forced from office in disgrace in 1964 and retired from public view.[15]

By June 1967, when Lyndon B. Johnson met with Soviet Premier Alexei N. Kosygin in Glassboro, N.J., the Arab-Israeli war that had occurred earlier in the month and the deepening American involvement in Vietnam had joined European security and nuclear weapons as chief issues in U.S.-Soviet relations. The meeting — perhaps not strictly a summit because Kosygin was only one member of the collective leadership that had succeeded Khrushchev — produced no solutions to these local conflicts. It did, however, lack the confrontational air of summits conducted during the Khrushchev years, leading commentators to speak of the "spirit of Glassboro." The encounter also allowed the two leaders to lay the groundwork for later strategic arms negotiations.

Nixon and Brezhnev: Era of Détente

Summitry as a means of managing U.S.-Soviet relations reached its peak during the Nixon administration. From 1969 until his hasty resignation from office in 1974 at the height of the Watergate scandal, Richard M. Nixon, together with Henry A. Kissinger, his national security adviser and later secretary of state, made détente — or the relaxation of tensions — the centerpiece of their foreign policy agenda. They were able to do so largely because détente was also a high priority for the Soviets.

The first of three summits held during Nixon's administration came in May 1972, when he became the first American president to visit Moscow. Following lengthy and largely secret preparations undertaken by Kissinger, Nixon met there with Leonid I. Brezhnev, who had emerged as the undisputed leader in the Kremlin. The two men signed 10 agreements, including the Strategic Arms Limitation Talks (SALT I) treaties. These consisted of a five-year Interim Agreement, which limited the numbers of certain offensive weapons, and the Anti-Ballistic Missile (ABM) treaty, of unlimited duration, which limited to two the number of defensive land-based nuclear weapons systems each country could deploy and barred the development, testing or deployment of any sea-, air-, space- or mobile land-based ABM system.

---

[15] For a description of the events leading up to the Cuban missile crisis, see Arthur M. Schlesinger, Jr., *A Thousand Days*, Fawcett Premier Books, 1965.

Richard M. Nixon and Leonid I. Brezhnev toasting after signing an agreement at Moscow summit in May 1972

While these two arms control agreements were the chief results of the summit, the Soviets also placed great importance on the Basic Principles of Mutual Relations, a statement of intent in which the Americans accepted for the first time the controversial concept of "peaceful coexistence," considered by many to be a catchword for Soviet expansionism. Raymond Garthoff described the meeting as "a remarkable event," that "reflected the desire of the leaders in both the United States and the Soviet Union to launch, for a number of shared and differing reasons, a relationship of détente." [16]

The two leaders followed up this unusually productive summit with a meeting in Washington in June 1973. This exchange produced several cultural and trade agreements and was intended to mark the beginning of periodic summits as a permanent forum for conducting East-West relations. Brezhnev marked his first visit to the United States with a televised address in which he proclaimed that the Cold War was over.

Watergate, the outbreak of war in the Middle East in October 1973 and growing American opposition to détente drastically undermined the last Nixon-Brezhnev summit, held in Moscow and Yalta from June 27 to July 3, 1974. The meeting produced a treaty limiting underground testing of nuclear weapons, but no progress on the SALT negotiations, which were stalled over differing views on how to place ceilings on multiple independently targetable re-entry vehicles, or MIRVS. American officials cited increasing evidence that the Soviets were continu-

---

[16] Raymond L. Garthoff, *Détente and Confrontation*, Brookings Institution (1985), p. 289.

Sitting in at the Summit

No president or Kremlin leader has been sufficiently fluent in his adversary's tongue to engage in strictly private discussions at the summit. The presence of interpreters is thus essential, but presidents and Soviet leaders have differed in their reliance on policy advisers. When he met with Khrushchev in Vienna in 1961, President Kennedy brought four top level advisers; Khrushchev, three.

For the first plenary discussion at the 1972 Moscow summit President Nixon brought along a phalanx of advisers, including his national security adviser, Henry Kissinger, who recalled the summit in his book, *White House Years*:

"The meeting took place in St. Catherine's Hall, a large, ornately gilded room, furnished sparsely with elegant candelabra and carved chairs around a long rectangular table covered in beige felt.... On the American side Nixon was in the middle, flanked by [Secretary of State William] Rogers and me; the full complement of White House and State Department aides was present, guaranteeing that Nixon would say nothing significant. The top Soviet leadership was seated with Brezhnev in the middle.... The table was divided in the middle — as if it were a frontier — by a row of bottles of fizzy Georgian mineral water and crystal glasses."

When Reagan and Gorbachev meet, they too will by no means be alone. Too much is at stake, and there are too many essential facts for any one leader to grasp entirely. "Pre-planning," explained Raymond Garthoff, "is used to insure against unsuccessful results and reduce the elements of uncertainty" present at any summit meeting. Drawbacks of summitry include "the fact that there is no higher authority to buck discussions up to if it doesn't produce results. There is also no place or time to refer questions back to, a useful device to play for time in case of disagreement," he said.

The final agenda for Geneva has yet to be defined. Beyond the obvious participants, Secretary of State George P. Shultz and National Security Adviser Robert C. McFarlane, it has not yet been announced who will sit with Reagan and Gorbachev during their discussions, nor whether any strictly private encounters will occur at all.

ing their military buildup to explain their reluctance to negotiate new arms limits — a theme Reagan later used to justify his defense spending increases. Barely one month after the summit Nixon resigned from the presidency.

Nixon's vice president and successor Gerald R. Ford carried on his policy of détente toward the Soviet Union, conducted in large part by Secretary of State Kissinger far from the public view. Ford met with Brezhnev once, in November 1974 in the Far Eastern Soviet city of Vladivostok. There they signed a framework for a successor to SALT I, setting equal limits on strategic bombers and missile launchers as well as the number of MIRVs.[17]

SALT II; Return to Cold War Rhetoric

Although five years were to pass before the next U.S-Soviet summit, Ford's successor, Jimmy Carter, supported both the policy of détente and the SALT process. By 1979 Brezhnev's health had deteriorated noticeably, and Carter acceded to the Soviet request they meet in Vienna that June rather than in the United States, as protocol would have had it. Virtually the only subject on the agenda was the SALT II treaty, which the negotiators had finally hammered out and which the two leaders signed during their meeting.

Carter's support was not enough to keep détente alive. By the Vienna summit, domestic opposition to SALT II was strong, and Carter's standing in the eyes of the American public was sinking fast. Both détente and the treaty received the coup de grâce in December, when Soviet forces invaded and occupied Afghanistan. Carter withdrew his support for SALT II and the Senate never ratified the treaty.

During the six years since the last U.S.-Soviet summit, Cold War rhetoric reached a level that had not been heard since the 1960s. Reagan's election victory in 1980, a year after the Vienna meeting, was also a victory for the opponents of the entire process of détente and arms control agreements of the preceding decade. It was only with Reagan's re-election in 1984 that a change in attitude toward such high-level meetings became apparent. But whether the change is substantive enough to produce a breakthrough in Geneva is far from clear.

Issues for Geneva

A S THE SUMMIT approaches, planners are still setting a formal agenda for discussions.[18] Reagan's U.N. address emphasizing resolution of regional conflicts indicated that the administration would like to broaden the agenda to include more than arms control. The White House had earlier defined a four-part agenda that included arms control issues, regional issues, bilateral questions and human rights. The Soviets have dismissed human rights as a topic of discussion. But whatever

---

[17] For background, see "Strategic Arms Debate," *E.R.R.*. 1979 Vol. I, pp. 401-20; "Politics of Strategic Arms Negotiations," 1977 Vol. I, pp. 349-72.
[18] Secretary of State Schultz is scheduled to meet with Gorbachev in Moscow Nov. 4-5 to finalize preparations for the Geneva meeting.

the formal agenda, arms control will dominate this summit, as it has in the past.

There is a new hitch to the old strategic arms limitation equation, Reagan's Strategic Defense Initiative. Soviet condemnation of the program has been unequivocal since Reagan announced it in March 1983. Gorbachev has said SDI must be canceled before there can be any progress either at the Geneva summit meeting or in the ongoing arms control negotiations. Reagan has steadfastly held to his position that he will not give up SDI.

Both sides have gone to great lengths to justify their respective positions on strategic defense.[19] According to Gorbachev, SDI is offensive rather than defensive in nature because it would destabilize the nuclear balance. He promises that the Soviet Union will counter the development of American space weaponry with a buildup of its own arsenal. But it is also clear that abandonment of Star Wars could save the hard-pressed Soviet economy from having to absorb the enormous costs of pursuing a similar research program, costs which would be all the heavier because of Russia's considerable technological lag.

Support for development of SDI is far from universal. The Union of Concerned Scientists said that SDI "would carry the nation — and the world — across a great divide. If the president's vision is pursued, outer space could become a battlefield." [20] Jimmy Carter echoed this sentiment calling the program "ill-conceived, a total waste of money and counterproductive," and said it posed "the key obstacle to success" at the Geneva summit.[21] SDI has also sparked controversy in Western Europe. "The early evidence strongly suggests that SDI carries with it a remarkable potential both to exacerbate existing transatlantic differences and create new tensions," wrote John Cartwright, a British participant in an Oct. 10 meeting in San Francisco of NATO officials. "There is a real danger of a transatlantic crisis brought about by a conflict of nuclear philosophies." [22]

During his Paris trip Gorbachev called for a 50 percent cut in strategic nuclear warheads — those capable of striking the other side's home territory. According to Soviet calculations, the United States has 3,360 "strategic nuclear delivery systems," the Soviet Union 2,504. The cut would apply to those figures.

---

[19] For administration views on SDI, see "The President's Strategic Defense Initiative," Government Printing Office, January 1985; the Soviet response is found in " 'Star Wars': Delusions and Dangers," Military Publishing House (Moscow), 1985.
[20] Union of Concerned Scientists, *The Fallacy of Star Wars* (October 1984), p. 5.
[21] Quoted in *The New York Times*, Sept. 29, 1985.
[22] Interim report, Special Committee on Nuclear Weapons, North Atlantic Assembly, October 1985.

The proposal also calls for a cut in "nuclear charges" — individual warheads, bombs and air-launched missiles — aimed at achieving a sublimit of 3,600 charges for each component of both sides' nuclear "triad," consisting of land-based missiles, bombers and submarine-based missiles. Although Reagan welcomed the idea of a cut in strategic weapons — his own START proposal had called for reductions and not merely limitations in each side's arsenal — he disagrees with the Soviets on which weapons should be defined as strategic, on the size of the cut and on the counting method applied to the proposed sublimits on "nuclear charges."

But the greatest gap between the two leaders' positions concerns strategic defense. While acknowledging that it would be unfeasible to ban laboratory research of exotic new weapons envisioned for the program, Gorbachev does want to ban the development and testing of "space strike weapons." According to critics, any testing of such weapons would violate the Anti-Ballistic Missile treaty signed by Nixon and Brezhnev at their first summit in 1972.

In mid-October Robert McFarlane announced that the administration would not be in violation of the ABM treaty if it went ahead with SDI. According to a new legal interpretation of a vaguely worded statement attached to the end of the document, he said, the treaty authorized both testing and development of systems "involving new physical concepts," such as those being studied for SDI. The new interpretation caused an uproar among arms control advocates here and within NATO. Retired Ambassador Gerard Smith, chief U.S. negotiator of that agreement, said the administration's about-face made "a dead letter" of the 13-year-old treaty and meant that "we in effect will be harpooning the whole ABM treaty just about six weeks before we go into a summit meeting, and directly after having received a new Soviet proposal on arms control." [23] Secretary of State Shultz attempted to quell the dispute by announcing Oct. 14 that the United States would continue to observe the "restrictive interpretation" of the ABM treaty.

The Soviet delegation to the strategic arms control negotiations in Geneva brought its new proposal to the table when the talks reconvened Sept. 30. But it seemed highly unlikely that the issue could be resolved in time for Reagan and Gorbachev to sign a formal agreement next month, as Nixon and Carter did when they met Brezhnev to sign the SALT agreements.

At best the two leaders may agree to a framework for further negotiations that would be conducted at a lower level, much as

---

[23] McFarlane was interviewed Oct. 6 on NBC News' "Meet the Press"; Smith responded at a news conference Oct. 11.

Ford and Brezhnev did when they agreed on an outline for SALT II at Vladivostok. Both U.S. and Soviet officials have suggested this possibility. Addressing the General Assembly shortly after Reagan on Oct. 24, Shevardnadze challenged the United States to come up with an arms control position that would allow the two leaders to reach "an agreement in principle." McFarlane also said that "some meeting of minds" on arms control was "conceivable" at the summit.[24] Officials of both nations have said Reagan and Gorbachev may sign a joint communiqué containing a statement of principles on arms control and defining a time period for future negotiations. Other military agreements reportedly being negotiated concern nuclear proliferation and chemical weapons.

Reagan Proposals on Regional Conflicts

It is also unclear whether there can be any progress on regional issues. Representatives of both countries have met several times in the past year to discuss developments in Afghanistan, the Middle East, southern Africa and the Far East. While these meetings have produced no apparent results, the topic of regional issues was assured a prominent place on the summit agenda by Reagan's proposal before the U.N. General Assembly to join with the Soviet Union to resolve five specific regional conflicts. Former summit participant Nixon had repeatedly emphasized this issue: "A summit agenda," he wrote, ". . . should have as its first priority not arms control but the potential flash points for U.S.-Soviet conflicts."[25] But as stated, the initiative was sure to be rejected by the Soviet Union, since all five countries — Angola, Ethiopia, Afghanistan, Cambodia and Nicaragua — are currently governed by Soviet allies facing armed opposition by insurgents.[26]

Reagan proposed a "regional peace process" consisting of negotiations between the warring parties in each of the countries. These direct negotiations would be supported by parallel U.S.-Soviet discussions. Once the conflicts were resolved and all foreign troops had withdrawn, Reagan added, the United States would "respond generously" — apparently with economic aid — by "welcoming each country back into the world economy."

Significantly, Reagan did not invite Soviet involvement in other regional conflicts, such as the Middle East peace negotiations. Shevardnadze concurred in his address to the General Assembly that "renewed efforts are also needed to extinguish regional hotbeds of tension," indicating that the door had not

---

[24] NBC television interview Oct. 24.
[25] Richard M. Nixon, "Superpower Summitry," *Foreign Affairs*, fall 1985, p. 6.
[26] The United States has provided aid to insurgents in Afghanistan and Nicaragua. For background on Cambodia, see "Cambodia, A Nation in Turmoil," *E.R.R.*, 1985 Vol I, pp. 253-72.

been closed on summit discussions of the issue. But given the differences in the two sides' conception of what constitutes a regional conflict it appeared unlikely that Reagan and Gorbachev would reach significant agreement.

One breakthrough in regional tensions did come Oct. 8, when Japan, the United States and the Soviet Union agreed to set up an emergency communications network designed to prevent civil aircraft from straying over prohibited air space. Prompted by the Soviet downing of a Korean Air Lines passenger plane two years ago, the agreement was expected to clear the way for a resumption of flights between the United States and the Soviet Union.[27] That hope was dashed in late October when the negotiations broke down over "considerable economic disagreement."

Trade is one area that may hold promise for progress in Geneva. In anticipation of February's Communist Party Congress, Gorbachev has already promised the ailing Soviet economy would undergo a "truly historic" transformation in the next 15 years, doubling both national income and industrial production and increasing productivity by 150 percent. He told a Central Committee meeting Oct. 15 the new five-year plan would provide for greater capital investment and expansion of several key sectors, including the machine-building and electronics industries.

Many experts say Gorbachev cannot hope to keep such promises without expanding trade with the West. According to Boris Rumer, an economist at Harvard University and formerly of the National Institute of Construction Industry in Moscow, the "decline in the production of machinery equipment is one of the chief problems in the Soviet economy today," and can only be reversed if the Soviet Union increases "significantly its import of machinery and equipment from the West." [28]

For its part, the United States continues to restrict the transfer of strategic and military technology to the Soviet Union but is actively seeking to expand the sale of non-strategic goods. Commerce Secretary Malcolm Baldrige has said the sale of non-strategic equipment to the Soviet Union may total $200 million this year, more than twice last year's rate.

New trade agreements would depend, however, on some improvement in the human rights situation in the Soviet Union, particularly the country's emigration policy and its treatment of

---

[27] KAL flight 007 was shot down Sept. 1, 1983, over Soviet territory, killing all 269 people aboard. Reagan had suspended flights to the United States by Aeroflot, the Soviet airline, Dec. 29, 1981, in retaliation for Soviet "repression in Poland," and Pan American World Airways voluntarily suspended its service to Moscow.

[28] Writing in *The Christian Science Monitor*, Oct. 7, 1985.

dissidents. Baldrige reportedly made this clear to Gorbachev during a trip to Moscow last May.[29] As the summit approached, it appeared that some noted dissidents, including Yelena Bonner, the wife of Nobel laureate Andrei Sakharov, might be allowed to leave the Soviet Union. But whether this signals an improvement in human rights practices or is merely a gesture aimed at gaining ground in Geneva remains to be seen.

---

[29] For background, see "Human Rights in the 1980s," *E.R.R.*, 1985 Vol. II, pp. 537-556.

Recommended Reading List
Books

Bialer, Seweryn, *Stalin's Successors*, Cambridge University Press, 1980.

Garthoff, Raymond L., *Détente and Confrontation*, Brookings Institution, 1985.

Hersh, Seymour M., *The Price of Power: Kissinger in the Nixon White House*, Summit Books, 1983.

Hough, Jerry F., *Soviet Leadership in Transition*, Brookings Institution, 1980.

Nye, Joseph S. Jr., *The Making of America's Soviet Policy*, Yale University Press, 1984.

Articles

Brown, Archie, "Gorbachëv: New Man in the Kremlin," *Problems of Communism*, May-June 1985.

Hough, Jerry F., "Gorbachev's Strategy," *Foreign Affairs*, fall 1985.

"An Interview with Gorbachev," *Time*, Sept. 9, 1985.

Nixon, Richard M., "Superpower Summitry," *Foreign Affairs*, fall 1985.

Reddaway, Peter, "Waiting for Gorbachev," *The New York Review of Books*, Oct. 10, 1985.

Shultz, George P., "Shaping American Foreign Policy," *Foreign Affairs*, spring 1985.

Ulam, Adam B., "Forty Years of Troubled Coexistence," *Foreign Affairs*, fall 1985.

Reports and Studies

Departments of Defense and State, "Soviet Strategic Defense Programs," October 1985.

Editorial Research Reports: "Presidential Diplomacy," 1971 Vol. II, p. 735; "Arms Control Negotiations," 1985 Vol. I, p. 145.

Fairbanks, Charles H. Jr., "Summit Diplomacy in East-West Relations," Foreign Policy Institute, School of Advanced International Studies, Johns Hopkins University, Oct. 18, 1985.

Office of Technology Assessment, "Anti-Satellite Weapons, Countermeasures, and Arms Control," September 1985.

—— "Ballistic Missile Defense Technologies," September 1985.

White House, "The President's Strategic Defense Initiative," January 1985.

Graphics: Illustration p. 1, Ray Driver; photo p. 5, the Soviet Embassy; photo p. 11, National Archives; photo p. 13, The White House.

ARMS CONTROL NEGOTIATIONS

by

Mary H. Cooper

Feb. 22
1 9 8 5

Editor's Update: The opening round of the three-part Geneva arms control talks ended in stalemate. At issue throughout the six-week session was the Strategic Defense Initiative, the Reagan administration's program of research into the feasibility of creating a land- and space-based weapons system to defend the United States from nuclear attack. Soviet negotiators held fast to their position that SDI be banned before discussing proposals to limit offensive nuclear weapons. The Americans rejected this view, saying that a ban on research cannot be verified and is thus not an acceptable issue for negotiations.

The negotiators in Geneva did not work in isolation. On March 10, 1985, just two days before the talks began, Soviet leader Konstantin Chernenko died after a long illness and was succeeded — as had been widely predicted — by Mikhail S. Gorbachev. While the transition in leadership brought no appreciable change in the Kremlin's stance at Geneva, Gorbachev soon announced that the Soviet Union would unilaterally halt deployment until November of SS-20 intermediate-range nuclear missiles aimed at Western Europe and challenged the United States to impose a similar freeze on its deployment of Pershing II and cruise missiles in Europe. The White House denounced Gorbachev's proposal as a propaganda ploy designed to foment dissent among the NATO allies and weaken the Americans' hand in Geneva.

Despite a lack of progress at the negotiating table, Gorbachev and President Reagan met in Geneva in November 1985 and again in Iceland in October 1986. In Iceland they nearly produced across-the-board agreements on arms control, including deep cuts in strategic nuclear weapons and the elimination of medium-range missiles from Europe.

The barrier that could not be overcome was SDI. As the price of their willingness to make concessions, the Soviets demanded strict limits on the program. Reagan, believing their purpose was to kill it, refused. Both Reagan and Gorbachev said the search for an arms-control agreement would continue. However, there was no agreement as to when the two leaders would meet again. Until then, it is back to Geneva for the negotiators of both nations.

ARMS CONTROL NEGOTIATIONS

A FTER a 13-month hiatus, the United States and the Soviet Union are about to return to the bargaining table in Geneva, Switzerland, to resume arms control negotiations. The talks, scheduled to begin March 12, will for the first time encompass three separate categories of arms: strategic nuclear weapons, intermediate-range nuclear weapons and — a category never before given special consideration — space weapons.

But no sooner was the agreement to resume negotiations announced than the prospects for their successful outcome were clouded by conflicting interpretations of the ambiguously worded announcement itself. The document to which both delegations agreed Jan. 8 specified that all three areas be "considered and resolved in their interrelationship." Subsequent statements by Soviet Foreign Minister Andrei A. Gromyko made clear the Soviet position that no agreement can be reached in any one area unless agreement is also reached in the other two. "If no progress were made in space," he said Jan. 13 in a television interview with Soviet journalists, "then none could be made in the question of strategic weapons." American spokesmen denied such iron-clad "linkage" was intended. "Interrelationships, yes," explained White House spokesman Larry Speakes, "but as far as linkage where one doesn't proceed without the other, no, that's not our position."

Another potential conflict that became immediately apparent centered around President Reagan's Strategic Defense Initiative, popularly known as SDI or, to its critics, "Star Wars." Now in the research stage, SDI envisions a new type of non-nuclear, space-based defense against nuclear attack that its supporters say would remove the enemy's incentive to use nuclear weapons. Advocates say the research program does not violate the terms of the 1972 Anti-Ballistic Missile (ABM) Treaty, which forbids the deployment of weapons in space, and say it should not be used as a "bargaining chip" in Geneva. Only if the program passes from the research stage to the development and deployment of weapons, they say, should SDI be a subject of negotiation. President Reagan reiterated this position in a recent interview. Asked if he would halt SDI research in return for Soviet concessions on offensive weapons, he replied: "No, I would want to proceed with what we're doing. . . ." [1]

[1] Interview with *The New York Times*, Feb. 13, 1985.

The Soviet Union is adamantly opposed to SDI and clearly intends to place the program at the top of its agenda in March. Far from being a benign defensive system, they say, SDI would guarantee the success of an American first strike against the Soviet Union. As such, it can only be interpreted as a destabilizing offensive weapons system and must be banned before it ever gets off the ground.

The selection of the negotiating teams is also an indication of each side's opening positions. On the U.S. side, the delegation will be headed by a newcomer to nuclear arms talks, Max M. Kampelman. On record as a hard-liner toward the Soviet Union and supporter of SDI, he will also lead the American team dealing with space weapons. John Tower, a former senator (R-Texas, 1961-85) and chairman of the Senate Armed Services Committee who supports Reagan's military buildup, will be the chief negotiator on strategic, or long-range, weapons *(see glossary, p. 33)*. The only delegation head with negotiating experience in the area to which he has been assigned is Maynard W. Glitman, a career diplomat who was deputy head of the delegation in previous talks on the intermediate-range nuclear force (INF).[2] He will lead the delegation on INF talks in Geneva.

Veteran arms negotiator Paul H. Nitze will play an important behind-the-scenes role. By far the most experienced arms control expert connected with the new talks, Nitze will be a "special adviser" to the proceedings. Hard-liners were encouraged by the selection of Kampelman and Tower. At the same time, however, supporters of arms control were encouraged by the surprise replacement of Edward L. Rowny, chief negotiator in the stalemated strategic arms reductions talks (START), and his relegation to a less visible advisory position.[3] Rowny, a retired general with strong conservative backing, has criticized past arms control efforts.

The Soviet delegation has greater experience in arms control negotiations. Delegation head and chief negotiator on strategic arms will be Viktor Karpov, who also led his party to the START talks. The space weapons team will be led by Yuli Kvitsinsky, former INF negotiator and co-author, with Nitze, of the ill-fated "walk-in-the-woods" proposal before those talks collapsed *(see p. 38)*. His place as chief negotiator for the INF

---

[2] The United States and the Soviet Union opened talks in Geneva in November 1981 aimed at limiting INF missiles based in Europe. Moscow broke off these talks two years later when the first American-made Pershing II and cruise missiles were deployed in Western Europe in accordance with a 1979 NATO decision *(see p. 16)*.

[3] The Reagan administration, critical of the strategic arms limitation talks (SALT) begun in 1969, proposed instead reducing the levels of these long-range nuclear weapons. START talks began in June 1982 but were suspended in December 1983 when Moscow refused to set a date for their resumption *(see p. 19)*.

Chernenko's Health

While official Soviet statements offer conflicting accounts of Konstantin U. Chernenko's state of health, the 73-year-old Soviet leader was last seen in public Dec. 27 and is reportedly suffering from emphysema and heart disease. Speculation on the eventual succession of a younger Kremlin leader has focused on 53-year-old Mikhail Gorbachev, the youngest member of the ruling Politburo. Gorbachev would be the first Soviet leader whose political formation was not directly shaped by World War II and the rule of Josef Stalin.

Whoever Chernenko's successor may be, however, the transition's impact on the Geneva talks may be minimal. Continuity in the Soviet position on arms control appears to be assured not only by the Politburo's final say in the matter but also by the active role that veteran negotiator Andrei A. Gromyko continues to play in the arms control process.

Should Chernenko die, his successor would be the fourth Soviet leader since Ronald Reagan was first elected to the White House. Leonid I. Breznev died in 1982 and was succeeded by Yuri V. Andropov, who died in February 1984. He was succeeded by Chernenko.

talks will be taken by Aleksei Obukhov, another experienced arms control negotiator.

President Reagan's Call for a 'New Dialogue'

In contrast to the skepticism with which he regarded arms control during his first term, Reagan welcomed the Geneva talks, saying he had "no more important goal" in his second term than to "achieve a good agreement — an agreement which meets the interests of both countries, which increases the security of our allies and which enhances international stability." [4]

At the same time, Reagan sought significant increases in defense spending for fiscal 1986, reinforcing his position that the United States should only enter into negotiations with the Soviet Union from a position of strength *(see p. 26)*. In addition, the administration has stepped up its campaign calling into question Soviet compliance with the terms of past arms control agreements. In a report to Congress, the administration cited 13 areas of "concern," but focused its attention on one "clear violation" of the 1972 ABM Treaty, a phased-array, early warning radar system now under construction near the Siberian city of Krasnoyarsk.[5] Calling the provision controlling deployment of phased-array radar "the linchpin of the ABM Treaty,"

[4] Statement issued Jan. 22, 1985.
[5] The unclassified version of the non-compliance report, required by the fiscal 1985 Defense Authorization Act, was released Feb. 1.

a senior administration official, who briefed reporters on condition he not be identified, termed Soviet non-compliance "a dagger pointed at the whole arms control process in the future."

With public opinion apparently solidly behind him and such misgivings about Soviet trustworthiness, why is Reagan embarking on new arms control negotiations? Kenneth Adelman, director of the U.S. Arms Control and Disarmament Agency, gave three reasons: "New arms control agreements, if soundly formulated, can serve U.S. security interests; entering into new negotiations does not in any way condone past Soviet behavior; and arms control gives us leverage and another way to get the Soviets to abide by existing agreements." [6]

Such an agreement would have to take account of changed expectations, as reflected in the administration's new "strategic concept," which couples the traditional aims of arms control negotiations in the short term with a longer-term vision of strategic defense. Deputy Secretary of State Kenneth W. Dam first presented the strategy, which other officials have since restated verbatim: "For the next 10 years, we should seek a radical reduction in the number and power of existing and planned offensive and defensive nuclear arms, whether land-based, space-based or otherwise. We should even now be looking forward to a period of transition, beginning possibly 10 years from now, to effective non-nuclear defensive forces, including defenses against offensive nuclear arms. This period of transition should lead to the eventual elimination of nuclear arms, both offensive and defensive. A nuclear-free world is an ultimate objective to which we, the Soviet Union and all other nations can agree." [7]

Continuing Push to Build Up U.S. Defenses

Even as the administration was elaborating its negotiating position for the coming talks, it was trying to build support in the United States and Europe for its defense modernization program, including SDI. This program, it argues, is necessary to persuade the Soviet Union to bargain in good faith. The administration requested that Congress approve a $2 trillion military budget over the next five years, beginning with $313.7 billion for fiscal 1986, which starts Oct. 1, 1985. Part of the money would be used to reinforce the arsenal of strategic nuclear weapons: the budget includes $3.2 billion for 48 land-based MX missiles,

---

[6] Adelman spoke at a State Department briefing Feb. 1. The arms control agency was set up in 1960 to advise the president and secretary of state on arms control.

[7] Dam spoke Jan. 14 before the Foreign Policy Association in New York. The new strategic concept was reportedly drafted by Paul Nitze and presented to Gromyko by Secretary of State Shultz at a meeting of the two in Geneva, Jan. 7-8. Nitze later reiterated the concept in a meeting Jan. 25 with reporters. See *The Washington Post*, Jan. 26, 1985.

President Reagan and Vice President Bush with the U.S. negotiating team; from left, chief Max M. Kampelman, John Tower and Maynard W. Glitman

$5.6 billion for 48 B1 bombers and $5 billion for a Trident submarine and Trident missiles.

Administration spokesmen, led by Defense Secretary Caspar W. Weinberger, maintain that Reagan's four-year-old program to "rearm America" is what led the Soviet Union back to the bargaining table and that efforts to reduce the Pentagon's budget will only undermine the American position in Geneva. Because of widespread bipartisan concern over the $200 billion federal budget deficit, however, the administration's defense budget request will undoubtedly be pared.[8] Reflecting this sentiment, Sen. Sam Nunn, D-Ga., told Weinberger during hearings before the Senate Armed Services Committee: "It's not a question of whether it will be cut, it's a question of how much it will be reduced."

Another subject of concern to the administration is the ongoing debate over the controversial MX missile. Dubbed the "peacekeeper" by Reagan because of its purported contribution to nuclear deterrence, the MX is a new, more accurate intercontinental ballistic missile (ICBM) armed with 10 nuclear warheads whose production has been delayed by congressional opposition.[9] The administration is trying to increase support for the program in Congress before it comes to a vote, possibly in March just as the Geneva talks are to open: "I must tell you, frankly," Weinberger told the Senate Foreign Relations Committee Jan. 31, "that cancellation of key programs, such as MX, will prolong negotiations, not facilitate them, and will reduce our ability to achieve arms reductions."

---

[8] For background, see "Federal Budget Deficit," *E.R.R.*, 1984 Vol. I, pp. 45-64; "Reagan's Defense Buildup," *E.R.R.*, 1984 Vol. I, pp. 309-328.

[9] Of the 100 missiles called for in the MX program, 21 are already under production. Under a complex formula agreed to in 1984, $1.5 billion earmarked for the production of 21 more MX missiles cannot be released until after March 1. Even then, the money cannot be spent until both the House of Representatives and the Senate vote their approval.

Further complicating the administration's effort to boost defense spending on Capitol Hill is the recent change in leadership on several key congressional committees. In particular, Rep. Les Aspin, D-Wis., newly elected chairman of the House Armed Services Committee, has suggested he may drop his support for the MX, a weapon he said may be unnecessary if Reagan's strategic defense initiative proves feasible.[10]

"Star Wars" itself has now overtaken the MX as the most controversial element of the administration's defense modernization program. In its preliminary research phase alone, SDI is expected to cost $26 billion, while some estimates of its final figure reach $1 trillion.[11] But budget concerns are only a small element of the growing criticism over SDI. While supporting the current research effort, former Secretary of State Cyrus R. Vance said he was "strongly opposed" to pursuing strategic defense beyond the research stage. "Once we cross the line from basic research to deployment," he told the Senate Foreign Relations Committee Feb. 4, "we have very radically changed the basic strategic doctrine." [12] He voiced the concern of many arms control advocates in Congress that the deployment of a strategic defense system in space would set off a new arms race. They fear that the Soviet Union would try to penetrate the defense with new offensive weapons and the United States would then be compelled to build even more elaborate defenses.

Up to now, the debate over SDI has been largely confined to the scientific community, where technical considerations are called into play either to boost or to debunk the program. Some of its supporters are physicists working in arms research facilities.[13] Others, however, oppose SDI as technically unfeasible. Some say that even if it were possible to extend a nuclear umbrella over the United States, SDI would pose grave dangers. According to a study conducted by the Union of Concerned Scientists: "If the president's vision is pursued, outer space could become a battlefield. An effective defense against a missile attack must employ weapons operating in space. This now peaceful sanctuary, so long a symbol of cooperation, would be violated. And the arduous process of arms control, which has scored so few genuine successes in the nuclear era, would also be imperiled — perhaps terminated — by the deployment of weapons in space." [14]

---

[10] Aspin has long supported the renegotiation of the ABM Treaty. See Les Aspin, "Missiles Become Protected," *The New Republic,* February 1981.

[11] The fiscal 1985 budget includes $1.4 billion for SDI; the administration has asked for $3.7 billion in fiscal 1986.

• [12] Vance served under President Carter from 1977 to 1980.

[13] See, for example, letters to the editor in support of SDI published in *The Wall Street Journal,* Jan. 17, 1985.

[14] Union of Concerned Scientists, *The Fallacy of Star Wars* (1984), pp. 5-6. UCS is a non-profit organization of 100,000 scientists and citizens concerned about the impact of advanced technology on society.

NATO, Soviet Concerns

THE DEBATE over SDI may be reawakening anti-nuclear sentiment in other countries, a worrisome prospect to administration supporters. The opposition Liberal Party in Canada in early February challenged the Conservative government of Prime Minister Brian Mulroney over its current negotiations with the U.S. government to modernize an early warning system in northern Canada. The Liberals said that the modernization would draw Canada into participation in SDI. Defense Minister Robert Coates denied that the new $1 billion North Warning System would be a part of SDI.[15]

Far more troubling to the administration is the effect an anti-SDI campaign among NATO's European members might have on the American position in Geneva.[16] So far the initiative has elicited no official opposition from the allied governments. Lord Carrington, NATO's secretary general, went so far as to say that it would be "the height of imprudence" for the United States to interrupt research on SDI.[17]

But SDI alarms many European observers who fear that the creation of an anti-ballistic defense over North America would encourage the United States to withdraw into a "Fortress America," abandoning Western Europe to its own defenses. With the United States safely protected behind its space-based shield, they say, Europe would become an attractive battlefield for a nuclear exchange. The governments of allied nations — West Germany, Britain, Italy, Belgium and the Netherlands — that supported a 1979 NATO decision to deploy 572 new intermediate-range nuclear weapons on their soil may have special cause for alarm.[18] The deployment began on schedule in December 1983, but it fueled a widespread anti-nuclear movement that undermined the ruling governments' political strength. The

[15] The United States and Canada are now negotiating an agreement to modernize the Distant Early Warning system — or DEW line — originally built to detect low-flying, strategic bombers that the Earth's curvature prevented U.S.-based radar from picking up from far away. It was allowed to deteriorate as the Soviet Union based its strategic arsenal ever more heavily on land-based ICBMs.

[16] NATO was formed in April 1949 as a military alliance against Soviet aggression in Europe in the wake of the Berlin blockade. It is made up of 16 countries: Belgium, Britain, Canada, Denmark, France, West Germany, Greece, Iceland, Italy, Luxembourg, the Netherlands, Norway, Portugal, Spain, Turkey and the United States.

[17] Lord Carrington, who served as foreign minister in the conservative government of British Prime Minister Margaret Thatcher, spoke Jan. 22 while visiting Ottawa.

[18] NATO's December 1979 "dual-track" decision called for U.S.-Soviet negotiations on intermediate-range nuclear forces. If negotiations were not successful, the decision called for the deployment in Europe of 464 ground-launched cruise missiles and 108 Pershing II missiles — each with a single nuclear warhead — beginning in December 1983. All 108 Pershings are to be deployed in West Germany, and 54 are reportedly in place now. Deployment of the cruise missiles has already begun in Britain, West Germany and Italy, and is scheduled to begin this year in Belgium and the Netherlands.

conservative government of West German Chancellor Helmut Kohl is particularly vulnerable. Already weakened by economic stagnation, the government faces elections in two years and can expect strong opposition from the country's peace movement.[19]

Only days after it was announced that U.S.-Soviet arms talks would resume, Belgian Prime Minister Wilfried Martens dismayed the Reagan administration by refusing to permit the cruise missile deployment scheduled in March. He said his government would decide by the end of that month when to begin deployment, but observers predicted that Martens, who is under pressure from anti-nuclear forces, would delay such a decision until after national elections are held in December. The Netherlands is exhibiting similar sensitivity to domestic anti-nuclear sentiment. The government there has delayed deployment of 48 cruise missiles until November.

As if NATO's jitters were not enough to jeopardize Reagan's plan to arrive in Geneva with a strong hand, U.S. allies in the southern Pacific dealt the administration an unexpected blow. First, New Zealand's Prime Minister David Lange, following up on a campaign promise to prohibit nuclear weapons in the country, announced his government would deny port access to a U.S. warship scheduled to arrive for joint naval exercises within the ANZUS alliance (Australia, New Zealand and the United States).[20] The United States, which for security reasons does not reveal whether or not Navy vessels at sea are carrying nuclear weapons, responded by canceling the exercises altogether. Days later, Australian Prime Minister Robert Hawke told the administration U.S. aircraft could not use Australian bases to monitor a test of the MX missile scheduled for this summer.

Pressure for Arms Control in Soviet Bloc

While pursuing arms modernization, the Reagan administration has consistently maintained that it was willing to resume arms control negotiations at any time the Soviet Union wished. It was, after all, the Soviet side that abandoned both the START and the INF talks in 1983, spokesmen maintain. First, Moscow broke off the INF negotiations in November to protest the initial NATO deployment of new Pershing and cruise missiles. The following month it failed to agree to a date for the next round of START talks. Soviet leader Konstantin U. Chernenko insisted as recently as last October that Moscow would not resume INF talks until the NATO weapons were

---

[19] For background, see "West Germany's 'Missile' Election," *E.R.R.*, 1983 Vol. I, pp. 149-168.

[20] The ANZUS defense treaty was signed in September 1951. Less structured than NATO, the treaty calls primarily for strategic consultation and periodic joint military exercises.

removed from Europe. In agreeing to return to Geneva, Moscow reversed its position. It also appears to have dropped its prior insistence on a moratorium on testing anti-satellite weapons as a condition for negotiations on space weaponry.

Since the agreement to resume negotiations, the Soviet Union has focused its attention on SDI, repeatedly asserting that no progress can be made on INF and strategic weapons unless some agreement can be worked out to prevent the "militarization of space." Some Western observers have deduced from such statements that Moscow is desperately trying to head off a new and highly expensive round of the arms race that it can ill afford. The Soviet economy has for the past several years suffered from repeated crop failures as well as depressed world prices for its oil exports.[21]

Secretary of State George P. Shultz expressed this view during recent testimony before the Senate Foreign Relations Committee. In contrast to the growing military and economic might of the West, he said, "the Soviets face ... profound structural economic difficulties, a continuing succession problem and restless allies; its diplomacy and its clients are on the defensive in many parts of the world." But this picture is not shared by all administration officials. Defense Secretary Weinberger told the same hearing Jan. 31 that the Soviet Union boasts a numerically stronger nuclear arsenal and is "dramatically improving" its quality, while "expanding the geographical reach" of its conventional forces.

History of Arms Control

THE GENEVA negotiations are but the most recent chapter in the turbulent history of arms control. Ever since the nuclear genie was let out of the bottle nearly 40 years ago, negotiators have tried in vain to halt the development of nuclear weapons.

The United States was the first country to explode nuclear devices and is the only country to have used them, destroying the Japanese cities of Hiroshima and Nagasaki in August 1945. Only by bringing Japan quickly to its knees, it was reasoned, could the Pacific war be ended without the additional loss of thousands of U.S. servicemen. Ten months later, on June 14, 1946, the United States presented a plan to the newly created

---

[21] For background on economic issues within the Soviet bloc, see "Communist Economies," *E.R.R.*, 1984 Vol. II, pp. 957-976.

United Nations to ban the production of nuclear weapons and to place all peaceful applications of nuclear technology under international control. The Baruch plan — named for its co-author, financier Bernard Baruch — called for the creation of an agency to oversee nuclear development and inspect member nations' facilities. The United States, which alone possessed the technology to produce nuclear weapons at that time, pledged to destroy its bombs as soon as the agency was established. The Soviet Union, however, insisted that the American arsenal be dismantled before it would agree to the agency's creation, and the Baruch plan became the first of many arms control proposals to fall victim to disagreements between the postwar superpowers.

The next two decades witnessed a steady worsening of U.S.-Soviet relations. It was during this so-called Cold War period of frosty diplomatic exchanges that the Soviet Union developed a nuclear capability of its own and rapidly built an arsenal of atomic weaponry to counter that of the United States. Both sides began modernizing their weapons, and the arms race was on. The first breakthrough in nuclear arms technology came as a result of reducing warhead size and weight. The bombs dropped over Japan were so heavy that they had to be transported by large bombers. By making them smaller and lighter, arms designers on both sides were able to load them instead onto rockets, which were a faster, and thus less vulnerable, means of delivering the bomb to its target. In time, both the United States and the Soviet Union developed intercontinental ballistic missiles (ICBMs), large rockets that could be shot up into the atmosphere to release their payload — the nuclear bomb — which would then follow a path determined by the physical law of "ballistic trajectory" toward its ultimate target halfway around the Earth.

The unprecedented danger and expense entailed in the spiraling arms race prompted both sides to propose several arms control initiatives during the 1950s and 1960s. This period saw considerable progress in areas not directly concerned with the armaments themselves. The bilateral Hot Line Agreement (1963) set up a direct link between the White House and the Kremlin to facilitate emergency communications and reduce the risk of war. Four multilateral agreements of the same period also were aimed at reducing the risk of nuclear conflict. The Antarctic Treaty (1959) banned "any measures of a military nature" on that continent; the Limited Nuclear Test Ban Treaty (1963) banned weapons tests under water, in the atmosphere and in outer space, including "the moon and other celestial bodies"; the Peaceful Uses of Outer Space Treaty (1966) went a step further and banned all nuclear weapons from

Arms Control: A Glossary

Anti-Ballistic Missile (ABM): A defensive system to intercept and destroy strategic ballistic missiles or their elements during flight, consisting of interceptor missiles, launchers and radars.

Cruise Missile: a small (18-ft.), jet-powered guided missile that can fly at very low altitudes to minimize radar detection.

Intercontinental Ballistic Missile (ICBM): A land-based, rocket-propelled missile with an intercontinental range (defined as over 5,500 kilometers under SALT). Usually launched from an underground silo, it is vulnerable to attack but is also the most destructive strategic weapon.

Intermediate-Range Nuclear Forces (INF): Land-based missiles and aircraft with ranges of up 5,500 kilometers that are capable of striking targets beyond the general region of the battlefield but not capable of intercontinental range.

Multiple Independently Targetable Re-entry Vehicle (MIRV): The portion of a strategic missile that carries a number of nuclear warheads, each of which can be directed to a separate target.

Mutual Assured Destruction: The ability of opposing sides to inflict an "unacceptable" de-

MX missile

gree of damage upon an aggressor after absorbing any first strike, or first offensive move of a nuclear war.

MX (Missile Experimental): A new, 10-warhead U.S. ICBM developed to replace the increasingly vulnerable Minuteman ICBM force and to counter the SS-18 and SS-19, Soviet ICBMs.

Short-Range Nuclear Forces: Land-based missiles, rockets and artillery capable of striking only targets in the general region of the battlefield.

Strategic Nuclear Forces: Ballistic missiles and bomber aircraft that have intercontinental range. U.S. strategic nuclear forces directly threaten Soviet territory and vice versa.

Submarine-Launched Ballistic Missile: Ballistic missiles carried in and launched from a submarine. These are harder to detect than land-based or air-launched missiles.

space; and signatories to the Nuclear Non-Proliferation Treaty (1968) agreed not to transfer nuclear weapons to nations that do not possess them. These agreed in turn not to embark on nuclear weapons programs of their own.[22]

Agreement to negotiate the far more difficult issue of existing weapons was longer in coming. After its humiliation in the Cuban missile crisis of 1962 — under U.S. pressure Russia withdrew its missiles from the island — the Soviet Union rapidly increased its nuclear arsenal. By the time agreement was finally reached to begin arms negotiations in 1968, each side already possessed nuclear arsenals capable of destroying the other. Deterrence was based on the mutual realization that a nuclear first strike could not destroy all the enemy's warheads and would merely provoke a retaliatory response. The concept, known as mutual assured destruction — or MAD — was to dominate the strategic thinking of both sides. President Johnson's defense secretary, Robert S. McNamara, gave top priority to the limitation of anti-ballistic missiles (ABMs). He believed they would be ineffective against an all-out attack and were destabilizing, in that each side was rushing ahead to develop newer offensive weapons to counter ABMs.

Delayed first by the Soviet invasion of Czechoslovakia in August 1968 and then by the election of a new president, Richard M. Nixon, the Strategic Arms Limitation Talks — SALT — finally began in Vienna April 16, 1970. After two years of hard bargaining, President Nixon went to Moscow and joined Soviet Communist Party Secretary Leonid I. Brezhnev on May 26, 1972, in signing the two accords that made up the first strategic arms limitation agreement — SALT I. The first accord, the ABM Treaty, reflected the shared belief that ABM systems are destabilizing and ineffective. The treaty — which is of unlimited duration but subject to review every five years — allowed each side only two ABM deployment sites — later amended to one — and strictly limited the technological development of ABM weaponry, including radar and interceptor missiles.[23]

SALT I's second component, an interim agreement on offensive strategic arms, was less sweeping in its effect. It froze the numbers of ICBMs and submarine-launched ballistic missiles (SLBMs) on each side for five years. The Soviet Union was left

---

[22] In addition to the United States and Soviet Union, the only country with acknowledged nuclear weapons are Britain, France and China. Several other countries possess the technical ability to produce nuclear weapons. See Joseph P. Yager, ed., *Nonproliferation and U.S. Foreign Policy,* The Brookings Institution, 1980. See also "Controlling Nuclear Proliferation," *E.R.R.*, 1981 Vol. I, pp. 509-532.

[23] By 1975 the United States had deactivated its ABM installation at Grand Forks, N.D., because it was considered to be of little military value by itself. The Soviet "Galosh" ABM system is deployed around Moscow.

with more missile launchers and land-based ICBMs than the United States, while the United States retained its technological superiority and numerical advantage in long-range strategic bombers.

It was this discrepancy in the nuclear balance, which allowed both sides to perceive themselves at a disadvantage, that was to spell eventual failure for the SALT process. The agreement also left unaddressed an important technological advance already under development. This was the multiple, independently targetable re-entry vehicle, or MIRV. A single missile could now be armed with several warheads, each aimed at different targets. MIRVs made simple missile counts obsolete at a single stroke and vastly complicated the already sticky problem of counting nuclear warheads. Although the Senate ratified SALT I by an 88-to-2 margin in September 1972, U.S. misgivings over the interim agreement were expressed in an amendment sponsored by Sen. Henry M. Jackson, D-Wash., that directed the president in future negotiations to accept arms levels equal or superior to those of the Soviet Union.

Technolgical improvements not restricted under SALT's numerical limits proceeded apace on both sides. Soviet advances included a new intermediate-range ballistic missile called the SS-20, the Tu-22M Backfire bomber, submarine-launched missiles and more accurate ICBMs with a higher throw-weight, or payload capacity. For its part, the United States deployed MIRVs to maintain its advantage in the number of nuclear warheads, expanded its Trident submarine-launched missile and B-1 strategic bomber forces, and began developing new weapons such as the MX missile and the long-range cruise missile, a small, guided aircraft similar to the buzz-bombs Nazi Germany used against England in World War II. Able to fly at low altitudes, the cruise missile can be launched from land, sea or air and is particularly difficult to classify under arms control agreements because it can be armed with either conventional or nuclear warheads.

Both sides continued to modernize their nuclear weapons while observing the numerical limits imposed by SALT I. On Nov. 24, 1974, Brezhnev and President Gerald R. Ford agreed to the framework for its successor, SALT II. The Vladivostok accord, named for the Soviet Pacific port city where the two leaders met, set an overall ceiling on the number of delivery vehicles, including strategic bombers, permitted each side. Of the 2,400 total, 1,320 missile launchers could be fitted with MIRVs. Both sides were allowed leeway to allocate their forces as they saw fit. The Soviet Union would continue to concentrate its nuclear warheads on ICBMs, while the United States distributed its arsenal more evenly among the strategic "triad" of land-based missiles, submarines and strategic bombers.

Once again, however, weapons designers in the military-industrial complex of both nations worked faster than the arms control negotiators. The Vladivostok agreement did not cover the American cruise missile or the Soviet Backfire bomber, presented as a medium-range bomber but considered capable of intercontinental missions as well. The impasse over these weapons was sidestepped under a compromise negotiating framework of September 1977, in which both sides agreed to observe the SALT I Interim Agreement until they could produce its successor.

The three-part SALT II accord that Brezhnev and President Jimmy Carter signed in Vienna on June 18, 1979, featured a Treaty on the Limitation of Strategic Offensive Arms. It set a limit of 2,400 on the total number of nuclear delivery vehicles and the following individual limits: 1,320 MIRV launchers (missiles and bombers carrying cruise missiles); 1,200 MIRVed ballistic missiles; 820 MIRVed land-based ICBMs; and 308 "heavy" ICBMs. No additional fixed launchers were permitted. It also banned any increase in the maximum number of warheads on existing types of ICBMs and limited the number of warheads allowed for each new type of ICBM to 10. Each SLBM was allowed to carry 14 warheads while an average of 28 long-range cruise missiles was permitted for each bomber. SALT II also banned the flight-testing and deployment of several missiles and the construction of new fixed ICBM launchers.

SALT II immediately came under fire from critics who said it enabled the Soviets to maintain nuclear superiority over the United States. For the next two years, as U.S.-Soviet relations deteriorated, the agreement was subjected to mounting criticism. In protest over the Soviet invasion of Afghanistan in December 1979, Carter himself stopped the ratification process by asking the Senate in January 1980 to "delay consideration" of SALT II. It was never ratified.

Arms Control Under Reagan Administration

Elected in the fall of 1980, Ronald Reagan came to office vowing to "rearm America." The SALT process was denounced as a failure and arms control figured hardly at all during the first 18 months of his administration. The Soviet Union, he and his officials repeatedly suggested, had deftly used the negotiations to slow U.S. weapons modernization while boldly forging ahead themselves to a position of military superiority over the United States.

While the strategic arms negotiations were placed on hold and

Other Arms Control Talks in Progress

In addition to the bilateral negotiations dealing with nuclear armaments, the United States and the Soviet Union have held negotiations to limit conventional forces and chemical weapons, as well as talks aimed at reducing tensions and averting the risk of war in times of crisis.

Mutual and Balanced Force Reductions (MBFR): Talks opened in Vienna in 1973 among 12 NATO and seven Warsaw Pact nations. Their aim is to enhance East-West security and reduce the likelihood of war in Europe by reducing each side's military manpower in Central Europe to a maximum level of 700,000 ground forces, or 900,000 air and ground force personnel combined. NATO claims the Warsaw Pact has a 170,000-man superiority over the West (960,000 compared with 790,000) in the area under consideration. Referred to as the "zone of reductions," the area includes West Germany, Belgium, the Netherlands and Luxembourg in the West, and East Germany, Poland and Czechoslovakia in the East. Issues blocking agreement involve on-site verification, a timetable for the reduction and the troop levels now deployed. Talks resumed Jan. 31.

Conference on Confidence- and Security-Building Measures and Disarmament in Europe (CDE): The goal of these 35-nation talks, which first opened Jan. 17, 1984, in Stockholm, is to reduce the possibility of an accidental nuclear confrontation resulting from miscalculation or a failure of communications. Its participants comprise the United States, Canada, the Soviet Union and all European countries except Albania. One recent product of these talks was the addition to the Washington-Moscow "hotline" of a high-speed facsimile capability that will allow the rapid transmission of photos and charts. The CDE talks are an outgrowth of the 35-nation Conference on Security and Cooperation in Europe (CSCE), which produced the Helsinki accords of 1975, under which both sides agreed to provide advance notification of large military maneuvers. Max Kampelman, who will lead the U.S. delegation in Geneva, headed the U.S. delegation to follow-up talks, held in Madrid and concluded in September 1983. NATO delegates to the Stockholm CDE talks have proposed additional measures for exchanging military information. This year's session opened Jan. 29.

Conference on Disarmament (CD): The 40-member Committee on Disarmament was established in 1979 to achieve a complete and verifiable ban on the production, stockpiling and transfer of chemical weapons. Although a prior agreement — the Geneva Protocol of 1925 — prohibits their use, it does not restrict the production or stockpiling of chemical and biological weapons and contains no provisions for verification. The United States has accused the Soviet Union of using such weapons in Southeast Asia and Afghanistan. On April 18, 1984, the United States introduced a draft treaty calling for a comprehensive and verifiable global ban on chemical weapons. The latest round opened Feb. 5.

the Pentagon was given the green light for increased military spending, the administration had to deal with the issue of intermediate-range nuclear forces in Europe. NATO in 1979 had announced its decision to pursue a "dual track" path to counter the Soviet Union's growing arsenal of intermediate-range missiles, the SS-4, SS-5 and the new SS-20, pointed toward Western Europe. NATO announced it would seek to draw the Soviet Union into negotiations and to begin deploying American-made Pershing II and cruise missiles on allied territory if agreement had not been reached by December 1983.

Secretary of State Alexander M. Haig and Soviet Foreign Minister Gromyko pledged in September 1981 "to spare no effort" to conclude an agreement before the NATO deadline. Talks opened in Geneva on Nov. 30 of that year. Only days earlier, Reagan had offered his own solution to the INF dilemma with his "zero-zero option": NATO would cancel deployment of the American missiles if the Soviet Union agreed to dismantle all its SS-4, SS-5 and SS-20 missiles.

But the Soviet position on INF proved irreconcilable with the U.S. contention that the SS-20s constituted a new and destabilizing class of weapons. Moscow rejected U.S. insistence on global limits of the SS-20 which, with a range of 5,000 kilometers, could threaten not only Western Europe but also American allies in Asia, including Japan. The Soviet Union insisted that British and French nuclear missiles be counted as part of NATO's arsenal; the United States refused, saying that these forces were purely national in scope and did not contribute to allied defense.

The two chief negotiators at Geneva attempted to resolve the impasse on their own during a private conversation in July 1982 later known as the "walk in the woods." U.S. chief negotiator Paul Nitze — founder of the Committee on the Present Danger and leader of the fight against SALT II — and his Soviet counterpart Yuli Kvitsinsky drove to a secluded mountaintop in the Jura range near the French border, ordered the driver to meet them at the bottom and started to walk down. According to one account: "Once they got down to business, Nitze and Kvitsinsky were sitting on a log. It was starting to rain. Nitze had brought along a typed outline of an agreement, from which he began to read aloud. Kvitsinsky listened for a while, then suggested some modifications. Incorporating these changes would make it a joint paper. Nitze asked Kvitsinsky if he realized that. 'Yes,' replied the Soviet. 'Let's go through with the rest of it.' " [24]

[24] Strobe Talbott, *Deadly Gambits* (1984), p. 127.

By the time they had reached their car, Nitze and Kvitsinsky reportedly had defined a compromise agreement that prohibited the Soviet Union from developing a long-range ground-launched cruise missile and froze SS-20s deployed in the Asian U.S.S.R. at current levels. In exchange, the United States would cancel deployment of the Pershing. Their efforts were to prove fruitless. Both governments disavowed the proposal and the stalemate persisted. On Nov. 23, 1983, Kvitsinsky announced the Soviet decision to "discontinue" the talks in protest against NATO's resolve to deploy the Pershing and cruise missiles on schedule the following month.

Meanwhile, after 16 months in office, Reagan outlined his first strategic arms control proposal. In an effort to distinguish it from the "failed" SALT process, Reagan named his proposal START, for Strategic Arms Reduction Talks. START's basic aim, as described by chief negotiator Edward L. Rowny, was "to break the mold of past negotiations which concentrated on limiting strategic offensive arms at high levels" and "to improve strategic stability through substantial reductions in the more destabilizing strategic offensive arms." [25] The initial proposal, which Reagan presented May 9, 1982, called for both sides to reduce the number of land- and sea-based missile warheads by about one-third to 5,000 and to reduce the number of deployed ballistic missiles to no more than 850, a cut of one-half for the United States, somewhat more for the Soviet Union.

Paul H. Nitze

Reagan subsequently modified his START proposal to accommodate the recommendations of the Commission on Strategic Forces — known as the Scowcroft commission after its head, former National Security Council member Brent Scowcroft. While reaffirming the goal of reducing each side's ballistic-missile warheads to 5,000, the president in June 1983 relaxed the overall limit of 850 deployed ballistic missiles. These changes were included in a draft treaty that the United States offered July 7.

Under pressure from congressional arms control advocates, Reagan in October incorporated into the U.S. bargaining position the "build-down" concept, which called for retiring older weapons as a corollary to modernization with the aim of reducing the total number of warheads over time. The Soviet Union, which had linked INF and START talks all along, rejected the

---

[25] Rowny spoke June 21, 1984, before the Royal United Services Institute of London.

modified proposal and, at the end of the negotiating round on Dec. 8, refused to agree to a resumption date for START.

Focus on 'Star Wars'

A S THE DATE for the Geneva talks approaches, the United States and Soviet Union have not altered their basic positions on either strategic or intermediate-range missiles. Officially, these remain as irreconcilable as they were when the two sets of talks were interrupted at the end of 1983.

Some observers speculate that the format to be followed in Geneva, establishing an "interrelationship" among the two categories of offensive weapons as well as strategic defense, may offer a means of breaking the stalemate. By merging the negotiations on INF and strategic forces, it is said, the two sides might satisfy Moscow's insistence on including the British and French INF arsenals — totaling some 140 missiles armed with 420 warheads — in NATO's overall weapons count.[25] These would seem less significant if the entire Euromissile issue were to be considered in the context of the 10,000 or so strategic weapons possessed by both sides.

Soviet Foreign Minister Gromyko seemed to indicate that a merger might be acceptable. "Earlier we conducted talks separately on strategic arms and on intermediate-range arms — and the two sides then agreed to try to conduct them this way because it might be easier this way to find accords — while it has now become absolutely clear that it is impossible to hold talks and to try to reach agreement on strategic armaments without solving also the question of intermediate-range weapons," he said during his Jan. 13 interview on Soviet television.

Whether or not this statement reflects Soviet interest in the merger idea, Reagan administration officials are reportedly opposed. The inclusion of INF with strategic weapons may give the NATO allies, who are closely involved in the INF talks, too great a say in the formulation of the U.S. position on strategic weapons. Given the West Europeans' strong desire for an arms control agreement between the superpowers, it is said, the United States would come under pressure to make concessions on strategic weapons.

The administration appears determined to continue its buildup of these weapons and to be wavering on its promise to abide

---

[25] *The New York Times*, Feb. 1, 1985.

by the terms of the unratified SALT II treaty. Reagan said in 1981 that the United States would not exceed the limits the treaty imposed on strategic weapons so long as the Soviet Union did likewise. But the administration's recent report on Soviet non-compliance charged Moscow with several treaty violations, and Reagan on Jan. 26 for the first time indicated the United States may decide to ignore SALT II when a new, 24-missile-bearing Trident submarine — the USS *Alaska* — puts to sea next October. Under the treaty's terms, the administration would have to retire an older, 16-missile Poseidon submarine or dismantle eight land-based Minuteman II ICBMs when the Trident is completed. Adelman of the Arms Control and Disarmament Agency has said recommendations will be made to the White House in October on whether to continue to abide by SALT II.

Meanwhile, weapons systems in all three areas of the American nuclear "triad" are being modernized. In addition to the Trident, which is quieter and thus more difficult to detect than older submarines, the sea leg of the triad will soon be reinforced by the long-range, highly accurate D-5 (also called the Trident II) submarine-launched missile. The Tomahawk cruise missile is also slated for deployment on board some 100 surface ships and submarines by the end of the decade. The stealth bomber, designed to evade detection by enemy radar, and air-launched cruise missiles incorporating stealth technology are also due for completion by the early 1990s. The MX, whose fate may be decided as the talks get under way, is only one of several new developments strengthening the land-based missile force.

Negotiating 'Star Wars,' the Non-Agreement

Judging from the barrage of Soviet criticism, the Soviet Union can be expected to concentrate its negotiating stance on preventing the Strategic Defense Initiative from proceeding beyond the research stage now in progress. Announcing the program on March 23, 1983, Reagan hailed the SDI concept as nothing less than visionary: "What if free people could live secure in the knowledge that their security did not rest upon the threat of instant U.S. retaliation to deter a Soviet attack, that we could intercept and destroy strategic ballistic missiles before they reached our own soil or that of our allies?" The purpose of SDI, he said, was to strengthen deterrence. The feasibility of such a non-nuclear defense system was expected to be determined by the early 1990s.

According to official descriptions, SDI would constitute a "layered defense" using different technologies to destroy attacking missiles during each phase of the ballistic trajectory. An ICBM could be destroyed during its "boost phase" shortly after launch; during the "post-boost phase" before the warheads are released; in the "mid-course phase" while the released warheads are soaring through space; or during the "terminal phase" as they re-enter the atmosphere *(see graphic, p. 43)*. A panoply of exotic-sounding weapons utilizing lasers and mirrors and based both on the ground and in space — hence the "Star Wars" connection — are envisioned.

SDI supporters, including Kampelman, insist that it must not be used as a "bargaining chip," to be dispensed with in return for Soviet concessions. "Strategic defense would compensate for the inevitable difficulties of verification and for the absence of genuine trust by permitting some risk-taking in [arms control] agreements," Kampelman and two co-authors wrote in a controversial article published shortly after his appointment to the Geneva talks. "This is another reason why strategic defense should not be traded in the forthcoming negotiations in return for promises that can be broken at any time." [26]

Repeating the concerns expressed by some American scientists, Soviet officials and academics condemn SDI out of hand. ". . . [I]ts creation will certainly increase the danger of the first (pre-emptive) strike and the probability of making wrong decisions in a crisis situation," a group of Soviet scientists wrote in a study issued last year. "That is why strategic stability will be diminished, although the two sides will retain a rough parity in their strategic armaments." [27] Another Soviet commentator predicted that SDI will further escalate the arms race. "The other side cannot shut its eyes to these war preparations, of course," arms control analyst Alexei Fedorov wrote. "It will do everything to make the Pentagon realize that [Soviet] ballistic missiles have not become 'a heap of junk' while the U.S. offensive strategic potential hangs over it like the sword of Damocles." [28]

Some observers believe the Soviet Union plans to resume testing and deployment of its anti-satellite (ASAT) systems. Like SDI, ASAT involves space weaponry. But while SDI would use space- and ground-based weapons to destroy attacking missiles, ASAT would destroy only satellites, including SDI satellites and existing communications and spy satellites. The Soviet Union has had an ASAT program since the early 1970s. But

[26] Zbigniew Brzezinski, Robert Jastrow and Max M. Kampelman, "Defense in Space Is Not 'Star Wars'," *The New York Times Magazine*, Jan. 27, 1985, p. 47. Brzezinski was national security adviser to President Carter. Jastrow, a physicist at Dartmouth College, founded the Goddard Institute for Space Studies. Following his appointment as chief U.S. negotiator, Kampelman reportedly tried to have his name removed as the article's co-author but was turned down by the newspaper.
[27] Committee of Soviet Scientists for Peace against Nuclear Threat, "A Space-Based Anti-Missile System with Directed Energy Weapons: Strategic, Legal and Political Implications," Institute of Cosmic Research, All-Union Academy of Sciences, 1984.
[28] Alexei Fedorov, "Is the 'Star Wars' Program a Defense Plan?" undated, Novosti Press Agency.

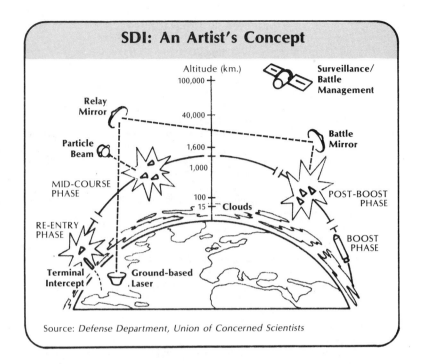

SDI: An Artist's Concept

Altitude (km.)

100,000

40,000

1,600

1,000

100

15 — Clouds

Surveillance/
Battle
Management

Relay
Mirror

Particle
Beam

Battle
Mirror

MID-COURSE
PHASE

POST-BOOST
PHASE

RE-ENTRY
PHASE

BOOST
PHASE

Terminal
Intercept

Ground-based
Laser

Source: *Defense Department, Union of Concerned Scientists*

after the United States began developing its own ASAT system, Russia in 1983 proposed a ban on further ASAT development.[29] No mention of such a ban has been made by the Soviets since October, leading some observers to believe they want to develop their system to counter SDI.

Because the eventual testing and deployment of the space-based components of SDI are prohibited by the terms of the 1972 ABM Treaty, negotiators involved in the space weapons category of talks in Geneva will discuss this as well as the alleged Soviet violations of that treaty. Meanwhile, some administration officials are openly discussing an approach to arms control that makes it hard to see why the negotiators should bother to meet in Geneva at all. In an article published just as the agenda for next month's talks was announced, ACDA Director Adelman wrote in support of "arms control without agreements."[30] According to this approach, each side would develop a strategic defense system, such as SDI, with the expectation that the other would do the same. President Reagan envisioned such a development when he offered to share SDI technology with the Soviet Union: if both sides constructed a viable strategic defense, he said, perhaps both would then dismantle their nuclear arsenals once and for all.

[29] The U.S. ASAT missile is designed to be launched in flight from an F-15 fighter aircraft. A congressionally imposed moratorium on space testing of the ASAT expires March 1, and the first test reportedly is set for June.
[30] Kenneth L. Adelman, "Arms Control With and Without Agreements," *Foreign Affairs*, winter 1984-85.

Selected Bibliography

Books

Goldblat, Jozef, *Agreements for Arms Control: A Critical Survey*, Stockholm International Peace Research Institute, 1982.
Gray, Colin S., *American Military Space Policy*, Abt Books, 1982.
Hecht, Jeff, *Beam Weapons*, Plenum Press, 1984.
Labrie, Roger P., ed., *SALT Handbook*, American Enterprise Institute, 1979.
National Academy of Sciences, *Nuclear Arms Control: Background and Issues*, National Academy Press, 1985.
Talbott, Strobe, *Deadly Gambits*, Alfred A. Knopf, 1984.
Union of Concerned Scientists, *The Fallacy of Star Wars*, Vintage Books, 1984.

Articles

Adelman, Kenneth L., "Arms Control With and Without Agreements," *Foreign Affairs*, winter 1984-85.
Brzezinski, Zbigniew, Robert Jastrow and Max M. Kampelman, "Defense in Space Is Not 'Star Wars'," *The New York Times Magazine*, Jan. 27, 1985.
Draper, Theodore, "Pie in the Sky," *The New York Review of Books*, Feb. 14, 1985.
Greb, G. Allen, and Gerald W. Johnson, "A History of Strategic Arms Limitations," *Bulletin of the Atomic Scientists*, January 1984.
Hedlin, Myron, "Moscow's Line on Arms Control," *Problems of Communism*, May-June 1984.
Lehrman, Lewis E., "The Case for Strategic Defense," *Policy Review*, winter 1985.
Newhouse, John, "Talks about Talks," *The New Yorker*, Dec. 31, 1984.
Nitze, Paul H., "Living With the Soviets," *Foreign Affairs*, winter 1984-85.

Reports and Studies

Carter, Ashton B., "Directed Energy Missile Defense in Space," Office of Technology Assessment, April 1984.
Congressional Budget Office, "An Analysis of Administration Strategic Arms Reduction and Modernization Proposals," March 1984.
Editorial Research Reports: "Reagan's Defense Buildup," 1984 Vol. I, p. 309; "West Germany's 'Missile' Election," 1983 Vol. I, p. 149; "Controlling Nuclear Proliferation," 1981 Vol. II, p. 509; "MX Missile Decision," 1981 Vol. I, p. 409.
International Institute for Strategic Studies, "The Military Balance 1984-1985," 1984.
U.S. Arms Control and Disarmament Agency, "Arms Control," September 1984.
U.S. Government Printing Office, "The President's Strategic Defense Initiative," January 1985.
U.S. Department of State, "Security and Arms Control: The Search for a More Stable Peace," October 1984.

Graphics: Illustration p. 21, Kathleen Ossenfort; photo p. 27, Bill Fitz-Patrick, The White House; photo p. 33, U.S. Air Force; illustration p. 43, Robert Redding.

GORBACHEV'S CHALLENGE

by

Mary H. Cooper

**Feb. 14
1 9 8 6**

Editor's Update: The inconclusive summit meeting in Iceland, Oct. 11-12, 1986, left Soviet-affairs analysts in the West wondering whether Mikhail S. Gorbachev's position had been weakened within the Kremlin by his inability to bring about an arms-control agreement. It was presumed that he had pushed hard for the meeting, even brushing aside harsh words from the United States over the Aug. 30 arrest of Nicholas S. Daniloff, Moscow correspondent for the magazine *U.S. News & World Report,* on spy charges. After strong U.S. protests, Daniloff was released and on Sept. 29 expelled from Russia, apparently in exchange for a Soviet U.N. official who had been arrested in New York City and charged with spying.

GORBACHEV'S CHALLENGE

MIKHAIL S. GORBACHEV will shortly complete his first year as leader of the Soviet Union. Recognized early as "a man in a hurry," Gorbachev, 54, has indeed accomplished a great deal since March 11, 1985, when he was named general secretary of the Communist Party. He has met with an American president at the first superpower summit in six years and placed his personal stamp on arms control negotiations. He has overhauled the Kremlin leadership, replacing older officials with men of his own generation. And he has initiated several bureaucratic and economic reforms aimed at improving the country's lagging economy.

It is still unclear whether Gorbachev's changes will prove to be more a matter of style or of substance. In any event, he has succeeded in creating an image different from his three immediate predecessors who were largely confined to the Kremlin by advanced age or illness. Gorbachev has exploited his relative youth, presenting himself as a vigorous leader capable of improving the Soviet way of life.

But the new leader may also be in a hurry to ensure his political survival. Even before his first anniversary at the top, Gorbachev will face a crucial test in the upcoming Soviet Communist Party Congress, a gathering of party delegates from all over the country held every five years. The congress, which begins Feb. 25, will elect a new Central Committee to represent it until the next congress and adopt a five-year plan, a set of production goals for the Soviet economy from 1986-90. This year the congress will also ratify a revised party program, a more general document defining Communist Party goals in all aspects of Soviet life.

Kremlin watchers will analyze both the congress pronouncements and comments in the Soviet media for signs that Gorbachev has indeed succeeded in consolidating his position or whether there may be challenges to his leadership. Indications about the feasibility of Gorbachev's economic reform proposals will also emerge from the congress. The congress will give Western analysts their best glimpse yet of his political standing within the Soviet Union.

Until now most appraisals of Gorbachev's performance have derived from his diplomatic initiatives. Even before he officially succeeded Konstantin U. Chernenko as party secretary last March, Gorbachev had impressed Western heads of state as a vigorous leader. British Prime Minister Margaret Thatcher called him "a man we can do business with" when he visited her country in December 1984. Although he was unable to reinvigorate the Western European anti-nuclear movement during his trip to France several months later, Gorbachev did reinforce Western perceptions of him as an effective and knowledgeable negotiator.

But it was his performance at the Geneva summit with Ronald Reagan last November that firmly established the new Kremlin leader's diplomatic credentials as well as his abilities as a formidable adversary in the superpower equation.[1] The first U.S.-Soviet summit since 1979 produced no breakthrough on nuclear arms control — Gorbachev continued to condition offensive weapons reductions on U.S. abandonment of the Strategic Defense Initiative (SDI) — and revealed no tangible shift in Kremlin thinking on the competitive nature of U.S.-Soviet relations.

The summit did, however, mark the resumption of dialogue between the two countries' leaders. They revived cultural and scientific exchange agreements that had been suspended in 1979 following the Soviet intervention in Afghanistan. Taking advantage of the apparent warming of bilateral relations, a group of some 400 U.S. business leaders met in Moscow in December with Gorbachev's trade representatives in the hope of improving commercial ties as well. Reagan and Gorbachev agreed to meet again this year and next. If he accepts the administration's invitation, Gorbachev will be the first Soviet leader to visit the United States since 1973.[2]

Gorbachev's latest diplomatic coup was a sweeping arms control proposal to eliminate all nuclear weapons by the turn of the century and obtain "a universal accord that such weapons should never again come into being." Presented Jan. 15, on the eve of the fourth round of U.S.-Soviet arms control negotiations in Geneva, the initiative marked a clear departure from the more passive response to American proposals that has characterized the Soviet negotiating stance in the past. Gorbachev clearly caught Washington by surprise: four weeks later, the administration still had offered no formal response except to reject once again a Soviet-supported moratorium on nuclear testing.

[1] For background, see "U.S.-Soviet Summitry," *E.R.R.*, 1985 Vol. II, pp. 821-840; and "Arms Control Negotiations," *E.R.R.*, 1985 Vol. I, pp. 145-168.
[2] The Soviets have not formally responded to Reagan's invitation to come in June or July but have indicated a preference for a September meeting and have conditioned the visit on progress in negotiations on medium-range missiles. According to the summit communiqué Reagan is to visit the Soviet Union in 1987. Leonid I. Brezhnev visited Richard Nixon in Washington in June 1973 at the height of détente.

Gorbachev Biography

Mikhail Sergeevich Gorbachev was born March 2, 1931, to peasants of Russian nationality in the region of Stavropol in the North Caucasus. The first Soviet leader to begin his political career after Stalin's reign of terror, Gorbachev did not escape the ravages of World War II and German occupation, during which he lost his father. Although his early education was interrupted by war, Gorbachev entered Moscow State University in 1950 at the age of 19. He joined the Communist Party in 1952 and participated in activities of the Komsomol, the party youth organization.

After receiving his law degree in 1955 Gorbachev returned to Stavropol where he worked full time in the Komsomol before moving to the party in 1962. In 1967 he received the title of agronomist-economist from the Stavropol Agricultural Institute.

Under the tutelage of Fedor Kulakov, first secretary of the Stavropol party organization, he rose quickly through the ranks and assumed his mentor's post at the relatively young age of 39 after Kulakov had been promoted to a post in Moscow. Gorbachev was named a full member of the Central Committee the following year, 1971.

Upon Kulakov's death in 1978, Gorbachev, now 47, was called to take his place in the Central Committee Secretariat to oversee agriculture. By 1980 he was also a voting member of the Politburo, becoming the youngest member of both ruling bodies. Gorbachev continued his rise throughout the succession battles that followed Brezhnev's death in 1982. Under Andropov he was given oversight responsibility for the whole economy and lower-level party appointments.

After nominating Chernenko as head of state on Andropov's death, Gorbachev effectively became second in command, extending his responsibilities to oversee foreign affairs and ideology. He led a government delegation to Britain in December 1984. Three months later, at the age of 54, he assumed the Kremlin leadership.

The Soviet proposal contains several new elements, notably the elimination of all nuclear weapons from Europe, including its own medium-range missiles as well as U.S. Pershing IIs and cruise missiles, within the next five to eight years. The Soviets have also dropped their longstanding demand that independently installed British and French medium-range nuclear weapons be counted as part of the U.S. European arsenal. Gorbachev is now calling for a freeze on these weapons. Moscow appears to have yielded on its previous insistence that no research be conducted in the field of strategic defense, as a condition for arms reduction.

Initial Reforms to Modernize Economy

While his diplomatic initiatives have received the widest attention in the West, Gorbachev's most significant moves have centered on domestic policy. As soon as he was named party chief, he began calling for economic reform in more strident terms than any Soviet leader in recent memory. Within three months, he had initiated a nationwide campaign to tighten worker discipline and rid the nation of alcoholism, recognized as a leading cause of low productivity. Gorbachev also announced plans to divert investment away from the construction of new factories and into the retooling of existing facilities as well as machine-building. These changes, he predicted, would allow a 4 percent annual growth rate of the economy without cutting back on military or social spending.

Gorbachev has also called for decentralization of certain aspects of economic planning. Initially introduced under Yuri V. Andropov in January 1984, the program would reduce the number of specific production targets for individual enterprises, allow their managers more power to determine wages and investments, and offer wage incentives as an inducement to workers to boost productivity and correct what Gorbachev called an "extremely confused, cumbersome and inefficient" system of incentives.

The decentralization program would not, he emphasized, diminish the role of central planning in the Soviet economy. Gosplan — the state planning agency — would continue to control decisions regarding investments, prices and production targets above the enterprise level. Rather, Gorbachev has said he would like to reduce the vast bureaucracy that lies between the strategic planners in Moscow and the individual enterprises.

Gorbachev's early emphasis on the economy was also reflected in the draft party program that will be before the congress this month. A principal goal is "making the Soviet economy the most sophisticated and powerful in the world." The Politburo — the country's top policy-making body — in October announced the creation of a new government bureau to oversee machine-building, one of the sectors Gorbachev has singled out for intensive investment. Another bureaucratic change was made in November when five agricultural ministries were merged into the new State Agro-Industrial Committee, charged with improving the country's lagging agricultural production.

The results of Gorbachev's first-year reforms are mixed. The partial decentralization of economic planning and the use of incentives — while far more limited in scope than those introduced in recent years in China and Hungary — have begun to yield positive results in certain areas and industries, particularly the notoriously inefficient services sector.[3] An especially successful experiment has been the distribution among the workers of all receipts above an enterprise's target, a modified form of profit-sharing that may be applied more widely.

But greater productivity, especially if it comes through increased automation and the development of the Soviet Union's high-technology sector, may lead to a loss of jobs, as it has in the West. The recent bureaucratic reorganization has already forced some 3,000 officials out of their jobs, prompting the first acknowledged use of unemployment insurance in the Soviet Union since the 1930s, when Stalin announced that joblessness had been eradicated from Soviet society. A government economist now predicts that current plans to modernize the economy may cost between 13 million and 19 million people their jobs.[4]

The tentative loosening of central control over the nation's economy has not been matched by a relaxation of state control over dissidents or emigration policies. While several Soviet citizens married to Americans have been allowed to join their families in the West since the November summit, there has been no significant increase in the number of Jews and other Soviet citizens allowed to emigrate.[5] Although noted human-rights activist Anatoly Scharansky left the Soviet Union Feb. 11, his release was part of an East-West spy swap and did not appear to indicate a shift in emigration policy.

Personnel Changes in Party Bureaucracy

If he is to reform the economy, Gorbachev must have the allegiance of the officials charged with running it. The most drastic change he has brought about over the past year has been the replacement of party and government personnel, giving credence to the comment Foreign Minister Andrei A. Gromyko reportedly made when he nominated Gorbachev to the position of general secretary: "Comrades, this man has a nice smile, but he's got iron teeth." Since coming to power, Gorbachev is

---

[3] For an example of services reform, see *The New York Times*, Jan. 21, 1985.

[4] Vladimir Kostakov, *Sovetskaya Kultura*, Jan. 4, 1986, cited in *The New York Times*, Jan. 9, 1986.

[5] More than 51,000 Jews emigrated in 1979. According to the New York-based National Conference on Soviet Jewry, only 1,139 Jews left in 1985, and 896 the previous year.

Boris N. Yeltsin   Nikolai I. Ryzhkov

thought to have replaced 45 of 159 regional party first secretaries and four of 15 republics' first secretaries. In addition, 19
of 59 government ministers have been replaced, while 37 of 113
seats on the Council of Ministers have been changed.[6]

The congress will elect a new Central Committee, usually
numbering around 300, and it appears certain that a clear
majority will support Gorbachev. This body, responsible for
implementing policy decided by the Politburo, has already seen
greater turnover under Gorbachev than it did during
Andropov's 15-month rule or Chernenko's 13 months in power.[7]
Many of Gorbachev's targets for early retirement are holdovers
from the Brezhnev era. Leonid I. Brezhnev, who emerged from
the collective leadership that succeeded Nikita S. Khrushchev
in 1964 to rule the Soviet Union until his death in November
1982, has increasingly been singled out in the Soviet press as an
unnamed "former leader" who allowed corruption to flourish
among party and government officials. As another sign of official distancing from the Brezhnev era, the late leader's son
Yuri was demoted from his position in the Ministry of Foreign
Trade in January.

The most visible evidence of Gorbachev's bloodless purge is
the Politburo. Just one month after gaining power, Gorbachev
added three new members: Yegor K. Ligachev, party secretary
in charge of high-level appointments and ideology, effectively
second in command to Gorbachev; Nikolai I. Ryzhkov, initially
charged with setting economic reform policy and later named

---

[6] Estimates reported in *The Washington Post*, Jan. 26, 1986.
[7] By the end of 1985, Gorbachev had retired at least 26 Central Committee members and
promoted 30 people to positions that make them eligible for membership in February.
Andropov retired 21 members and named 26 new members, while Chernenko retired just
eight and placed 13 on the Central Committee. See *Soviet World Outlook*, Advanced
International Studies Institute, Dec. 1, 1985.

premier; and Viktor M. Chebrikov, head of the K.G.B. Like Gorbachev, all three were protégés of Andropov and supported his economic reforms and discipline campaign, which Gorbachev has revived.

In a personnel change of special interest to the United States, Andrei A. Gromyko, who presided over the postwar course of U.S.-Soviet relations during 28 years as foreign minister, was named president of the Soviet Union at a July session of the Supreme Soviet, or parliament. Although his new title carries little weight, Gromyko retains his seat on the Politburo, where he will continue to have a voice in policy making. The new foreign minister is Eduard A. Shevardnadze, 57, who is credited with weeding out corruption as party secretary in his native Georgia, one of 15 republics that make up the Soviet Union. Although he had no previous foreign policy experience, Shevardnadze has impressed Western observers as a capable diplomat whose relaxed demeanor is in keeping with Gorbachev's own style of leadership.

The same occasion saw the retirement from the Politburo of Grigory V. Romanov, the Leningrad party chief and Brezhnev protégé who is thought to have posed the greatest challenge to Gorbachev's rise to power. Ryzhkov replaced Nikolai A. Tikhonov, the 80-year-old Soviet premier, in October, and Moscow party chief Viktor V. Grishin, another member of the old guard, was replaced in December by Boris Yeltsin, a Gorbachev ally who has strongly criticized Grishin's handling of city affairs.

Economic Concerns

THE BUREAUCRATIC stagnation that set in during the Brezhnev era may well be the most difficult challenge Gorbachev faces. "Leonid Brezhnev made the Soviet Union a true superpower," William G. Hyland, editor of *Foreign Affairs*, wrote. "But there was a price. Stability became stagnation: the economy ran down; the leadership began to atrophy." [8] Andropov, the one leader who even attempted to invigorate the economy through bureaucratic reforms, died before he had the chance to carry them out. Gorbachev, his political heir, has revived some of these initiatives.

The need for change has been openly recognized in the Soviet Union in recent years. According to a widely circulated report by Soviet economists, economic growth fell from an annual rate

---

[8] William G. Hyland, "The Gorbachev Succession," *Foreign Affairs*, spring 1985, p. 801.

of 7.5 percent in the late 1960s to 2.5 percent in the first part of this decade.[9] By the first quarter of 1985 it had sunk to 2 percent.

The Soviet Union has long depended heavily on oil and gas exports to earn foreign currency needed to pay for vital imports, especially grains. Although last year's harvest was not as poor as those of recent years, food production continues to lag behind consumption needs. The currency situation will likely grow worse with the recent fall in world oil prices. The Soviets have for several years experienced a drop in oil production due to poor management, inadequate transportation facilities and the depletion of reserves in the Tyumen region of western Siberia, where over half the nation's oil is produced.[10] Currency earnings from exports, over half of which is oil, fell from a $4 billion surplus in 1984 to a deficit of $6 billion in 1985.

The decline in oil production has hurt the Soviet Union's Eastern European economic partners who have relied on cheap Soviet oil to fuel their factories.[11] Since 1982 the Soviets have curtailed their supply of oil to Eastern Europe and have stepped up their demand for high-quality finished goods in exchange for Soviet energy and raw materials. At a December meeting of Comecon, the Soviet-dominated Council for Mutual Economic Assistance, these demands were contained in a 15-year agreement that also called for energy conservation and a doubling of labor productivity in the member nations. For some, notably Poland, the diversion of high-quality exports away from Western markets will make it even harder to obtain the hard currency earnings they need to pay off foreign debts.

Recent efforts to improve the living conditions of Soviet citizens have begun to pay off, according to official accounts. Wages are said to have increased in all sectors, while state subsidies of consumer items, housing, transportation and social services have continued to hold down the cost of many goods and services. But the system's ability to meet Soviet consumer demands is limited to essential goods and services. According to one analysis, a loaf of white bread costs about the same for a worker in Moscow as for his counterpart in Washington, D.C., in terms of equivalent work time. The Muscovite enjoys a clear advantage in terms of rent (one-quarter the Washingtonian's cost) and subway fare (one-half), but a color television or a

[9] "The Novosibirsk Report," *Survey* (London), spring 1984.
[10] Soviet oil output has fallen steadily from 4.31 billion barrels in 1983 to 4.29 billion in 1984 to 4.16 billion last year. See *The Washington Post*, Jan. 31, 1986.
[11] For background, see John M. Kramer, "Soviet-CEMA Energy Ties," *Problems of Communism*, July-August 1985. In addition to the Soviet Union, the members of Comecon are Bulgaria, Czechoslovakia, East Germany, Hungary, Poland, Romania, Cuba, Mongolia and Vietnam.

Soviet Consumer Goods and Services
Planned Production Growth, 1986-2000

	Average Annual Increase	
	1986-1990	1991-2000
All non-food goods	5.4%	3.3-3.9%
Light industry	3.9	5.3
Textiles	2.6-4.1	1.8-3.1
Knitwear	4.1-4.9	3.7-4.4
Footwear	2.8	1.2
Consumer goods	6.4	3.9-4.4
Radios	3.1-4.8	1.8-3.2
Color TVs	10.9-11.8	3.2-4.1
Refrigerators	1.9-3.5	1.3-2.9
Sewing machines	10.8	3.4
Washing machines	5.1-7.0	0.5-1.6
Printed matter	4.2	3.3
Consumer-purchased services	5.4-7.0	4.1-5.9

Source: Wharton Econometric Forecasting Associates based on the Soviet Union's "Comprehensive Program for the Development of Consumer Goods Production and the Service Sphere for the Years 1986-2000."

small car costs over 10 times what it does here, while a bottle of aspirin is 50 times as expensive.[12]

Setting New Growth, Productivity Goals

The Kremlin last October published a plan to increase investments in non-food consumer goods and services in order to raise the quality and variety of goods and improve living standards. The plan envisions a 5.4 percent annual growth rate in consumer goods and a 5.4 to 7 percent rate for consumer-paid services, well over the 4 percent growth forecast for national income *(see box, above)*. While the program provides few indications as to how this growth will be achieved, the timing of its release shortly before the party congress suggests that this sector will receive greater emphasis than it has in the past and will figure highly in Gorbachev's campaign to raise labor productivity. "If more and better consumer goods and services are available for purchase, the incentive value of wages will increase, and wage policy will be a more effective instrument for increasing labor productivity," Daniel Bond of Wharton Econometric Forecasting Associates reasoned.[13]

---

[12] Mervyn Matthews, "Poverty in the Soviet Union," *The Wilson Quarterly,* autumn 1985.
[13] Daniel L. Bond, "Soviet Plan for Consumer Goods & Services," *Centrally Planned Economies Current Analysis,* Nov. 21, 1985, p. 10.

The two principal documents that must be ratified by the party congress are the party program and the five-year plan. The draft party program, the first to be issued since 1961, presents in general terms the economic goals the new leadership has set for the country. It calls for Soviet economic output to double by the year 2000 — the equivalent of a 4.7 percent annual growth rate for the period — to be achieved largely through the application of new technologies and scientific breakthroughs to Soviet industry and agriculture.

This goal is spelled out in detail in the 12th five-year plan, released Nov. 9. The first draft of the plan, drawn up under Chernenko, was returned to the planners last May and rewritten. The current, more optimistic five-year plan, bears Gorbachev's stamp. The new plan's "central objective" is "to increase the growth rates and efficiency of the economy on the basis of accelerating scientific and technological progress, the technical modernisation and re-equipment of production, intensive utilisation of the created production potential, perfecting the system of management and the economic mechanism and achieving on this basis a further rise in the Soviet people's well-being." [14]

In contrast to recent five-year plans, whose growth targets fell to reflect the decline in actual output, the new plan foresees a slowdown only in industrial output. National income, agricultural production, consumption and investment are all expected to increase. Investment targets confirm the party's emphasis on modernization through the "development of electronics, nuclear power engineering, comprehensive automation, production engineering and the processing of new materials." The plan predicts that high technology will produce "no less than two-thirds of the increment in social labour productivity" to be achieved by 1990.[15] Output in machine-building and metalworking — sectors that include computer equipment, robotics and other machinery that allow for automation in industry — is slated to increase by 40 to 45 percent.

Modernization is also expected to raise agricultural production by 14 to 16 percent a year. Considered an overly ambitious target by Western analysts, the gains in food output are to be obtained with better farming techniques and crops improved through biotechnology and genetic engineering.

Potential Opposition to Economic Plans

The party congress is likely to ratify both the party program and the five-year plan without major modifications. But the

[14] "Guidelines for the Economic and Social Development of the USSR for 1986-1990 and for the Period Ending in 2000," Novosti Press Agency Publishing House (Moscow, 1985), p. 21.
[15] *Ibid*, p. 26.

traditional show of approval for the new leadership's economic goals may not accurately reflect dissent within the party.

Opposition to elements of the new plan may come from ideological conservatives and the military. Since his elevation to the Politburo, Yegor Ligachev has countered Gorbachev's enthusiastic predictions of a reinvigorated economy with more conservative pronouncements of his own. In particular, he has cautioned that any economic reforms will occur "within the framework of scientific social-ism" and will not entail the "shifts toward a market econ-omy or private enterprise" that have marked China's re-cent economic policy.[16] These comments may be aimed at re-assuring members of the older generation of the new leader-ship's adherence to the central tenets of Marxism-Leninism, but given Ligachev's position as second in command, they could be construed as a veiled warning against proceeding too fast on economic reforms.

Yegor K. Ligachev

The Soviet military may take a dim view of Gorbachev's reform proposals because they divert investment funds from the defense economy. Reagan's Strategic Defense Initiative, based on esoteric technology that has only begun to be developed in the United States, represents a huge challenge to the Soviet Union's relatively backward technological base. If the United States does not abandon SDI as part of an arms control agree-ment, Gorbachev will come under increasing pressure from his own high command to pour more money into defense.

Signs of the Soviet military's cool attitude toward Gorbachev are evident, ranging from a pessimistic appraisal of the Novem-ber summit by Marshal Sergei F. Akhromeyev, chief of the general staff, to the stiffly formal greeting given Gorbachev on his return to Moscow by his defense minister, Marshal Sergei L. Sokolov. Unlike his predecessor, the late Marshal Dmitri F. Ustinov, who was a full member of the Politburo, Sokolov is only a candidate, or non-voting, member.

Despite the military's apparently diminished political power under Gorbachev, defense accounts for a huge segment of Soviet

---

[16] Quoted in *The New York Times*, Dec. 23, 1985.

economic activity, and the bureaucracy responsible for it cannot be ignored. The Kremlin does not reveal data on defense spending, but the CIA estimates that military spending has absorbed some 12 to 14 percent of the Soviet gross national product over the past two decades of the arms race. "High priority is manifest in other ways, too," explained David Holloway, a military analyst at the University of Edinburgh, Scotland. "The defense sector receives the best machinery and instruments, and the best workers and managers; it can commandeer scarce supplies from civilian industry; and planning bodies will deal more quickly with its requests and orders." [17]

Foreign Policy Goals

BECAUSE IT HAS RECEIVED priority treatment in the allocation of resources, the Soviet military is considered to be on a technological par with the West in conventional and nuclear weapons production. Despite Reagan administration claims that the Soviet military has been conducting research on its own version of SDI,[18] most Western analysts say the development of electronic and laser components needed to construct such a complex "shield" against an offensive nuclear attack would place a tremendous strain on Soviet technological capabilities.

According to a report released by the Paris-based Organization for Economic Cooperation and Development (OECD), "[t]here is a striking technological gap between the USSR and the West in the development of computers.... In technical capabilities and performance, currently produced Soviet general-purpose computers are similar to those marketed in the United States a decade earlier." [19]

U.S. trade policy toward the Soviet Union has been aimed at maintaining this gap. As a member of the Coordinating Committee for Multilateral Export Controls — CoCom[20] — the United States embargoes or limits the transfer of military items, nuclear reactors and their components as well as a wide range of machinery and equipment made for civilian use but having the

---

[17] Holloway testified Dec. 5, 1985, on Soviet military trends before the House Foreign Affairs Subcommittee on Europe and the Middle East.
[18] See, for example, "Soviet Strategic Defense Programs," Department of Defense and Department of State, October 1985.
[19] Morris Bornstein, "East-West Technology Transfer: The Transfer of Western Technology to the USSR," (OECD, 1985), p. 39.
[20] CoCom includes all NATO members except Iceland and Spain — Belgium, Britain, Canada, Denmark, France, Greece, Italy, Luxembourg, the Netherlands, Norway, Portugal, Turkey, the United States and West Germany — as well as Japan.

Soviet Leadership Organization

Communist Party of the Soviet Union

Communist Party Congress: Some 5,000 party delegates from all over the country normally meet every five years to ratify five-year plans and other party programs and to elect members of the Central Committee. Officially the supreme authority in the party. This year's congress will be the 27th such meeting.

Central Committee: About 300 members elected by the party congress to represent it between sessions. The Central Committee meets about every six months to approve policy formulated by the top bodies, the Central Committee Secretariat and the Politburo, whose members it elects.

Central Committee Secretariat: Headed by the party's general secretary, currently Gorbachev, the Secretariat is the party's executive branch, made up of about 10 officials charged with overseeing various facets of the country's political and economic life.

Politburo: Responsible for formulating policy, the Politburo consists of about 10 full, or voting, members and several candidate, or non-voting, members. It is headed by the general secretary and may include other Secretariat members.

Government Organization

Council of Ministers: Top governing body, charged with carrying out policy decisions made by the party leadership. Its chairman is the head of government.

Supreme Soviet of the U.S.S.R.: Like the Central Committee, the country's bicameral legislature meets twice a year. It has no policy-making role, however, and passes into law proposals made by the party leadership. Members are elected every five years.

Presidium: Government administrative body representing the Supreme Soviet between meetings, headed by the president. Below these three bodies, various ministries, state committees and agencies complete the government structure.

---

potential for military application. Computer technology, industrial machinery and electrical equipment fall within the last category of goods the West tries to keep out of Soviet hands. The United States also withholds most-favored-nation status, or favorable tariff treatment, from the Soviet Union and all its Comecon partners except Hungary and Romania.[21] An additional law, the Jackson-Vanik amendment, prohibits the Soviet Union from obtaining favorable tariff treatment as long as it denies Soviet Jews the right to emigrate to Israel.

---

[21] The Trade Agreements Extension Act of 1951 denied most communist nations most-favored-nation (MFN) status. Hungary (1978), Romania (1975) and China (1980) were exempted under a provision of the Trade Act of 1974 allowing communist countries whose emigration policies are deemed sufficiently liberal to obtain MFN status.

Gorbachev has made relaxation of U.S. trade restrictions with his nation a high-priority item in superpower relations. Addressing the delegation of U.S. businessmen in Moscow to discuss broader trade ties, Gorbachev said Dec. 10 that until the United States lifts its trade restrictions, "there will be no normal development of Soviet-U.S. trade and other economic ties on a large scale. This is regrettable but we are not going to beg the United States for anything." As an example of the American "policy of boycotts, embargoes, 'punishments' and broken contracts," Gorbachev complained that "the volume of U.S. imports from the U.S.S.R. is roughly equal to what your country imports from the Republic of Ivory Coast."

Despite its growing trade deficit with the world as a whole, the United States does in fact enjoy a surplus with the Soviet Union. According to the Commerce Department, U.S. imports from the Soviet Union totaled a mere $410 million in 1985, while the United States exported $2.15 billion to the Soviet Union. Most of these exports were agricultural goods, particularly corn.

For all Gorbachev's complaints of U.S. unfairness, the prospect of increased East-West trade presents him with a dilemma. He needs the West's advanced technology to meet his goals. But any significant opening to the West may expose the Soviet economy to the potentially destabilizing rigors of competition that the nation has guarded against by limiting its trade relations to the other planned economies of Comecon. When it comes to economic reform, wrote Jerry Hough, a well-regarded Soviet analyst, "... the industrial managers are ambivalent: they would support a change in social policy and a widening of their prerogatives vis-à-vis the workers ('decentralization' is often a code word for this), but they have no desire for the harsh discipline of the market, let alone for the pleasure of competing with Toyota." By broadening commercial ties with the outside world, the leadership also risks losing its grip on Soviet society. "While it would be advantageous to have Tadzhik salesmen selling Soviet computers in Teheran," Hough queried, "what ideas would they bring home, especially when they studied the local culture enough to advertise effectively?" [22]

Shift Away From East-West Policy Focus

The Reagan administration has announced no plans to request significant changes in trade restrictions, prompting Gorbachev to say Dec. 10 that "if the United States persists in its current policy, we will produce what we need on our own or buy it elsewhere." The search for more cooperative trading

[22] Jerry F. Hough, "Gorbachev's Strategy," *Foreign Affairs*, fall 1985, p. 42.

partners may explain some foreign policy shifts evident since Gorbachev came to power. The replacement of Gromyko with Shevardnadze, some analysts say, may signal a shift in focus from preoccupation with U.S.-Soviet relations to a broader approach, with special emphasis on Asia.

Shevardnadze visited Japan in January, the first time a Soviet foreign minister had visited the Asian economic giant in 10 years. Enemies during World War II, the two countries have never signed a peace treaty because of a dispute over four Soviet-occupied islands north of Japan. Although the visit did not produce a resolution of the territorial dispute or a long-term economic cooperation agreement, it may have opened the way for improved relations between the two countries and increased Soviet access to Japan's advanced technology.

Eduard A. Shevardnadze

The new Kremlin leadership has also continued the thaw in relations with China initiated by Andropov. The "three obstacles" identified by China — the presence of Soviet troops along the border separating the two nations, the Soviet presence in Afghanistan and the occupation of Cambodia by Moscow's ally Vietnam — still prevent the complete normalization of relations. For their part, the Soviets distrust China's economic modernization campaign and opening to the West. Because the two nations' communist parties have no official ties, the appearance of a Chinese delegation at the Soviet party congress would be seen as a sign of reconciliation.

Gorbachev has been less successful on other fronts. While he maintains good relations with India, neither Indian Prime Minister Rajiv Gandhi nor the other leaders of the Asian democracies have shown enthusiasm for a Soviet proposal to form a regional security council. The plan is widely seen as an effort to create tensions between the United States and its Asian allies.

The Kremlin's activities in the Middle East have also had mixed results. After establishing diplomatic relations with the sultanate of Oman and the United Arab Emirates in an effort to improve its standing among the moderate Arab nations, Gorbachev suffered a diplomatic setback with the outbreak in mid-January of civil war in Soviet-backed South Yemen. Although the rebellion was settled by early February with the succession of another Moscow-supported leader, the incident clearly caught the Kremlin by surprise and unprepared to control events in its closest ally in the region.

Perhaps as a result of his emphasis on domestic issues, Gorbachev seems to have adopted a more cautious foreign policy in general than his predecessors, especially Brezhnev, who spoke at length at the last party congress in 1981 ·of Soviet commitment to Third World national liberation movements. Soviet efforts to gain footholds in sub-Saharan Africa and Latin America have proved costly and often ineffective, however, and Gorbachev may have decided to weigh such efforts against needs closer to home.[23] Although Soviet troops in Afghanistan launched a series of offensives against U.S-supported resistance forces last year, Gorbachev told the Supreme Soviet last November that he seeks a political settlement of the six-year war there and the eventual withdrawal of Soviet forces.

New Implications for U.S. Policy Decisions

The signs of change emanating from the Kremlin mean that the United States faces fundamental policy decisions in the areas of trade and arms control. Some observers say the West should do all it can to exacerbate Soviet economic troubles. ". . . [B]y denying to the Soviet bloc various forms of economic aid, [the West] can help intensify the formidable pressures which are being exerted on their creaky economies," wrote Richard Pipes, professor of history at Harvard University. "This will push them in the direction of general liberalization as well as accommodation with the West, since this is the only way of reducing military expenditures and gaining access to Western help in modernization." [24]

The Reagan administration has been divided over the issue. Some White House officials support legislation that would authorize the president to cut off commercial bank loans to Soviet-bloc nations. In December, Secretary of State George P. Shultz accused them of "wanting to start an economic war against the Soviet Union." [25] The bill is aimed at preventing actions such as last November's agreement by a group of U.S. lenders to extend the Soviet Union a $400 million, low-interest loan. Earlier last year American banks had led international syndicates that lent the Soviets $200 million and lent East Germany $1.1 billion.

---

[23] For an analysis, see Charles Wolf, Jr., "The Costs of the Soviet Empire," *Science*, Nov. 29, 1985.
[24] Richard Pipes, "Can the Soviet Union Reform?" *Foreign Policy*, fall 1984, p. 61.
[25] Quoted in *The Wall Street Journal*, Jan. 15, 1986.

SCIENCE WARS

OVER STAR WARS

by

William Sweet

**Sept. 19
1 9 8 6**

Scientists Divided Over Star Wars

The cuts that Congress has proposed in President Reagan's Strategic Defense Initiative (SDI) or "Star Wars" program signal a new mood on Capitol Hill. In 1984 and 1985, buoyed by the President's enthusiasm and the optimism expressed by SDI officials and scientists, Congress approved sharp funding increases for the program.[1] This year, however, the budget request for SDI took a beating in both the Senate and House Armed Services committees. While Congress is considered unlikely to enact a fiscal 1987 budget before the November congressional elections, it almost certainly will settle eventually on a figure of about $3.5 billion for Star Wars — about $1.3 billion less than Reagan requested.[2] Still, many members of Congress complain that even that cut is not deep enough. Last spring, 48 senators signed a letter saying that the SDI budget should be held to 3 percent over its 1986 level.

More important than the exact magnitude of the cuts, in the estimation of a Hill aide who has followed the fortunes of SDI

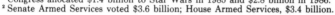

[1] Congress allocated $1.4 billion to Star Wars in 1985 and $2.8 billion in 1986.
[2] Senate Armed Services voted $3.6 billion; House Armed Services, $3.4 billion.

In the latest Star Wars test, a sensor-equipped satellite tracked and destroyed another satellite by colliding with it.

closely, is a new wariness in Congress about the fast-paced, expensive program. At a time of mounting interest about whether the president might accept restrictions on the Star Wars program in exchange for a Soviet agreement to make deep cuts in offensive missiles, SDI officials no longer exude confidence that their claims about the effectiveness of proposed missile defense systems will be uncritically accepted in Congress. Typical of the new mood on the Hill was the statement made by Sen. Daniel J. Evans, R-Wash., on June 19, when a petition from 1,400 scientists opposed to SDI was presented to Congress. "Clearly there are powerful reasons to conduct a healthy ballistic missile defense program," Evans said. However, he added, "these possibilities do not militate in favor of a precipitously paced program. We need to look no further than the waste and abuse in recent military spending to find reasons for prudence in SDI funding."

Evans' statement focuses on the fiscal situation, surely an important factor to an extremely cost-conscious Congress in the first year of Gramm-Rudman-Hollings budget cuts. Another factor contributing to the new cautiousness about the Star Wars program is the *Challenger* space shuttle disaster and the string of missile mishaps that ensued. The accidents, which left the United States temporarily without the capability to lift any large payload into space, raised the question of when it would be possible to launch the components for a huge missile defense system, assuming an effective system could be built. The disasters also raised questions about the reliability of technological systems in general, undermined the notion that the United States could do anything it tried to do and tarnished the reputation of Air Force Lt. Gen. James A. Abrahamson, who ran the shuttle program before taking over as head of the SDI program in April 1984.

Adding to Congress' skepticism about the Star Wars program has been testimony from thousands of reputable scientists, mostly physicists and computer experts, that they do not believe an effective anti-missile system could be developed in the foreseeable future. Robert Park, public affairs director for the American Physical Society (APS) in Washington, said he thinks that the overwhelming factor in changing Congress' mood "has been the reaction from the scientific community." [3] It is "obvious from the budget action that congressional opposition to Star Wars has been stiffening, and I think in general it is the scientific community that has produced that," Park said. Commenting on reports that many scientists have dropped in on their members of Congress to express opposition to Star Wars, Park said that this has indeed had an impact

---

[3] APS has 37,000 members and is the largest association representing U.S. physicists.

because "scientists don't often do that."

As the lobbyist for the main organization representing U.S. physicists, Park may be overstating their influence — and understating the extent to which they are willing to lobby personally to promote their interests. But there is no denying that the movement among scientists against Star Wars

Nobel laureate Hans A. Bethe coauthored a report concluding that Star Wars would be costly and vulnerable to attack.

has been an unusual phenomenon, unexpected and strikingly spontaneous. Zellman Warshaft, an electrical engineer at Cornell University who has participated in the movement against Star Wars, calls it "unprecedented" and a "watershed." [4]

Early Star Wars Critics Were Physicists

If the opposition to Star Wars among scientists seems now to be a virtual grass-roots mass movement, it was not always that way. Debate originally was confined to a small circle of physicists. Soon after Reagan proposed in March 1983 to launch a crash program to render nuclear weapons "impotent and obsolete," the first reactions came mainly from physicists who were recognized experts on arms control and had well-established positions on missile-defense systems. In 1984, Sidney Drell, associate director of the Stanford Linear Accelerator Center and current president of the American Physical Society, did a study with colleagues at the Stanford Center for International Security and Arms Control, in which they found that the SDI program could not be reconciled with the 1972 Treaty on Anti-Ballistic Missile (ABM) Systems. [5] The treaty prohibits the development, testing or deployment of ABM systems launched from sea, air or space.

Also in 1984, Hans A. Bethe of Cornell University and Richard L. Garwin of International Business Machines Corp. (IBM) were among the authors of a study sponsored by the Union of Concerned Scientists (UCS). It concluded that any conceivable space-based missile-defense system would require deployment

---

[4] Quoted in Seth Shulman, "Stopping Star Wars," *Science for the People*, January-February 1986, p. 11.

[5] See Sidney D. Drell, Philip J. Farley and David Holloway, *The Reagan Strategic Defense Initiative: A Technical, Political and Arms Control Assessment*, Ballinger, 1984.

of an extremely large number of very expensive space stations, which in turn would be highly vulnerable to attack by space-based mines.[6] Bethe is a Nobel prize-winning physicist who headed the theory division in the Manhattan Project, the project that produced the first atomic bomb; Garwin is a respected veteran of the H-bomb programs who is consulted frequently by the government on weapons development issues.

The position adopted by elder scientific statesmen like Bethe, Drell and Garwin was greatly resented by some young scientists working on exotic new Star Wars technologies and by their mentor, Edward Teller. Teller, a key figure in the design of the first hydrogen bomb, told William Broad of *The New York Times* in May 1984 that Bethe "sees the future in a too easy manner. He was there at the birth of quantum mechanics [the current theory of the atom] and he was there when we constructed the first atomic bomb. Yet he now says there won't be anything new under the sun." [7]

In December 1984 Robert Jastrow of Dartmouth College, a former National Aeronautics and Space Administration (NASA) official and strong supporter of Star Wars, wrote an article for *Commentary* magazine taking issue with the UCS report on many technical grounds and accusing physicists like Garwin of bending scientific truth in order to support their political position on Star Wars.[8] The Jastrow article provoked a lively exchange of letters in *Commentary,* which spilled over into the pages of *Physics Today* after the magazine ran a review by Garwin of Jastrow's book, *How to Make Nuclear Weapons Obsolete.*[9]

The net impact of the Jastrow-Garwin feud is not easily assessed. Jastrow's assault on the scientific truthfulness of Garwin and the scientists associated with UCS was widely resented in the physics community and may to some extent have backfired. But Garwin and his associates also were forced to retreat from some of the claims they had made in the initial UCS study, which damaged their credibility and prompted some observers to ask whether it was really necessary and wise to argue about Star Wars in great technical detail. Philip W. Anderson, a retired Bell Laboratories physicist and Nobel laure-

---

[6] See UCS, *The Fallacy of Star Wars,* Viking, 1985.
[7] William J. Broad, *Star Warriors,* Simon & Shuster, 1985, p. 36.
[8] See Robert Jastrow, "The War Against Star Wars," *Commentary,* December 1984, pp. 19-25, and March 1985 issue for an exchange of letters between Jastrow and his critics.
[9] The book was published by Little, Brown in 1985. Garwin's review appeared in the December 1985 issue of *Physics Today* and letters from Garwin, Jastrow and their respective supporters in January, March and July 1986 issues. *Physics Today* is published by the American Institute of Physics and is circulated to about 80,000 physicists who are members of U.S. professional societies.

ate, commented on the controversy as follows: "Fortunately, most of the scientific issues that come up in discussing Star Wars are very simple ones. . . . If you go through the enormously detailed kinds of calculations on specific configurations which Richard Garwin and his fellow opponents of SDI felt necessary to convince the stubborn, you leave yourself open to the kind of errors of factors of two or four . . . which then — to the lay person — seem to weaken the whole structure [of the anti-Star Wars argument]." [10]

University Scientists Launch Petitions

The first petitions opposing Star Wars began to circulate in college and university science departments in spring 1985 after the SDI program began to solicit proposals from the academic community and SDI officials publicly interpreted submissions as evidence of political support for the program. James A. Ionson, director of the SDI Innovative Science and Technology Program, said in a March 1985 meeting with university researchers that academic participation in SDI would give the program "prestige and credibility" and "influence Congress to be more generous in funding the program." Massachusetts Institute of Technology President Paul E. Gray denounced the statement during commencement exercises that June, calling it a "manipulative effort to garner implicit institutional endorsement for SDI."

Not content with the effort to dissociate scientific participation from political support, physicists and computer scientists at Cornell University and the University of Illinois (Champaign-Urbana) independently wrote petitions pledging signatories not to accept funds for Star Wars research. The language of the two petitions proved to be very similar, and when the two groups learned of each other, they were able to agree quickly on a common formulation. Steering clear of technical argumentation, the petition simply called the Star Wars program "ill-conceived and dangerous." It concluded with a pledge "neither to solicit nor accept SDI funds." Thus, it said, "we hope together to persuade the public and Congress not to support this deeply misguided and dangerous program."

Last March, a second petition opposing Star Wars began to circulate at industry and government laboratories with initial signatures from eminent scientists at Bell Laboratories, IBM, Lawrence Berkeley Laboratory, Argonne National Laboratory, Brookhaven National Laboratory, Los Alamos Scientific Laboratory and the National Institutes of Health. It, too, shunned technicalities and simply characterized SDI as a crash weapons

[10] Philip W. Anderson, "The Case Against Star Wars," *Princeton Alumni Weekly,* Sept. 25, 1985, p. 10.

Star Wars Research on Campus

From 1980 to 1986, funding for college and university research sponsored by the Defense Department more than doubled, growing about twice as fast as the overall federal academic research budget, according to the National Science Foundation. At the same time, in 1986 the Pentagon still only accounted for one-sixth of the federal academic research budget.

Within the Defense Department research budget, the "Star Wars" Strategic Defense Initiative (SDI) is the biggest single component, awarding contracts to colleges and universities as well as federal and industry laboratories. One branch of the Star Wars program that provides a lot of money for university research is SDI's Innovative Science and Technology Program. Its budget is growing by leaps and bounds.

In fiscal 1986, the program's budget jumped from $28 million to $96 million, and in President Reagan's fiscal 1987 budget request it was slated to go to $167 million. By the beginning of this year, the program had received more than 3,000 research proposals from colleges and universities.

James A. Ionson, an astrophysicist who heads the science and technology program, promised that SDI work "performed on a university campus will not be classified ... and subject to any control or restrictive clauses or security classification," but researchers have been skeptical. Last year, when experiments on a free-electron laser at the Lawrence Livermore National Laboratory were dramatically more successful than expected, the SDI program classified the results after the fact, over the researchers' protests.

University researchers also have been concerned about the recategorization of some research in progress as SDI research, which sometimes has been done without notice. Some university professors have been startled to find their names on lists of projects funded by SDI and were resentful when this was interpreted as indicative of support for Star Wars.

Opponents of the Star Wars program fear that they might be penalized for their position, an anxiety that was not alleviated when Defense Under Secretary Donald Hicks said at his July 1985 confirmation hearing: "I am not particularly interested in seeing department money going to someplace where an individual is outspoken in his rejection of department aims, even for

development program masquerading as a scientific research program, initiated without adequate review from the science community. In contrast to the Cornell-Illinois petition, the second one did not require signatories to promise not to accept SDI funds; such a pledge would be an impractical demand for most researchers at government and large industry labs.

Yet another petition of sorts began to circulate last March, circulating, in the form of a questionnaire written by William A. Shurcliff, a retired Harvard University physicist, sent to the 1,500 members of the National Academy of Sciences. Shurcliff

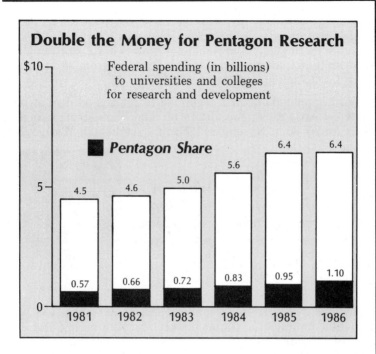

Double the Money for Pentagon Research

$10 —

Federal spending (in billions)
to universities and colleges
for research and development

■ *Pentagon Share*

				6.4	6.4
			5.6		
		5.0			
5 —	4.5	4.6				
0.57	0.66	0.72	0.83	0.95	1.10
0 —
1981	1982	1983	1984	1985	1986

basic research." After coming under heavy fire, Hicks backed off only to the extent of saying he thought Pentagon support for basic research should be independent of the researchers' political views.

University researchers who would like to do SDI work fear that anti-SDI majorities might succeed in banning such research on their campuses. Anti-SDI petitioners have denied that this is their goal, but one faculty at least — at Tufts University — already has voted to ban SDI research from the campus. Sidney Hook, a research fellow at the Hoover Institution on War, Revolution and Peace in Stanford, Calif., complained last October on the op-ed page of the *The New York Times*: "The effort to enlist scientists against defense research is being used to intimidate those willing to serve their government. . . . Such tactics assault the academic freedom of those who disagree."

initiated a similar survey in the late 1960s to question academy members about their position on the proposed supersonic passenger plane and used the results to help persuade Congress to ditch the project. His SDI survey hardly met scientific standards of objectivity: He made no secret of his intention to make political use of the results, and the sample of respondents was self-selecting. Still, about a third of the academicians replied, and "by majorities of more than 20-to-1," Shurcliff reported, "the responding members declared that the proposed Star Wars program would not provide an effective shield, would not defeat a high-altitude attack, would not prevent delivery of A-bombs by other methods . . . and would not protect our European allies. In overall attitude toward the Star Wars program, 20 members were for it and 461 against it."

With opponents of SDI beginning to get a good deal of publicity by early 1986, supporters of Star Wars started to rally their forces. At a November 1985 SDI seminar in Washington,

Physicist William A. Shurcliff found a group of National Academy of Science members opposed Star Wars, 461-20.

sponsored by the Global Foundation of Coral Gables, Fla., participants produced a statement saying: "We accept the concept of a strategic defense against nuclear missiles. We therefore support research to establish the feasibility of such a strategic defense. . . . We find defense morally preferable to the current strategy of naked offensive confrontation." While this statement was issued with just a dozen or so signatures, in contrast to the anti-SDI statements that already were picking up hundreds of signatures, the signatories included some very distinguished scientists, including Alvin M. Weinberg of the Institute for Energy Analysis, Eugene P. Wigner of Princeton University, and R. V. Jones of the University of Aberdeen, who was assistant director of British scientific intelligence in World War II and is a respected expert on air defenses.

Last June, a group calling itself the Science and Engineering Committee for a Secure World issued a challenge to the 1,600 laboratory scientists who by that time had signed the anti-SDI petition circulating at labs. The 80 founding members of the group included names not previously associated with the Star Wars cause in addition to well-known SDI supporters such as Jastrow, Teller and Teller's protégé Lowell Wood, who heads an important SDI research group at Lawrence Livermore National Laboratory. Wood said the 1,600 anti-SDI petitioners represented just "one half of 1 percent" of the scientists and engineers working in technical fields in the United States.[11]

---

[11] Another pro-SDI group to announce itself in June of this year was "Former Soviet Scientists" — 30 Soviet emigré scientists who sent an open letter to Congress urging the United States to support Star Wars and not make concessions on the program to the Soviet Union.

Physicists Clash with SDI Officials

For their part, officials of the Star Wars program sought from the start to maintain good relations with the scientific community, and this was also true of scientists in the program who were keen to retain their reputations in the science community for being truthful and objective. For example, when Gerald Yonas, the chief scientist of SDI, described the program in a lengthy article for a science magazine in 1985, one of the most striking things about the article was the modesty of the claims he advanced and the forthrightness of his disclaimers. He said that integration of a multi-layered defense system would require computers, software and communications "far beyond existing capabilities" and that defending a system against attack would pose "a difficult challenge and may be pivotal to the outcome of the entire ballistic missile defense endeavor." [12]

When the anti-SDI petitions first appeared, SDI officials initially dismissed them as insignificant. In late 1985, Gen. Abrahamson said opposition to Star Wars in the science community was confined "to a few diehards," while George A. Keyworth II, the White House science adviser at that time, said scientists opposing Star Wars were "politically motivated." Energy Secretary John S. Herrington dismissed the debate in the science community as just "a little squabble." [13]

Scientists were quick to react. On Nov. 22, 1985, Park of APS drew attention to the statements by Abrahamson and Keyworth in an electronic news bulletin for physicists. Park noted that the Cornell-Illinois petition had garnered more than 2,000 signatures and commented that Abrahamson and Keyworth seemed to be "living on a different planet." By last May, 3,700 faculty members and 2,800 graduate students had signed the petition, including majorities in 59 leading physics departments.

Skeptical about the implied claim from SDI officials that Star Wars had the support of a "silent majority" in the science community, the Union of Concerned Scientists commissioned pollster Peter D. Hart to do a survey of APS members. The results, which were released last March, indicated that professional physicists opposed SDI by a margin of 2-to-1, though many saw merits in some aspects of Star Wars research. The margin of opinion in the general public, by comparison, has been much more closely divided. *(See box, pp. 76-77.)*

When APS held an annual meeting in Washington at the end of April, relations between the Star Wars program and the

(continued on p. 78)

---

[12] Gerald Yonas, "Strategic Defense Initiative: The Politics and Science of Weapons in Space," *Physics Today*, June 1985, p. 31.
[13] The Energy Department produces the nation's nuclear weapons and administers one of the key Star Wars development programs, the nuclear-pumped X-ray laser program.

How Physicists Rate th

How much would you say you know about the issues surrounding the Strategic Defense Initiative (SDI) — a great deal, quite a bit, some, just a little, or hardly anything?

Great deal/quite a bit	61%	Just a little/ hardly anything	9%
Some	29	Not sure	1

For each of the following systems the United States might develop for its national security, do you think it represents a step in the right or wrong direction?

	Right direction	Wrong direction	No effect	Not sure
MX missile	18%	50%	19%	13%
Trident submarine	63	11	8	18
Cruise missile	45	26	10	19
SDI	29	54	6	11
Midgetman missile	25	19	8	48
Stealth bomber	39	24	10	27

For each of the following three phases in which SDI might be implemented, is this something you would strongly favor, mildly favor, mildly oppose or strongly oppose?

	Favor	Oppose	Not sure
Proceeding with basic SDI lab research	77%	21%	2%
Developing and testing SDI systems	43	49	8
Deploying SDI systems	23	62	15

SOURCE: March 1986 survey by Peter D. Hart Research Associates Inc. for the Union of Concerned

Star Wars Program

For each goal listed below, how likely do you think it is that an SDI system could meet the goal?

	Very likely/ probable	50-50	Improbable/ very unlikely	Not sure
Provide an effective point defense for hardened military targets such as U.S. missile silos.	45%	21%	27%	7%
Provide an effective defense for selected population centers?	25	17	52	6
Provide an effective population defense for the country as a whole?	16	11	67	6

What percent of Soviet warheads launched in a massive attack do you think would be able to penetrate and get through the best designed strategic defense system?

Zero	1%	41-49.............	—
1-10..............	32	50	12
11-20.............	14	51-60..............	2
21-30.............	11	61-100.............	7
31-40.............	3	Not sure..........	18

Do you think America's offensive nuclear capability is adequate or insufficient to serve as an effective deterrent to a Soviet nuclear attack?

Adequate.................................... 81%
Insufficient.................................... 8
Other/not sure................................ 11

sts.

(continued from p. 75)
physics community were visibly strained. An SDI official showed up to give a technical briefing at one session, and participants reported that the atmosphere was civil. But at a second session, devoted to the impact of SDI on the physics community, the SDI officials who were supposed to participate canceled and gave conflicting explanations for their absence. At the session, which drew a large number of graduate students, several physicists expressed concern that they might no longer be able to promise their students careers outside military research in light of the fact that so much federal research money was Star Wars-related. Virtually all participants in the session expressed a desire for more information about how Star Wars money was affecting university research *(See box, pp. 72-73)*. And one participant, Charles Schwarz of the University of California (Berkeley), said that he had decided to stop teaching physics for the time being because he believed that under current circumstances it would inevitably lead students into military work.

Nuclear Age Heralds Weaponry Debate

B ecause of their role in conceiving, designing and building the first atomic bomb, physicists have been deeply involved in the discussion of nuclear weapons issues ever since the nuclear age began in 1945. But their influence has varied depending on their standing with the public and their relationship with the incumbent presidential administration. Also, their influence has been greater when defense issues being debated have had a big technical component. In the years immediately after World War II, physicists were held in awe and their influence was great. But after the first Soviet atomic and hydrogen bombs, there was a reaction against physicists, who now were held responsible for having introduced a grave threat. After the Soviet Union launched the first missile into space in 1957 and temporarily was perceived as being ahead in the arms race, physicists once again were invited into the corridors of power, and for the next decade they were well represented in a highly institutionalized process of science advising to the White House. In 1973 President Nixon abolished the President's Science Advisory Committee because of dissatisfaction with the advice he was getting, thus ending what scientists sometimes look back upon as a golden age.[14]

[14] For a more detailed account of the role of scientists in nuclear controversies, see Congressional Quarterly, *The Nuclear Age*, 1984, chapter 2.

Bomb Brings Fear of Surprise Attack

The first group of physicists to systematically consider the implications of nuclear weapons was a committee established by scientists working on the Manhattan Project in Chicago in 1945 and chaired by project member and Nobel laureate James Franck. The committee's report predicted that uncontrolled development of nuclear weapons would lead ineluctably to a situation in which peoples would live in mortal fear of surprise attack. For this reason it recommended that the bomb should not be used without notifying the Soviet leadership of its existence with a view to seeking means of international control. The report was locked up on alleged security grounds by Manhattan Project officials and never reached President Truman, the intended recipient.

In the early 1950s, a debate broke out among physicists about whether it was necessary and advisable to proceed with development of a hydrogen bomb, and for the first time physicists became openly divided into two camps. Some thought that the United States should seek to win the nuclear arms race, and some thought the arms race should be limited. J. Robert Oppenheimer, who had been scientific director of the Manhattan Project, led a camp that wanted to delay H-bomb development pending an attempt at negotiations with the Soviet Union. Teller led those who wanted to build the bomb right away.[15] After President Eisenhower took office, charges were revived that Oppenheimer represented a security risk because of his ties with communists in the 1930s, and in a dramatic proceeding he was stripped of his security clearances, effectively ending his role as a high-level adviser. Teller testified against him in the hearing.

Oppenheimer is thought to have fallen into official disfavor not only because of his opposition to the hydrogen bomb but also because he favored, more generally, reducing U.S. reliance on nuclear weapons for defense. This ran directly counter to the Eisenhower administration's emergent doctrine of "massive retaliation," the policy rule that the United States would respond to any Soviet attack — whether nuclear or non-nuclear — with an all-out nuclear attack.

When the Soviet Union began to deploy a missile force in the 1960s, it was apparent that its nuclear arsenal would soon equal or surpass the U.S. arsenal. The Kennedy administration's doctrine of "mutually assured destruction" (MAD) — the notion that neither side would dare attack the other with nuclear weapons because such an attack would provoke an equally devastating counterattack — replaced massive retaliation as the foundation of nuclear weapons policy. A very strong consensus in elite circles favored the view that reliance on MAD was the

---

[15] See Herbert York, *The Advisors: Oppenheimer, Teller and the Superbomb*, W. H. Freeman, 1976.

best possible path to peace and security as long as nuclear weapons existed. The doctrine was vulnerable to two lines of criticism, however. First, it seemed to leave the United States vulnerable to Soviet pressure or attack in situations in which nuclear retaliation could not be credibly threatened. And second, it seemed to leave the American people living with the threat of nuclear extermination in perpetuity — a prospect nobody was happy about.

First ABM Debate: Will It Work?

The possibility of a surprise missile attack was so frightening that the search for a defense was begun even before such missiles were first tested. The first contracts for feasibility studies on an ABM system were let by the Army and Air Force in 1955, two years before the Soviet Union launched Sputnik, the first Earth satellite, showing that the Soviets would soon have missiles capable of reaching the United States.

After Sputnik, then Senate Majority Leader Lyndon B. Johnson accused the Eisenhower administration of not working hard enough to develop an ABM system. In 1964, as president, Johnson found himself the target of similar charges from Sen. Barry Goldwater. But despite technical efforts and political pressure, work on ABM systems was not promising. In 1965 the Joint Chiefs of Staff — giving up on winning political support for a comprehensive defense against a Soviet missile attack — recommended building a smaller system oriented to defense against so-called primitive Chinese nuclear weapons. In 1968, under pressure from Republican presidential candidate Richard M. Nixon on the ABM issue, the Johnson administration announced it would proceed with a light anti-Chinese system called Sentinel.

The decision to build Sentinel set the stage for a political struggle in which physicists played a key part. The Federation of American Scientists, founded in 1946 by veterans of the Manhattan Project, and the Council for a Livable World, founded in 1962 to channel funds to members of Congress who supported arms control, both organized briefings and prepared documentary material opposing the Sentinel program. "Probably the most influential document in convincing scientists to oppose the ABM, however, was an article on the subject by Hans Bethe and Richard Garwin published in the March 1968 *Scientific American,* according to the conclusions of two students of the controversy.[16]

The anti-ABM scientists generally emphasized the relative ease with which such a system could be circumvented, the

---

[16] See Joel Primack and Frank von Hippel, *Advice and Dissent: Scientists in the Political Arena* (1974), pp. 59-60.

vulnerability of the radars needed to run it, the impossibility of testing it and the intrinsic difficulty of "hitting a bullet with a bullet," as the standard stock phrase went. In drumming up public concern, however, they were much helped by a decision of Director of Defense Research and Engineering John Foster to recommend placing eight of the proposed ABM sites near major cities — a decision made because he and Paul Nitze, then deputy defense secretary, wanted to keep open the option of expanding the system to defend cities against Soviet attack. The trouble was that the Sentinel system was to rely on nuclear-armed interceptors, raising the specter of an accidental nuclear explosion near a major city — and that is what captured the public's imagination in cities such as Seattle, Chicago and Boston, where scientists actively opposed the plan. In a meeting in Libertyville, Ill., in December 1968, the manager of the ABM program, Army Lt. Gen. Alfred Starbird, flatly denied that there could be an accidental nuclear explosion. But his statement had little impact compared with that of a map passed out at the meeting by Argonne Laboratory scientists showing a 60-square-mile area that would be flattened if an explosion did occur.

The campaign mounted by the scientists was remarkably effective in mustering citizen pressure on Congress, and by the time Nixon took office, influential voices in Congress already were calling for reconsideration of Sentinel. In March 1969 Nixon announced that the plan to base the ABM system near cities had been scrapped and that the system — renamed Safeguard — would be redesigned to protect Minuteman intercontinental ballistic missile (ICBM) silos against a pre-emptive Soviet strike. Even so, the Senate allowed work on Safeguard to proceed only when Vice President Spiro T. Agnew cast a tie-breaking vote in August 1969, and only when the administration provided assurances that the ABM system was a vital bargaining chip in the Strategic Arms Limitation Talks (SALT), which it had just agreed to enter with the Soviet Union.

From SALT I to Star Wars Decision

The SALT talks led to the negotiation of the 1972 ABM treaty, which banned the testing and deployment of ABM systems, but permitted each side to have two regional systems. The United States built one such system in North Dakota to defend missile silos but rapidly concluded that it was ineffective and closed it. The Soviets retained a system to defend Moscow, providing grist for those who would argue in the following years that Soviet leaders were not giving up on missile defense and that their ultimate intention was to have the capability of fighting and winning a nuclear war.

Believers in ballistic missile defense in the United States did not give up after SALT I, though their efforts did not receive much public attention. Particularly active were Air Force Gen. George Keegan and Army Lt. Gen. Daniel O. Graham, both former chiefs of military intelligence and both firmly convinced that the CIA systematically underestimated Soviet capabilities. Keegan and Graham had opportunity to advance their views as members of a committee established in June 1976 by George

Reagan's decision to launch SDI reportedly was made largely under the influence of Edward Teller.

Bush — director of intelligence at that time — to review the CIA. The thrust of the committee's report, as Defense Secretary Donald H. Rumsfeld put it shortly before leaving office in January 1977, was that known Soviet capabilities indicated "a tendency toward [nuclear] war fighting."

During the Carter years, Keegan and Graham associated themselves with the Coalition for Peace through Strength, a bipartisan group formed in 1978 to lobby for a military buildup, and during the 1980 election they were close to the Reagan campaign. Meanwhile, a steady stream of articles appeared in *Aviation Week & Space Technology* and other defense-oriented publications suggesting that the Soviets were working hard on exotic new ABM systems such as "particle beam weapons" and various kinds of lasers. Political scientists such as William Van Cleave at UCLA and Colin Grey at the Hudson Institute argued that the United States should adopt nuclear war-fighting strategies to match the presumed Soviet strategy.

Ironically, the group most active in pushing for a military buildup in the Carter years, the Committee on the Present Danger, did not stress the ABM issue, and after Reagan took office its director, Nitze, emerged as one of the more dovish members of the Reagan team. Keegan, Graham and Van Cleave, despite prominence in the transition, ended up on the sidelines, where they continued to lobby for missile defenses. Reagan's 1983 decision to launch SDI reportedly was highly personal, made largely under the influence of Teller and without much consultation with anybody else. Richard D. DeLauer, then director of defense research and engineering at the Pentagon, was not shown a copy of the speech announcing the decision until eight hours before it was delivered.[17] Later that year, DeLauer told Congress that the proposed SDI system posed eight major problems, each of which would require an effort equal to or greater than the effort mounted to land men on the moon.

Technology Choices Behind Star Wars

The Star Wars debate among physicists has focused largely on whether an effective system could be built and, if such a system were possible, how soon the United States would be capable of building it. Hardly any physicist would claim that an effective system never could be built, but many argue that it would not be possible to build one before early in the next century and that arms control, in the meantime, is a more promising way of trying to make the world safer.

Estimates of when an effective missile defense system might be built depend greatly on what kind of system is under discussion. When Reagan launched SDI, he was reported to have been inspired largely by Teller's enthusiastic account of work done on a highly innovative X-ray system that would be powered by a nuclear explosive. In the proposed system, at first warning of a missile attack, submarines would launch missiles into space, the missiles would deploy satellites carrying bundles of metal rods surrounding hydrogen bombs, the rods would be electronically focused on the incoming missiles, the hydrogen bombs would explode and the rods would channel lethal X-rays from the explosives, destroying the missiles — all this in a matter of minutes.

The first underground test results of the X-ray system initially were reported to be impressive but later were found to be dubious. Meanwhile, even before Reagan's 1983 speech, a leading pro-Star Wars group had become deeply divided about the merits of the X-ray system. The group, sponsored by the Heritage Foundation in Washington and headed by Graham, finally decided in favor of relatively conventional rocket interceptors based in space, to the dismay of Teller, the leading advocate of the pop-up X-ray system.[18] Teller argued, like Garwin, that any system based in space could be destroyed by enemy space mines.

---

[17] See Robert Scheer, "Teller's Obsession Became Reality in Star Wars Plan," *Los Angeles Times*, July 10, 1983.
[18] See Gen. Daniel O. Graham, "High Frontier: A New National Strategy," High Frontier, Washington, D.C., 1982.

In a June 1986 Star Wars test above White Sands Missile Range in New Mexico, a moving target vehicle was intercepted and destroyed by a radar-guided vehicle.

Flashy Tests of Interceptors, Satellites

By fall 1985, published reports in the press were indicating that the Star Wars program was contemplating a multi-tiered system with as many as seven layers. The system would reportedly employ both rockets and directed-energy systems, which include various kinds of lasers and devices for firing subatomic particles such as neutrons, and it would be dually based on Earth and in space. Schematic drawings typically showed lasers casting beams through the atmosphere to a system of space-based mirrors, which in turn would reflect the lethal beams onto Soviet missiles immediately after their launch from the Soviet Union.

A panel set up to evaluate the computer software and hardware that would be required to control such a system ended up bitterly divided about whether adequate technology could be devised or not. Other issues in hot dispute included the amount of power needed to produce beams of the required lethality, the precision of the mirrors, methods of targeting and retargeting mirrors and, not least, the question of whether distortion of the beams by the atmosphere could be overcome. Gen. Abrahamson regularly made enthusiastic statements about progress in the program, claiming for example that new technology would permit refocusing of the mirrors without mechanically changing the shape of the mirrors and that similar techniques could be used to overcome atmospheric distortion, but such claims often were disputed by people doing research on the technologies in question.

Meanwhile, the Star Wars program arranged for a series of flashy tests designed, apparently, to inspire confidence in the program. In 1984, a heat-seeking interceptor successfully destroyed a dummy warhead in space, a test designed to show that a bullet could, in fact, hit a bullet. In June 1985 a laser beam from Earth was bounced off the shuttle in space; in September 1985 a beam from a chemical laser was used to ignite a stationary missile. In the most recent test, earlier this month, two satellites were launched into parallel orbits and then one tracked the other and destroyed it by colliding with it. Within the SDI program, the demonstration program initially was called "Beacon," for Bold Experiments to Advance Confidence, and later "Star," for Significant Technical Achievements and Research.

Restructuring Around Two Technologies

In November 1985 Gen. Abrahamson held a press conference, which was announced on very short notice, to describe, it was said, some of the "incredible" advances made by Star Wars researchers. In the midst of the long, rambling briefing, Abrahamson in fact announced a major restructuring of the program to narrow its focus on the two technologies considered most promising: infrared heat-seeking rocket interceptors

In a September 1985 Star Wars test, a beam from a chemical laser was used to ignite a stationary missile.

somewhat similar to interceptors that have been tested in space for use as anti-satellite weapons, and free-electron lasers, a type of laser so new and advanced that initial studies of the Star Wars program sometimes did not discuss them in detail. Abrahamson made it clear that chemical lasers were being radically downgraded, and apparently there also would be less emphasis on "rail guns" — an innovative way of using electromagnetism to fire projectiles at extremely high speeds. He left the status of the X-ray laser project somewhat indeterminate.

Shortly before Abrahamson's press conference, and at about the time of Reagan's summit meeting with Mikhail Gorbachev, Abrahamson had indicated in a speech that he expected to receive an order from the president to streamline the program. Abrahamson's statement was striking because it expressed confidence in the president's intentions at a time when other administration officials appeared to be in the dark about what agreement Reagan might reach with Gorbachev. A highly placed source with the free-electron laser program at Lawrence Livermore says it is his understanding that Reagan told Abrahamson, after the summit, to produce a technical breakthrough by 1988. Members of the Livermore free-electron laser program were told their budget would be quadrupled.

Despite Abrahamson's claim about research progress, SDI officials became noticeably more cautious in 1985 about the aims of the program. By the end of the year they regularly emphasized that it was not their intention — whatever Reagan had said about rendering nuclear weapons impotent and obsolete — to design a leakproof defense. One reason for their caution may have been the publication in late 1985 of *Star Warriors* by *New York Times* reporter Broad. In extensive interviews with researchers at Lawrence Livermore Laboratory, Broad did not find a single researcher who considered a leakproof defense achievable.

In March of this year, another report on Star Wars research began to circulate on Capitol Hill, where it attracted a good deal of attention. Prepared by three Senate staffers, the study arrived at the following major findings:

● "While some significant progress has been achieved ..., none of it could be described as 'amazing.' Interviews with key SDI scientists involved in the research revealed that there have been *no major breakthroughs* which make a mid- to late-1990s deployment of comprehensive missile defenses more feasible than it was three years ago."

● "In fact, the 'schedule-driven' nature of the current research program, which requires that a development decision be made by the early 1990s, has aroused significant concern among scientists at the national laboratories."

● "Much of the progress that has been achieved has resulted in a greater understanding of program difficulties, which are much more severe than previously considered." [19]

Douglas Waller, an author of the report, believes that it had an impact on the Hill because it was based on the views of individuals who are basically supportive of the Star Wars program. Together with the grass-roots movement against Star Wars among physicists, which Waller said "surprised everybody," the report was a contributing factor in the House and Senate committee proposals to cut the president's request for the SDI budget, according to Waller.

The physicists' movement may indeed be "unprecedented," as Warshaft of Cornell has claimed, but if so, it is unprecedented only in scope. Already in 1968-69, it will be recalled, a similar movement persuaded citizens in Illinois that they might do better to listen to independent experts from Argonne Lab-

---

[19] The report was prepared by Douglas Waller, James Bruce and Douglas Cook, aides to Sens. William Proxmire, D-Wis., J. Bennett Johnston, D-La., and Lawton Chiles, D-Fla.

oratory than to government officials like Gen. Starbird, the man who had the job then that Gen. Abrahamson has today.

Selected Bibliography

Books

Carter, Ashton B., and N. Schwartz, eds., *Ballistic Missile Defense,* Brookings Institution, 1984.

Chayes, Abram, and Jerome B. Wiesner, eds., *ABM,* Harper and Row, 1969.

Newhouse, John, *Cold Dawn: The Story of SALT,* Holt, Rinehart and Winston, 1973.

Articles

Bethe, Hans A., Richard L. Garwin, Kurt Gottfried and Henry W. Kendall, "Space Based Ballistic Missile Defense," *Scientific American,* October 1984.

Fletcher, James C., "Technologies for Strategic Defense," *Issues in Science and Technology,* fall 1984.

Keyworth, George A., "The Case for Ballistic Missile Defense," *Issues in Science and Technology,* fall 1984.

Panofsky, Wolfgang K. H., "Strategic Defense Initiative: Perception vs. Reality," *Physics Today,* June 1985.

"Weapons in Space," *Daedalus,* spring 1985: Vol. I, Concepts and Technologies; Vol. II, Implications for security.

Reports and Studies

Armstrong, Scott, and Peter Frier, "Strategic Defense Initiative: Splendid Defense or Pipe Dream," Foreign Policy Association Headline Series, No. 275, Foreign Policy Association (New York), 1985.

Jones, R. V., "New Light on Star Wars," Policy Study No. 71, Centre for Policy Studies (London), June 1985.

Office of Technology Assessment, "Strategic Defenses: Ballistic Missile Defense Technologies, Anti-Satellite Weapons," Princeton University Press, 1986.

Union of Concerned Scientists, "The ASAT/SDI Link," Cambridge, Mass., 1986.

Graphics: Photo p. 65, Defense Department; photos p. 67, National Aeronautics and Space Administration; photo p. 69, Russ Hamilton; chart p. 73, Robert Redding; photo p. 74, Richard Howard; photos pp. 82, 84 and 86, Defense Department.

CHEMICAL WEAPONS
Push for Controls

by

Harrison Donnelly

July 11
1 9 8 6

CHEMICAL WEAPONS

For the first time in years, arms-control experts are holding out cautious hope that an effective international agreement can be worked out to rid the planet of chemical weapons. At their Geneva summit meeting last November, President Reagan and Soviet leader Mikhail S. Gorbachev agreed to intensify the efforts of their two countries to establish the framework for a worldwide chemical weapons treaty *(see p. 96),* which negotiators have been discussing for nearly two decades. There is informed speculation that despite formidable technical obstacles, the two leaders may decide to push through an agreement. According to this line of thinking, a chemical warfare agreement would prevent them from coming away empty-handed at a follow-up summit, possibly later this year, in the event they cannot break the continuing deadlock over a nuclear arms control treaty.[1]

If the United States, the Soviet Union and the other members of the 40-nation disarmament conference currently meeting in Geneva cannot reach an agreement, however, the outlook for restricting or outlawing chemical weapons is bleak. The specter raised by chemical weapons in World War I seemed to vanish when they were not used in World War II, but it is returning. Modern chemical weapons are far more lethal than the gases used in World War I; a tiny drop of some substances on the skin can produce a rapid, agonizing death. Together with agents of biological warfare, they are capable of rendering battlefields and vast surrounding areas almost unimaginably deadly for both soldiers and civilians. "American service members are more likely to be attacked with chemical weapons today than at any time since World War I," the Pentagon's top chemical-warfare specialist said recently.[2]

While the superpowers consider a new treaty, they continue to maintain formidable chemical arsenals. The Russians, who suffered terribly from chemical weapons in World War I, have developed a large array of munitions filled with lethal compounds. U.S. intelligence reports that the Soviet army trains intensively for fighting in a chemical environment, and appar-

---

[1] For background, see "Arms Control Negotiations," *E.R.R.*, 1985 Vol. I, pp. 145-168, and "U.S.-Soviet Summitry," *E.R.R.*, 1985 Vol. II, pp. 821-840.
[2] Thomas J. Welch, deputy assistant to the secretary of defense for chemical matters, at a Pentagon news briefing, June 12, 1986.

ently has made extensive use of chemical weapons against anti-communist guerrillas in Afghanistan.

The United States has vowed never to be the first country to use chemicals in war, and has not acquired any more such weapons since President Nixon stopped production in 1969. But it still has a considerable chemical stockpile, albeit one that U.S. officials say is smaller than the Soviet Union's and in deteriorating condition. Arguing that only an improved chemical capability will deter the Soviets from using chemicals in a future war, the Defense Department is preparing to begin production of a new class of chemical weapons.

Issues relating to chemical weapons also are taking on a growing political importance. It took five years of effort by the Reagan administration before Congress in 1985 agreed to allow the final states of production of new chemical weapons known as "binary" munitions. Liberal arms-control advocates hope to overturn that position this year. In Europe, where the idea of chemical wars stirs up disturbing memories, the U.S. munitions plan could become the subject of a new wave of anti-American agitation. America's allies in the North Atlantic Treaty Organization (NATO) have shown misgivings about the new program, backing it only after the United States agreed to withdraw its current stock of chemical munitions from West Germany.

The chemical arms question extends beyond the United States, Russia and Western Europe. The U.S. intelligence community estimates that 16 nations already have chemical warfare capabilities, and six others are close to acquiring them.[3] Military planners in the Third World do not all seem to have the abhorrence for chemical weapons that is so widely felt in the West. Egypt, Vietnam and Ethiopia have been accused of using chemicals on the battlefield in recent decades, and Iraq is known to have used chemical weapons in its continuing war with Iran.

The dangers posed by chemical weapons may someday seem relatively tame compared with the killing potential of biological weapons — diseases and poisons produced by living organisms. The United States has charged that the Soviet Union supplied a fungus-produced toxin called "yellow rain" to its allies in Southeast Asia and that they used it against insurgents in mountain villages *(see p. 97)*. While there is a continuing

---

[3] U.S. officials have declined to name the countries they include on their list. Other than the United States and the Soviet Union, the only countries with confirmed possession of chemical arms are France and Iraq. According to a February 1985 article in *Chemical and Engineering News*, a trade publication, other likely possessors include Egypt, Syria, Libya, Israel, Ethiopia, Burma, Thailand, China, North Korea, Vietnam and Taiwan.

Kinds of Chemical-Biological Weapons

Armies today have access to a much wide variety of lethal agents, almost all of them much more deadly than any used in World War I. Generally they are not gases but liquids, dispersed as mists or vapors. Modern arsenals may include:

Blister agents. Mustard, Lewisite and related products burn body surfaces, producing painful skin wounds. They can kill if inhaled, by blistering the lungs.

Blood agents. Hydrogen cyanide and cyanogen chloride, which when inhaled, kill by blocking the blood cells' ability to convey oxygen.

Nerve agents. Of the same chemical family as modern pesticides, these "organophosphorous" compounds kill by inhibiting the action of an enyzme essential to the nervous system. Exposure results in paralysis and heart failure. Most can be absorbed through the skin, and so need not be inhaled to cause death. The most common nerve agents are the "G" class — tabun, sarin and soman, developed around World War II — and "VX," developed in the 1950s.

Toxins. These are poisonous substances extracted from living creatures. The large number of biological poisons with possible military uses include saxitoxin, from shellfish, and mycotoxins, from fungus.

Incapacitants. Some chemicals can be used to debilitate opponents without killing them. The U.S. Army has BZ, a mind-altering psychedelic, while the Soviets are thought to possess chemicals that cause opponents to fall asleep.

debate over whether yellow rain really existed, there is a widespread belief that biological weapons could unleash a destructive power comparable to nuclear war. Advances in genetic engineering may enable scientists to develop new organisms so dangerous that they could become, in the words of Nobel laureate Joshua Lederberg, "the most efficient means for removing man from the planet." [4]

U.S. and Soviet Chemical War Capabilities

At the heart of the debate over chemical issues lies the question of the relative strength of the U.S. and Soviet chemical stockpiles. Although little information is publicly available about the Soviet chemical arsenal — and what is known is subject to conflicting interpretations — it seems clear that Moscow views chemical weapons as an integral part of modern war. While estimates of the stockpile vary widely, most analysts calculate that it is about 350,000 tons of lethal agents.

[4] Remarks before the Conference on Disarmament in 1970. See "Genetic Breakthroughs," *E.R.R.*, 1986 Vol. I, pp. 1-20.

As portrayed in reports issued by the General Accounting Office, the Defense Intelligence Agency, and the Chemical Warfare Review Commission,[5] the Soviet Union has weapons for delivering the chemicals in many different military situations. These include artillery pieces for use at the front and medium-range missiles for attacks on rear support areas. The U.S. government reports said that a separate wing of the Soviet military structure, the Military Chemical Forces, may have up to 100,000 personnel assigned to related offensive and defensive tasks, and estimated that the Russians maintain 32 chemical munitions depots in Eastern Europe alone.

The U.S. chemical stockpile probably is smaller. Again, exact figures are secret, but a well-known chemical expert has estimated that there are about 8,000 tons of nerve agent and mustard available in bombs and shells.[6] A larger amount of lethal compounds is stored in bulk form. However, Pentagon officials stress that a large part of the existing stockpile is no longer usable — either because it has lost its lethal potency, is leaking or is not suited for present weapons systems. Only 28 percent of the current supplies could be used at all, according to the Defense Department, and only 7 percent is in a form suitable for immediate deployment.

The Chemical Warfare Review Commission was less pessimistic about the current state of the stockpile.[7] But the presidentially appointed panel did conclude in its June 1985 report that long-term deterioration of the weapons would effectively eliminate the U.S. stockpile by the mid-1990s. Critics of proposals for new chemical weapons respond that current supplies could remain usable much longer if properly maintained. "Clearly sometime they will have to be replaced, but the question is when," said John Isaacs of the Council for a Livable World. "It's better to keep the weapons we have going than to produce a whole new generation of weapons." [8]

Defensive measures are the other aspect of chemical capacities. Modern armies have developed a panoply of devices that can effectively protect combat personnel even from the ex-

---

[5] "Chemical Warfare: Many Unanswered Questions," General Accounting Office, 1983; "Soviet Chemical Weapons Threat," Defense Intelligence Agency, 1985; and "Report of the Chemical Warfare Review Commission," June 1985.

[6] Estimate by Professor Julian Perry Robinson of the University of Sussex, England. Figures quoted in briefing materials supplied by the Council for a Livable World, a Boston-based organization that supports arms control.

[7] President Reagan appointed the eight-member commission March 11, 1985, to provide an independent appraisal of the chemical warfare posture. Democrats in Congress accused him of stacking it with individuals who supported his contention that the arsenal should be rebuilt. The members were Walter J. Stoessel Jr., former under secretary of state, chairman; ex-Reps. Barber B. Conable Jr., R-N.Y., and John N. Erlenborn, R-Ill.; ex-Secretary of State Alexander M. Haig Jr.; former national security adviser Zbigniew Brzezinski; John G. Kester, a lawyer and former Pentagon official; retired Army Gen. Richard E. Cavazos; and Philip Bakes Jr., Continental Airlines president.

[8] Isaacs is director of the council's Washington, D.C, office. He and others quoted in this report were interviewed by the author unless otherwise indicated.

tremely potent nerve agents. The Soviets not only have provided individual protective suits for soldiers, but have designed their tanks and personnel carriers to keep out surrounding poisons. The United States, which has spent some $4 billion on chemical defensive measures since 1978, provides sophisticated protective gear for individuals, although its vehicles generally are not chemical-proof. While protective devices can prevent immediate combat deaths on a mass scale, they carry a high cost. Even the high-tech garments available to NATO troops are hot and bulky, and greatly limit sight and hearing. In warm weather, troops might be able to fight for only a short time before becoming exhausted.

Debate Over Development of Binary Arms

To remedy the perceived chemical imbalance, Pentagon officials have for more than a decade advocated development of binary munitions. Although these weapons have been the subject of intense debate in Congress, they do not represent a fundamental intensification of lethal technology. They are designed to deliver the same nerve agents that existing unitary chemical weapons do. The difference is that unitary weapons are filled with the lethal compounds themselves, while binary weapons are composed of two or more chemicals, each less dangerous in itself. The compounds are kept separated until the shell or bomb is fired, at which point they are automatically combined to form the more deadly product. The chief argument for binary weapons is that they are safer to store and transport than other chemical weapons.

One of the two binary weapons approved by Congress last year — the "Bigeye" bomb — has been sharply criticized in many quarters for technical failings.[9] The goal of the Bigeye program is to provide a chemical weapon that can be dropped by aircraft on enemy air bases. But overcoming Soviet air defenses poses a significant problem for the Bigeye system. Attacking aircraft are expected to approach their targets at high speeds and low altitudes, creating high temperatures that could cause the bombs to explode. To prevent that, defense planners have had to devise tactics that could expose pilots to intense anti-aircraft fire and cause the bombs to misfire. In a report specifically on the Bigeve,[10] the General Accounting Office

---

[9] The other was a 155 millimeter artillery shell *(see p. 107).*
[10] "Bigeye Bomb: An Evaluation of DOD's Chemical and Developmental Tests," May 1986.

sharply criticized the bomb and called for the Pentagon to reconsider its backing of the project. Defense officials plan to continue pushing for the Bigeye, however.

Technical objections to the Bigeye were one reason that binary munitions were the only major weapons system sought by the administration to be rejected by Congress in Reagan's first term. In 1982, 1983 and 1984 the House refused to approve funds for production of the munitions. In 1985, however, Congress agreed to authorize $148 million for production of binary weapons. Even so, the lawmakers barred final assembly of the munitions until December 1987, required that existing stocks of unitary weapons be destroyed by 1994 and that NATO approval be obtained before production begins.

The NATO requirement has served to focus attention on European concerns over the new weapons. NATO defense ministers, meeting in Brussels, voted May 22 to back the weapons, although several of the attending European officials objected. Rep. Dante B. Fascell, D-Fla., chairman of the House Foreign Affairs Committee, among others, has claimed that the way for approval was cleared by a private deal arranged between Reagan and West German Chancellor Helmut Kohl.

The agreement was that the United States would remove its chemical weapons from West Germany in exchange for West German approval of the binary weapons. Critics have complained that the decision amounted to unilateral chemical disarmament in Europe, since the binary weapons would not be stored on European soil. Pentagon officials point out that they had already been required by Congress to remove and destroy the existing unitary weapons by 1994.

Progress and Obstacles in the Negotiations

Nations have long been willing to say that chemical weapons were terrible and should be abolished, but unwilling to agree on how to enforce a ban on production and use. Both a 1925 treaty outlawing chemical arms, known as the Geneva Protocol, and a 1972 treaty banning biological weapons[11] lack procedures for verifying that their conditions are not secretly being violated. The Geneva disarmament conference has struggled since 1968 with the question of how to verify a chemical treaty.

---

[11] Delegates from 28 countries, including the United States, meeting in Geneva in 1925, drafted and signed a Protocol for the Prohibition of the Use in War of Asphyxiating, Poisonous or Other Gases, and of Bacteriological Methods of Warfare. The treaty was ratified before World War II by all the major powers except Japan and, ironically, the United States, which has been a principal sponsor of the Geneva conference. While the 1925 treaty mentioned bacteriological warfare, it was outdated by subsequent laboratory discoveries. A treaty attempting to restrict all known biological agents was drawn up in 1972, the U.N. Convention on the Prohibition of Bacteriological and Toxin Weapons. It was ratified by the U.S. Senate in 1974, along with the Geneva Protocol.

Yellow Rain Controversy

"Yellow rain" — the biologically produced poison allegedly used by the Soviet Union and its allies in Southeast Asia — has been a central element in recent debates over chemical and biological weapons. Reagan administration officials repeatedly have pointed to evidence of yellow rain as justification both for a new U.S. chemical weapons program, and for caution in seeking a chemical arms-control agreement with the Russians.

Since the late 1970s, U.S. officials and some outside experts have argued that Laotian and Vietnamese forces, supplied by the Soviet Union, were attacking rebellious villages in Laos and Cambodia with a lethal toxin produced from certain types of fungus. Dispensed from airplanes in the form of a yellow cloud, the toxin trichothecene was alleged to have killed thousands of people by inducing skin blistering, bloody vomiting, diarrhea and hemorrhaging.

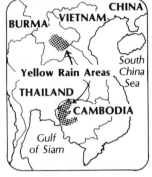

Support for the U.S. claims has come from two sources. One is laboratory studies, which have found levels of trichothecene on leaves and rocks from the areas said to have been attacked by yellow rain, as well as in the blood and urine of people exposed to the attacks. According to the State Department, the fungi that produce trichothecene do not occur naturally in Southeast Asia, so the toxin must have been introduced into the environment as a weapon. Refugees told of the deaths of many villagers who had been exposed to yellow rain.

Some scientists quickly challenged the yellow rain theory, however. Led by Harvard biochemist Matthew Meselson, they raised the possibility that the cases of trichothecene poisoning were a natural phenomenon resulting from the consumption of moldy food. The trichothecene-bearing yellow spots on leaves and rocks, Meselson said, were drops of bee feces on which mold had grown. In Southeast Asia, as in some other parts of the world, swarms of bees on occasion release so much fecal material that it seems to be raining. As for the testimony of victims, critics suggested that the refugees might have been trying to curry favor with U.S. officials by agreeing with their questions about toxic attacks.

Evidence recently released by the British and Canadian governments has undermined a key point in the administration's case — that there is no natural source of the toxin in Laos and Cambodia. Samples collected by researchers of the two countries have shown that some people in the region who had never been exposed to yellow rain attacks had measurable levels of trichothecene in their blood. The State Department and other supporters of the yellow rain theory have not abandoned their case, however.

The impetus for breaking the deadlock came from the Reagan-Gorbachev meeting last fall. One of the few concrete results of their encounter was a commitment to speed up chemical control negotiations. "The two sides agreed to intensify bilateral discussions on the level of experts on all aspects of such a chemical weapons ban, including the question of verification," said the joint summit statement. In addition, Gorbachev has indicated qualified acceptance of the U.S. position on one of the many remaining verification issues. His statement on the issue was part of his Jan. 15 proposal calling for the abolition of nuclear weapons by the year 2000.

Some analysts see political pressures on the two men as the key factor in making a chemical treaty possible. Having begun the summit process, each wants to show it has been worth the effort. "The prospects for arms control of chemical weapons look more promising. Both Reagan and Gorbachev need to demonstrate progress, to look serious on arms control," said Brad Roberts of the Georgetown University Center for Strategic and International Studies (CSIS), a specialist on chemical weapons issues. "So there is pressure for an agreement — but they probably won't be able to resolve their differences over nuclear weapons. So they will look for an area where the differences aren't very big. The opportunities are there in the field of chemical weapons."

But the difficulties of verifying a chemical treaty are immense. For one thing, the nerve agents that make up most of the modern chemical arsenal are quite similar to pesticides. It is possible to turn a pesticide factory into a weapons facility by altering a few chemical processes. As a result, any weapons treaty will require regulation of the worldwide chemical industry. So nations with substantial pesticide production, such as Japan, have a vital interest in a treaty even though they do not have any chemical weapons.

The key U.S. statement in the longstanding Geneva negotiations was outlined by Vice President George Bush on April 18, 1984. Bush presented a proposal containing two basic principles that have gained general acceptance — that chemical weapons stockpiles and production facilities should be destroyed within 10 years, and that "on-site" inspections be made by outside observers to ensure adequate verification. The proposal also contained a controversial provision — to require that a nation open chemical facilities to inspection whenever another nation suspected it was producing chemical weapons. The Soviets have been extremely reluctant to accept this proposal.

The Legacy of Ypres

Throughout the history of battle, men have searched for chemical and biological means to supplement the destructive force of weapons powered by muscle or gunpowder. Over the centuries they tried everything from creating lethal smoke by burning poison-soaked rags to hurling the infected bodies of men or animals into an enemy camp. But generally their efforts did not have much impact on the course of war.

It was not until the development of the European industrial economy in the 19th century that the means for chemical killing on a mass scale became available. The process developed in Germany for synthesizing fabric dyes, for example, created large quantities of poisonous chlorine gas as a byproduct. While chemical weapons were not used in the wars of that era, there was growing concern that they might be in the future. That anxiety culminated in the Hague Gas Declaration of 1899, in which 25 nations, not including the United States, pledged to abstain from using "asphyxiating or deleterious gases" against their enemies.

At the outset of World War I, most military planners were reluctant to consider chemical weapons. Even after the German General Staff agreed to undertake an experiment with chlorine gas, it was so skeptical of the military value of chemicals that it declined to provide extra troops to exploit any opening in enemy lines the gas might create. But there was no question about the efficacy of the first gas attack, launched by the German army along a four-mile front held by British, French and Canadian troops in the Ypres area on the French-Belgian border, April 22, 1915. Within minutes, the Allied troops were reeling in terror from the deadly green clouds of chlorine. If the Germans had had enough troops to sustain their surprise success, they might have changed the course of the war. But they did not, and by that night Allied forces had regrouped and stabilized the front.

The Allied armies soon developed primitive protective equipment, and within six months the British retaliated with a gas attack. Then in December the Germans struck with phosgene, a choking gas capable of penetrating their enemies' protective masks. Still later, after the masks had been improved, the Germans used vomit gas to force soldiers to remove their masks and expose their lungs to phosgene. Finally, in July 1917, three months after America's entry into the war, the Germans introduced the most effective chemical weapon of the war — mustard gas, which causes painful blisters on the skin. Gas masks were virtually useless against mustard, and no effective

Storing, Destroying Current Stocks

Whatever the United States decides to do about production of new chemical weapons, it will be faced with some difficult choices concerning its current supplies of lethal chemicals. The nation's existing chemical stockpile is stored in 10 locations: eight depots in the continental United States and one on Johnston Island in the Pacific, as well as undisclosed sites in West Germany. The cost of maintaining the supplies, which are buried in underground bunkers, is about $65 million a year.

Although there are sharp debates over the condition of the current stockpiles, in most cases the stored weapons are not seen as environmental threats to the surrounding areas. The major exceptions are the rapidly deteriorating M-55 rockets, which are beginning to leak their highly toxic contents. The rockets have been a particularly troubling issue for residents of Richmond, Ky., who have deep fears about the 70,000 rockets stored in the nearby Lexington-Blue Grass depot.

The 1985 law that authorized production of new binary weapons also required the Pentagon to adopt a plan for destruction of existing chemical weapons by 1994. According to the Chemical Warfare Review Commission, most scientists now believe that the nerve gases and other components of the U.S. arsenal could be incinerated safely. The hot question, however, is where to do the incineration.

One option would be to build a single facility for destruction. But that would require transportation of large quantities of highly toxic materials around the country — an undertaking that could generate strong opposition from areas through which the weapons were moved. To a somewhat lesser degree, the same problem also applies to the idea of regional destruction plants.

Pentagon officials announced July 1 that they were leaning toward building destruction facilities at each depot. If implemented, that decision would eliminate the transportation problem, but could involve very high costs. The Defense Department estimates that future costs of destroying the weapons will be $1.9 billion. But the review commission predicted that costs would be up to three times that amount, and other estimates have approached $20 billion. A final decision on a destruction plan is not due until the end of the year.

defense was developed against it. From then until the end of the war, both sides made increasingly heavy use of gas.

Still, the verdict on chemicals was not settled by the war's end. Gas casualties were substantial — an estimated 1.3 million — but only 7 percent of those who were gassed died as a result. However, untold numbers were disabled for a lifetime. The most severely affected force was the Russian army, which suffered 35 percent of all the war's gas casualties. Among the American casualties, according to a report of the surgeon gen-

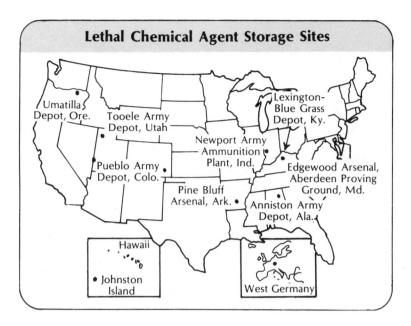

Lethal Chemical Agent Storage Sites

Umatilla Depot, Ore.

Tooele Army Depot, Utah

Pueblo Army Depot, Colo.

Newport Army Ammunition Plant, Ind.

Pine Bluff Arsenal, Ark.

Anniston Army Depot, Ala.

Lexington-Blue Grass Depot, Ky.

Edgewood Arsenal, Aberdeen Proving Ground, Md.

Hawaii

Johnston Island

West Germany

eral after the war, about 2.7 percent were gas victims but only 2 percent of those victims died of their injuries.[12]

Moral abhorrence over the use of chemicals — together with the continuing ambivalence of military planners about the value of such weapons — led to the adoption of an international ban on their use in 1925. The Geneva Protocol, signed by the representatives of 28 nations including the United States and the Soviet Union, outlawed the use of poison gases in war, except in retaliation. However, the agreement ran into trouble in the U.S. Senate, where lobbying opposition from the chemical industry and the military services was strong. The Senate did not formally ratify the agreement until 1974. Gas was used occasionally in the years after the protocol was signed, notably in 1936 by Italian troops in Ethiopia and Japanese soldiers in China after their invasion in 1937. In addition, advances in the production of agricultural pesticides led to German development of lethal nerve gases.

There are a number of theories as to why the armies in World War II did not use lethal chemicals. Supporters of the current U.S. chemical program contend that fear of retaliation prevented Germany from using its ample chemical supplies on the battlefield. However, Germany did use poison gas to kill many of the six million Jews who met death in concentration camps before the war ended. Critics of chemical weapons argue that it was their lack of military usefulness that prevented either side from unleashing them against the other. During the war Presi-

---

[12] Report of the Surgeon General of the U.S. Army to the Secretary of War (Government Printing Office), 1920.

dent Roosevelt appointed a commission to consider U.S. use of chemical weapons. "We told the president that chemical weapons would not affect the outcome of the war — they would merely prolong the fighting," said Saul Hormats, a chemical weapons expert who served on the panel.[13] In 1943, Roosevelt proclaimed that the United States would never be the first to use chemical weapons.

After the war, the interests of chemical weapons planners shifted to the idea of "non-lethal war" — using chemicals to incapacitate enemy soldiers without killing them. Not much came of the efforts, although the Army did acquire a large stock of a psychedelic chemical called BZ. BZ was later determined to be too unreliable for battlefield use, particularly after experiments in Vietnam showed it had a disconcerting tendency to turn enemy soldiers into uncontrollable killers. Far more significant in Vietnam were the military's reliance on two different kinds of chemical agents — tear gas and herbicides. Tear gas and other supposedly non-fatal "crowd control" compounds were used to drive Vietcong troops out of their hiding places. Agent Orange and other herbicides were used to defoliate jungle and agricultural regions, in order to deprive enemy forces of concealing cover and food.

Both chemical usages provoked strong criticism. The United Nations condemned tear gas use as contrary to the Geneva Protocol. Agent Orange was found to contain dioxin, an extremely toxic chemical whose long-term health effects are still being debated. U.S. soldiers in Vietnam who were exposed to it have argued, before the Veterans Administration and in courts, that it was responsible for health problems they later developed.[14] In response to public opposition to U.S. chemical policies — as well as to the continuing outcry over the death of some 6,000 sheep following the 1968 accidental release of nerve gas from the Army's Dugway Proving Ground in Utah — President Nixon announced Nov. 25, 1969, that he was ordering a halt to production of biological weapons, and he reaffirmed that the nation would never be the first to use chemical weapons. The declaration marked the end of new U.S. chemical weapons production, although current stocks were retained and research programs continued.

Manfred Hamm of the Heritage Foundation observed, "No military man likes chemical weapons. Our neglect of chemical weapons is a reflection of military ambivalence about them."

[13] Hormats recently retired after 37 years with the U.S. Army's Edgewood Arsenal in Maryland.

[14] See "Agent Orange: The Continuing Debate," *E.R.R.*, 1984 Vol. II, pp. 489-508. Also see, especially for U.S. use of tear gas in Vietnam, "Chemical-Biological Weaponry," *E.R.R.*, 1969 Vol. I, pp. 451-470.

Chemical Weapons

Part of the reason for that caution is that many soldiers have the same moral repugnance for chemical weapons that civilians do. The insidious character of chemical weapons seems to violate a military code that goes back to the days of chivalry and man-to-man combat.

Chemical weapons have a number of deficiencies. The most obvious is their unpredictability — the effectiveness of chemicals depends on weather and other uncontrollable factors. The risks of chemical use are particularly great in densely populated Europe, where a stray breeze could kill friendly civilians. Chemical weapons also must be judged in competition with more conventional armaments. Each chemical-filled shell or rocket that is fired represents a sacrifice of other kinds of destructive capability. "You're wasting firepower with poison gas," said Hormats. "There are a hell of a lot of better munitions."

Potential Uses in a Future European War

Despite those potential drawbacks, military planners in both East and West see specific military uses for chemical weapons. For the Soviet Union, the value of chemicals is based on its fundamental strategic principle for a conventional war — the rapid advance. According to many military analysts, including David C. Isby, an expert on Soviet military power, the Soviet army is primarily equipped and trained for offensive action.[15] Chemical weapons could contribute significantly to any fast-moving Soviet attack in Central Europe. Surprise use of chemicals could open up defensive gaps in the first hours of the war. Chemical attacks on key NATO command centers could disrupt defensive coordination, while contamination of port facilities could slow arrival of vital reinforcements.

Soviet use of chemicals would weaken Western defense capabilities in other ways as well. Already numerically inferior, NATO ground troops would find it even harder to resist if burdened with cumbersome and debilitating protective garments. Attacks on NATO air bases would force fliers and ground crews into protective gear, slowing the rate at which planes could depart for combat missions, reducing NATO's ability to control European air space and probably depriving its ground forces of vital close air support.

Western commanders probably would not have as much to gain from chemical use. The main purpose of chemical arms would be to discourage the other side from bringing them into play. A key assumption of supporters of the U.S. chemical modernization program is that only the threat of retaliation "in

---

[15] See Isby's *Weapons and Tactics of the Soviet Army*, 1981.

kind" — with the same type of weapons — will keep the Soviets from using chemicals. Another view holds that the threat of retaliation with nuclear weapons would be enough to prevent a Soviet chemical attack. France has indicated that it will respond with nuclear weapons if chemically attacked. However, NATO planners have been trying strenuously in recent years to reduce their dependence on nuclear defenses, and it is not clear that the West would risk a nuclear exchange in response to Soviet use of chemicals.

If chemicals did become a factor, NATO leaders presumably would not expect to kill large numbers of Soviet troops with chemicals, given their ample protective equipment. Instead, the goal would be to force their troops to don anti-chemical gear and thus handicap their fighting ability. "The deterrent effect of chemical weapons is that you impose the same combat conditions on your opponent," said Hamm. "You make them wear protective suits once they start using the stuff, thus degrading their own performance."

Deadly New Terrors

For all the potential dangers posed by the U.S. and Soviet chemical stockpiles, most strategic analysts do not see much chance of an all-out conventional war being fought in Central Europe any time soon. But smaller conflicts are occurring and are likely to continue in many other parts of the world, and the prospects for use of chemical weapons is greater. "The sad fact is that a half century of widely accepted international restraint on the development of chemical weapons is in danger of breaking down," Secretary of State George P. Shultz said last year.[16]

The most basic reason for the spread of chemical weapons is that the technology of making them is readily available to many nations. Pesticide, fertilizer and pharmaceutical factories, which in some cases can be converted to production of lethal agents, are increasingly found in developing countries. In contrast to the raw materials needed for producing nuclear weapons, the compounds used in making chemical weapons are easy to obtain.

In addition, the constraints which work to prevent chemical arms use in Europe are considerably weaker in other regions. With a few notable exceptions the Third World has had little experience with chemical weapons, and the people do not nec-

---

[16] Speech before the National Academy of Sciences, March 6, 1985.

essarily share the powerful moral revulsion that Europeans do. After all, the victim of a chemical attack is no more dead than a casualty of more common weapons.

Iraq appears to have made the most use of chemical weapons in recent years. Although the Iraqi government has denied employing chemicals, both the United States and the United Nations say they have conclusive evidence that it has.[17] The U.N. and U.S. reports say that chemicals, including both mustard and nerve agents, were produced in Iraq, possibly with pesticide equipment supplied by West Germany, and were used against the Iranians first in 1984 and sporadically since then.

U.S. troops in training

Other chemical attacks in recent decades have been shrouded in secrecy. Egypt may have employed lethal agents against rebels in Yemen in the 1960s. U.S. officials suspect Ethiopia has used such weapons against separatist guerrillas. Along with allegedly using chemicals against insurgents in Laos and Cambodia, Vietnam has been accused of using chemicals to repel Chinese troops during their 1979 border clashes.[18]

The United States and other developed countries have little control over Third World chemical proliferation. Especially after the relatively mild steps taken against Iraq — the United States acted to curb chemical exports to both Iraq and Iran — some governments may conclude they can include chemicals in their war plans without having to worry about tough international sanctions — such as might be imposed under a chemical non-proliferation agreement. Until there is a U.S.-Soviet agreement on eliminating existing chemical stocks, however, most other countries are likely to oppose any non-proliferation program. Alternatively, nations that supply international chemical markets could act on their own to control exports of

---

[17] The United Nations report on Iraq's chemical attacks, entitled "Report of the Specialists Appointed by the Secretary-General to Investigate Allegations by the Islamic Republic of Iran Concerning the Use of Chemical Weapons," was released March 26, 1984. The U.S. State Department officially accused Iraq of chemical use in a statement it issued March 5, 1984.

[18] See Sterling Seagrave, *Yellow Rain,* 1981.

products with potential military uses. The United States announced June 5 that it was limiting chemical exports to Syria. Officials from a number of supplier nations, convened by the Australian government, have been meeting privately over the past year on ways to restrict sensitive products.

Biological Weapons in Gene-Splicing Age

Until recently, thinking about the military applications of biology was dominated by two main ideas. One was that there was a clear line separating biological weapons — disease-causing living organisms — from non-living chemical agents. The other was that biological weapons were not very useful in modern war. They were slow in taking effect; soldiers infected with fatal viruses or bacteria might continue to fight on for some time. Even worse, they were extremely risky, since a disease that killed enemy soldiers might soon spread to friendly troops or civilians.

Military experts did not ignore the possibilities of biological weapons. For two decades after World War II, the U.S. Army conducted extensive biological experiments, testing ways to wage "germ warfare" as well as methods for defending the civilian population against it. Supposedly harmless bacteria were secretly released over cities, and human volunteers were exposed to pathogenic agents. In some cases, the tests led to illness and death among unsuspecting citizens.[19]

By 1969, though, experts at the National Security Council had concluded that biological weapons offered no real advantages. Nor was any retaliatory capacity deemed necessary, since a biological attack on the United States was widely seen as leading to a nuclear response. Those conclusions cleared the way for Nixon's proclamation renouncing biological weapons, and ordering the destruction of existing germ-war supplies. A similar perception by military experts around the world led to the approval three years later of the United Nations Convention on the Prohibition of Bacteriological and Toxin Weapons. The treaty, which has been called one of the strongest arms-control agreements ever approved, called for a total ban on development, production or use of biological weapons, "whatever their origin or method of production." Unlike the 1925 Geneva Protocol, the treaty did not even allow even for retaliatory use of biological weapons. However, it lacked any procedures for verification.

The progress of genetic engineering has undermined key assumptions about biological weapons. Using recombinant-

---

[19] The extent of this testing came to light in 1977 Senate hearings and in a report, "U.S. Army Activity in the U.S. Biological Warfare Programs," dated Feb. 24, 1977. For background, see "Chemical-Biological Warfare," *E.R.R.*, 1977 Vol. I, pp. 393-412.

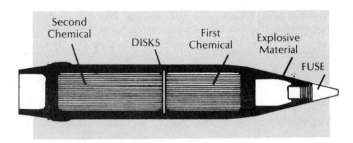

155mm. Binary Munition

Second Chemical   DISKS   First Chemical   Explosive Material   FUSE

1 After artillery shell is fired, disks rupture and chemicals mix

2 The fuse detonates explosive material, spreading the lethal chemicals over a wide area

DNA technology developed mostly in the past decade, scientists are able to manipulate the basic hereditary information of organisms. They can take specific genes from one species and insert them into the genetic material of another to create a creature with a new set of characteristics. While the techniques were developed for peaceful purposes, their potential for military applications are ominous.

One military application of genetic engineering might be to expand production of toxins, which are poisons produced by organisms. Toxins already occupied a gray area between chemical and biological weapons, but their importance was limited by production difficulties. Tons of living creatures had to be processed to produce small quantities of toxin. With gene-splicing, organisms could be altered to make militarily significant amounts of toxins. Another use would be to tailor diseases to increase their killing power or make them easier to store and deliver. In addition, mass quantities of vaccines could be produced, making it possible to inoculate the domestic population before launching a biological attack.

The dangers of genetic engineering are particularly troubling in light of what U.S. officials say is a concerted Soviet effort to develop new biological weapons. The most dramatic evidence was an outbreak in 1979 of anthrax, a deadly disease common to cattle, in the Soviet city of Sverdlovsk. According to U.S. intelligence officials, an explosion at a nearby biological-warfare laboratory released anthrax spores into the environment, leading to the death of up to 1,000 people. The Soviet government denies the charge, saying that the outbreak was caused by the eating of meat naturally tainted by the disease. Other evidence comes from Russian emigre scientists, who report that vast resources are being spent on developing genetically engineered weapons.

Recommended Reading List

Books

Hersh, Seymour M., *Chemical and Biological Warfare,* Bobbs-Merrill Co., 1968.

Isby, David C., *Weapons and Tactics of the Soviet Army,* Jane's Publishing Inc., 1981.

Seagrave, Sterling, *Yellow Rain,* M. Evans and Co., 1981.

Articles

Bernstein, Barton J., "Why We Didn't Use Poison Gas in World War II," *American Heritage,* August-September 1985.

Douglass, Joseph D. Jr. and H. Richard Lukens, "The Expanding Arena of Chemical-Biological Warfare," *Strategic Review,* fall 1984.

Hamm, Manfred R., "Deterrence, Chemical Warfare, and Arms Control," *Orbis,* spring 1985.

Kucewicz, William, "Beyond Yellow Rain: The Threat of Soviet Genetic Engineering," *The Wall Street Journal,* April 23, 25, 27 and May 1, 3, 8, 10, 18, 1984.

Meselson, Matthew et al., "Yellow Rain," *Scientific American,* September 1985.

Roberts, Brad, "Chemical Weapons: A Policy Overview," *Issues in Science and Technology,* spring 1986.

Smith, R. Jeffrey, "GAO Blasts Bigeye Chemical Weapon," *Science,* June 20, 1986.

Tucker, Jonathan B., "Gene Wars," *Foreign Policy,* winter 1984-85.

Reports and Studies

Chemical Warfare Review Commission, "Report," U.S. Government Printing Office, June 1985.

Council for a Livable World, "Binary Nerve Gas Production," February 1986.

Defense Intelligence Agency, "Soviet Chemical Weapons Threat," Defense Department, 1985.

Editorial Research Reports: "Chemical-Biological Warfare," 1977 Vol. I, pp. 393-412; "Agent Orange: The Continuing Debate," 1984 Vol. II, pp. 489-508; "Genetic Breakthroughs" 1986 Vol. I, pp. 1-20.

General Accounting Office, "Chemical Warfare: Many Unanswered Questions," April 29, 1983; "Bigeye Bomb: An Evaluation of DOD's Chemical and Developmental Tests," May 1986.

Senate Armed Services Committee, March 1, 1985, hearing on "Binary Chemicals," in "Department of Defense Authorization for Appropriations for Fiscal Year 1986," Senate Hearing 99-58, part 3, U.S. Government Printing Office.

U.S. Department of State, "Chemical Warfare in Southeast Asia and Afghanistan," March 22, 1982.

Graphics: Maps, illustrations by staff artists; photos, U.S. Air Force.

THE STRATEGIC PACIFIC

by

Mary H. Cooper

April 25
1 9 8 6

THE STRATEGIC PACIFIC

When leaders of the seven principal non-communist industrial countries meet in Tokyo May 4-6 for their annual summit conference,[1] world attention will inevitably follow. The vast Pacific Basin's economic and strategic importance will again be brought to the forefront of American public thought, which recently has fastened almost solely upon events in the Mediterranean. While the thrust of the conference is economic, especially Japan's role in international trade and finance, U.S. security interests in the Pacific are not left aside, even if they do not appear on the formal agenda. The Pacific Basin, in President Reagan's words, "is where the future of the world lies."[2] As if to underline the importance he ascribes to Asia, Reagan will make a side trip to Indonesia and attend a meeting of the Association of Southeast Asian Nations on the island of Bali before going on to Tokyo.

America's vision of a new, dominant Pacific era is nonetheless marred with trouble spots. The economic boom experienced by several of the countries has also brought political unrest, especially in the Philippines and South Korea. Often a growing middle class is demanding greater political freedom than the governments are willing to cede. The downfall of Ferdinand E. Marcos as president of the Philippines ended 20 years of despotic rule that is widely blamed for destroying the Pacific island nation's once burgeoning economy and driving many of its citizens into the arms of an insurgency that seeks to set up a communist government.

The growth of the insurgency despite the overwhelming support shown newly elected President Corazon Aquino has renewed concern about the fate of two U.S. military bases in the Philippines. For the removal of Subic Bay Naval Base and Clark Air Base — the two largest U.S. military installations outside the United States — remains a central demand of the insurgents. The Pentagon has proposed other sites for Pacific bases, but no new basing arrangement would offer the same combination of proximity to the East Asian mainland and vital sea lanes, large capacity and cheap labor as Clark and Subic. Moving the bases would mean dispersing U.S. forces among several smaller

---

[1] The countries are the United States, Britain, Canada, France, West Germany, Italy and Japan. This will be the 12th annual conference. Last year's meeting was held in Bonn.
[2] See "Dawn of the Pacific Era," *E.R.R.*, 1985 Vol. II, pp. 497-516.

sites separated by long distances. Finally, construction costs as well as the cost of procuring more ships, aircraft and other weapons necessary to maintain the effectiveness of the Pacific forces would be exorbitant, possibly prohibitive, in an era of budget constraint in Washington.

The question of bases extends beyond the immediate region to other parts of what military and foreign policy planners call the Pacific theater. It comprises both the Pacific and Indian Oceans, as well as the volatile Persian Gulf, and the countries along their shores. The Soviet Union has reinforced its conventional and nuclear arsenals in its territories in Northeast Asia as well as in Vietnam, its principal Southeast Asian ally. To counter this perceived threat, Japan appears ready to assume a stronger defense posture than in the past, but pacifist and anti-nuclear sentiments are increasing among allies, particularly New Zealand, posing new limits to U.S. naval maneuverability in the South Pacific.

Uncertainty in Post-Marcos Philippines

But the political developments with the greatest immediate impact on U.S. strategic interests stem from the Feb. 25 downfall of Ferdinand E. Marcos.[3] His successor, Corazon Aquino, is in a race with time to restore stability to the 7,000-island nation and rebuild the economy, devastated by a $26 billion foreign debt, 20 percent unemployment and extreme poverty. While constitutional and military reform are essential components of Aquino's program to dismantle the corrupt political structure erected by Marcos over the past two decades, she has identified economic recovery as the main key to the survival of democracy.

The New People's Army (NPA), by most reports a completely indigenous communist movement organized by a handful of combatants in 1969, has grown to at least 12,000 and controls about one-fifth of the land area of the Philippines.[4] Despite Aquino's release of hundreds of communist detainees and her promise to offer amnesty to the insurgents, the NPA has continued its attacks in the countryside and the prospects for national reconciliation remain uncertain.

In addition to land reform, the insurgents and their political branch, the National Democratic Front (NDF), demand the removal of the U.S. bases from the Philippines. "We in the NDF don't believe that any country, any power, has any right to establish a military base in our country," declared Antonio Zumel, a member of the National Democratic Front. "... [W]e

---

[3] For background on Marcos' rule, see "Political Unrest in the Philippines," *E.R.R.*, 1983 Vol. II, pp. 801-820. Marcos left the country under U.S. pressure following tainted presidential elections Feb. 7 in which he claimed victory and the subsequent defection of his top military staff to the Aquino camp.

[4] The Philippine government estimates the guerrilla forces at 12,000 to 16,000, while the NPA claims to have 30,000 fighters.

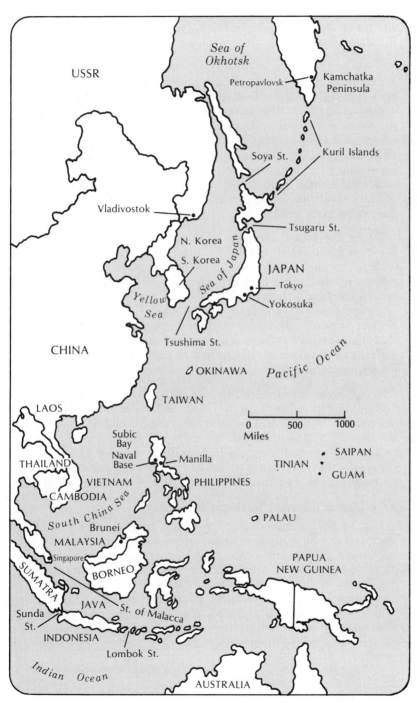

don't want the American bases in our country. We don't want any other foreign base in our country. We will never allow the Russians or any other foreign power to establish bases in our country." [5]

President Aquino has said she would honor the terms of the agreement allowing the United States to operate the bases until it expires in 1991. The bases — which are the second largest employer in the Philippines — are also a source of badly needed revenue for the economy, providing an estimated $350 million a year. On April 10, Aquino announced that the decision on the bases' future will be made by the Filipinos through a referendum that would be held after negotiating the renewal of a military treaty with the United States. These negotiations are due to begin in 1988.

Citing the bases' strategic importance, the Reagan administration has offered increased military aid to the Philippines, with an implicit aim toward crushing the insurgency if efforts toward reconciliation prove fruitless. In his recent visit to Manila — the first Cabinet-level visit since Aquino came to power — Defense Secretary Caspar W. Weinberger said that while the United States would also provide economic assistance, "I think that it's necessary to have some military assistance to continue with the reorganization, strengthening and modernization of the Philippine armed forces." [6]

The Reagan administration has asked Congress to approve $100 million in military aid for fiscal 1987 and about $80 million in economic assistance. Last year Congress turned down a similar request and authorized far more in economic aid ($125 million) than in military aid ($55 million). Aquino has repeatedly stated her preference for economic development as a means of removing the root cause of the insurgency's growth, poverty.

American and Soviet Strategic Interests

Led by the postwar boom in Japan, most countries of the Pacific Basin have made impressive economic gains. In particular, South Korea, Hong Kong, Singapore and Taiwan — the "four tigers" — have followed in Japan's footsteps as important consumers of industrial raw materials from the Third World and producers of manufactured goods for the industrial West. Today, the region has replaced Western Europe as America's chief trading area. [7] Protecting these vital markets remains a primary goal of U.S. strategy.

[5] Interviewed on the "MacNeil/Lehrer News Hour," Public Broadcasting System, Feb. 18, 1986.
[6] Weinberger spoke at a news conference in Manila April 4 during a 14-day defense-related tour of allied countries in East Asia.
[7] However, among individual nations, Canada is America's chief trade partner.

Collective Defense Treaties

Philippine Treaty: United States, Philippines (signed Aug. 30, 1951).

ANZUS: United States, New Zealand, Australia (signed Sept. 1, 1951).

Southeast Asia Collective Defense Treaty (SEATO): United States, Britain, France, New Zealand, Australia, Philippines, Thailand (signed Sept. 8, 1954). It was formally disbanded in 1975 but the nations pledged to honor related obligations to take "common action to maintain peace and security of Southeast Asia and the Paciffic."

Japanese Treaty: United States, Japan (signed Jan. 19, 1960).

Republic of Korea Treaty: United States, Republic of Korea (signed Oct. 1, 1953).

In addition to preserving the flow of trade, the United States has defined as its strategic interest the freedom of sea travel between the Pacific Ocean and the Persian Gulf. Most countries on the Pacific rim, including Japan, depend almost entirely on imports from the Persian Gulf states to fuel their industries. Oil tankers destined for Japan must pass through the war-torn gulf and then a series of straits — potential "choke points" — between the Indian Ocean and South China Sea.

Political stability in the Pacific has long been a U.S. goal, especially since World War II. The impasse of the Korean War (1950-53) and the U.S. withdrawal from Vietnam (1975) have frustrated America's aim. But it has been, and continues to be, pursued through multilateral and bilateral alliances and security treaties *(see above)* in combination with a permanent U.S. military presence in the Pacific.

East Asia's spectacular growth has been accompanied by an unprecedented military buildup by the Soviet Union in its Pacific territories. The Soviet Union began increasing its forces in Asia in 1969, but the buildup has accelerated since 1979. That year Russia began diverting some of its forces from its border with China to the Soviet Far East and created a separate Far Eastern theater of military operations.[8] The Soviet Pacific fleet has tripled in size since the mid-1970s to become the largest of the country's four fleets. Its maneuverability has been enhanced by access to the facilities which Americans built but abandoned at Cam Ranh Bay in Vietnam, now the largest Soviet naval forward-deployment base outside the Soviet Union.

During the same period Russia introduced in its Far Eastern territory intermediate-range nuclear missiles capable of reaching China and Japan. According to Western estimates, 170 SS-

[8] See "Soviet Military Power 1986," Defense Department, March 1986.

20 intermediate-range nuclear missile launchers are in the region and possibly one-third of the country's combat forces — including about 2,700 combat aircraft and strategic bombers — are deployed there. In 1978, the Soviets began posting additional troops on four islands in the Kuril chain north of Japan, which Russia has occupied since World War II. Japan's claim to these islands has kept the two countries from signing a peace treaty. Weinberger told the Japanese during his Pacific tour, "The Soviets have moved beyond what anyone might reasonably define as a defensive posture, and have assembled a clearly offensive arsenal [on the islands]."

The Soviet Union has not matched its military strength with diplomatic skill. Last year it did conclude a one-year fishing agreement with the South Pacific island of Kiribati, giving the Soviets their first tenuous foothold in that region. But they can count only two strong allies in East Asia — North Korea and Vietnam — and the economic weakness of these allies, standing in sharp contrast to the robust market economies of the region, cannot be lost on other developing countries.[9]

Even China, a Soviet ally until 1960, has turned to the West for technological expertise, finance and even some military assistance.[10] Despite a March 1986 Sino-Soviet agreement to double bilateral trade by 1990, the United States and Japan remain far ahead of the Soviet Union in terms of trade with China. Although further Soviet expansion is hardly ruled out, the Kremlin's desire for additional client states in the region may be tempered by the high cost of its current alliances.

Soviet military and economic aid to Vietnam, which maintains 150,000 troops in neighboring Cambodia, is expected to double between 1986 and 1989 to $1.6 billion a year. Since Mikhail S. Gorbachev became the Soviet leader in March 1985, Moscow has demonstrated a desire to reduce tensions with its East Asian neighbors. Trade and technical exchanges with China are growing, while the chill in relations with Japan has thawed somewhat following Soviet diplomatic initiatives this year. But remaining political differences appear likely to prevent these diplomatic forays from damaging U.S. standing with these two Pacific giants.

Deterrence Aim in Pacific, Indian Oceans

The basic strategy to protect U.S. interests in the Pacific is the same as in other other areas of the world. As stated by

---

[9] The Soviet Union has a mutual defense treaty with North Korea and a treaty of friendship with Vietnam. It also provides military and economic assistance to Cambodia and Laos.

[10] See "China: Quest for Stability and Development," *E.R.R.*, 1984 Vol. I, pp. 269-288, and "Sino-Soviet Relations," *E.R.R.*, 1977 Vol. I, pp. 81-100.

Weinberger, "We seek to prevent war by maintaining forces and demonstrating the determination to use them, if necessary, in ways that will persuade our adversaries that the cost of any attack on our vital interests will exceed the benefits they could hope to gain. The label for this strategy is deterrence. It is the core of our defense strategy today, as it has been for most of the postwar period." [11]

Just as in Western Europe, this strategy is formulated with one primary adversary in mind — the Soviet Union — as it has been for the past four decades. As in Europe, it is implemented by "forward deployment" and by the formation of alliances with countries in the area to share the burden of collective defense. But in other ways the Pacific theater is quite unlike Europe, where the allied members of the North Atlantic Treaty Organization (NATO) lie close together and land forces make up the bulk of defenses. The Pacific command, covering 60 percent of the Earth's surface, relies on naval and air forces.

Countries bordering the Pacific and Indian oceans, as well as the Persian Gulf and Arabian Sea, are all within the Pacific theater. They are highly diverse, and their relations with the two superpowers are often not clearly defined. Not all U.S. allies in this region share the American view that the Soviet Union is the main threat to their security. Some consider China the greater menace. South Korea is clearly most concerned about North Korea, whose forces are poised along the 38th parallel, while Thailand perceives its main threat from the Vietnamese who occupy neighboring Cambodia.

Strategy Evolution

A merica's interest in the Pacific as a lucrative market has been evident since Commodore Matthew Perry opened Japan to trade in 1853. But it was only at the close of the 19th century that the United States greatly expanded its presence in the Far East and set the stage for its permanent military presence in the Pacific. The United States seized the Philippines from Spain during the Spanish-American War (1898) and annexed the islands. That same year the Hawaiian Islands, Guam and several other Pacific islands came under American control, leaving this country with a colonial empire thousands of miles from its shores. New territories, at great distances from home, required naval bases and a substantial Pacific fleet.

[11] Caspar W. Weinberger, "U.S. Defense Strategy," *Foreign Affairs*, spring 1986, pp. 676-677.

After World War I, Japan set out on its own expansionist course. Japan's invasion of China in 1932 led ultimately to the extension of World War II to the Pacific in 1941. After Japan's defeat in 1945, "containing" the Soviet Union within its postwar borders replaced Japanese military expansionism as the chief U.S. security concern in the region. This concern was heightened in 1949, when Mao Tse-tung expelled the Nationalist government to Taiwan and established a communist government, initially allied with the Soviet Union, in mainland China.

The United States has twice committed troops to conflicts in the Pacific since then, first in Korea and then in Vietnam. In neither war could it claim absolute victory. The Korean peninsula was divided in 1945 according to the locations of the forces that liberated it from 35 years of Japanese occupation, the Soviets to the north of the 38th parallel and the Americans to the south. Two years after Syngman Rhee was elected president of the newly created Republic of Korea (South Korea) in 1948, the Truman administration defined a U.S. "defense perimeter" in the Pacific. In January 1950, Secretary of State Dean Acheson said in a National Press Club speech that countries lying outside the perimeter — running from Alaska, along the Aleutian Islands, Japan, the Ryukyu Islands to the Philippines — would be responsible for their own self-defense and could not count on U.S. help in case of attack.

Republicans in Congress later charged that South Korea's exclusion invited the invasion from the north, which came in June 1950. The Democratic People's Republic (North Korea) invaded the south in an effort to reunify the peninsula under the communist regime of Kim Il Sung. The invasion set off a war that was to last three years and cost some 500,000 lives. The United States quickly won United Nations' backing and sent in defense troops under the command of Gen. Douglas MacArthur.[12] Ultimately, the North Koreans were forced to withdraw to the 38th parallel, but tensions between the two Koreas persist and 40,000 U.S. troops remain stationed in the south.

While the Korean War ended in an impasse, the Vietnam War turned into a U.S. military defeat. The United States first committed combat forces in Vietnam in March 1965 and nearly 10 years later pulled out the few remaining troops upon the fall of Saigon. The conflict, ending in reunification of Vietnam under communist control, claimed the lives of 58,000 Americans and hundreds of thousands of Vietnamese.[13] The Vietnam de-

---

[12] For background on the war and its aftermath, see "Divided Korea," *E.R.R.*, 1968 Vol. I, pp. 301-320; and Joseph C. Goulden, *Korea: The Untold Story of the War* (Times Books, 1982).

[13] For background on U.S. involvement in Vietnam, see "Vietnam War Reconsidered," *E.R.R.*, 1983 Vol. I, pp. 189-212; and Stanley Karnow, *Vietnam: A History* (Viking, 1983).

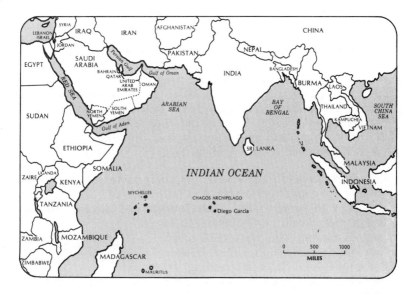

feat, accompanied by widespread anti-war protests at home, had a lasting effect on military strategy in the Pacific. "After the Vietnam war," wrote Adm. Robert L. J. Long, the Pacific commander-in-chief from 1979 to 1983, "the United States military figuratively turned its back on the Pacific." [14]

Forward Deployment and 600-Ship Navy

While the U.S. military presence in the Pacific dropped significantly after Vietnam, events in the Middle East and Southwest Asia placed additional strain on the remaining forces. The U.S. naval presence in the area was for many years limited to the Middle East Force, an intelligence-gathering unit first set up in 1949 at Bahrain on the Persian Gulf. But when Britain announced in 1968 that it would withdraw all its forces from "east of Suez" by the end of 1971, the Navy also began conducting peacetime patrols in the Indian Ocean, drawing on both the Atlantic and Pacific fleets. [15]

After the Iranian revolution of 1979, and particularly after the Soviet invasion and occupation of Afghanistan in 1979, these patrols were transformed into a continuous U.S. naval presence in the area under the Pacific command. The U.S. Navy established a facility on the British-owned island of Diego Garcia in the Indian Ocean 2,500 miles south of the Strait of Hormuz, through which oil tankers must pass en route from the Persian Gulf. The Soviet Union also maintains a permanent naval squadron of 20 to 30 ships in the Indian Ocean.

The downfall of the shah of Iran, the chief U.S. ally in the Middle East, also prompted the creation in 1980 of the Rapid

[14] Robert L. J. Long, "Coping with Distance — and a Bear on the Prowl," in *The Almanac of Seapower 1984* (Navy League of the United States, 1984), p. 59.
[15] See "Indian Ocean Policy," *E.R.R.*, 1971 Vol. I, pp. 187-206.

Deployment Force, trained and equipped specifically to intervene quickly in the Middle East. On Jan. 1, 1983, the force was
renamed Central Command, becoming the first new U.S. unified command since World War II, and receiving the
responsibility of coordinating all U.S. military operations in the
Southwest Asia region. Most of the force is based in the United
States, however, and only a few ships of the Middle East Force
are still deployed in the Arabian Sea.

As U.S. forces in the Pacific gradually increased after 1973,
Soviet deployments also grew, so that by the end of the decade,
according to some military calculations, the two superpowers
had a rough military equivalence in
East Asia and the western Pacific.
Since taking office, President Reagan
has emphasized defense spending, especially to increase the Navy's battle
force to 600 ships by the end of the
1980s, and enlarge the number of carrier groups from 12 to 15. The 600-
ship Navy carries a high price tag.
From fiscal 1980 through 1985, Navy
Department spending grew from $69.9
billion to $100.3 billion.[16]

John F. Lehman Jr.

The Reagan administration has
brought about changes in strategy as
well as spending. Navy Secretary John F. Lehman Jr. has set
forth a "forward offensive strategy" for naval action in the event
of war. U.S. naval forces — primarily carrier groups — would
move quickly from forward positions to attack enemy ships
before they could reach the high seas.[17] In the Pacific, protecting critical sea lanes, or choke points, is a strategic priority.
These include the Soya, Tsugaru and Tsushima straits which
control passage to and from the Sea of Japan and through which
Soviet ships sail from Vladivostok, Russia's main Pacific naval
base.

This forward offensive strategy has its critics. Adm.
Stansfield Turner and Capt. George Thibault say the strategy
poses such a great risk to carrier battle groups that commanders
would be unlikely to implement it. The ships would be vulnerable to attack from numerous weapons both at sea and from
shore as they approach in full view of the enemy. Particularly

---

[16] For spending needs ahead, see Congressional Budget Office, "Future Budget Requirements for the 600-Ship Navy," September 1985.

[17] Each carrier battle group consists of an aircraft carrier, its air wing of 80 to 90 aircraft
and several escort cruisers or destroyers equipped with anti-submarine warfare to protect
the vulnerable carrier from enemy submarine attack.

tempting, they say, would be the use of a tactical nuclear weapon against the battle group.[18]

Adm. William J. Crowe, chairman of the Joint Chiefs of Staff and former Pacific commander, has cited the growing Soviet submarine fleet as a source of danger to U.S. forces on the high seas. "We're already beginning to see them range farther and farther from their bases, and we're going to see them in the eastern Pacific, as well as the western Pacific," he said.[19] A study conducted by the Washington-based Center for Defense Information challenges this reading of Soviet naval capability and purpose. It concluded that the Soviet navy is designed to perform only limited tasks: to protect its ballistic missile submarines in coastal sanctuaries and defend the Soviet coasts from attack by carrier-based aircraft and amphibious assault.

In the Pacific, according to the study, Soviet nuclear submarines are concentrated in the Seas of Japan and Okhotsk, which lie between the Soviet Pacific bases of Petropavlovsk on the Kamchatka peninsula and Vladivostok. Beyond these coastal waters, the authors of the study argue, the Soviet navy is ill-adapted to function. "The Soviet Union and its allies," it concluded, "continue to lack the forces necessary to challenge Western superiority on the high seas." [20]

Defense Treaties; Push for Allied Help

While military strategy counts heavily on maintaining U.S. forces in the Pacific, the United States is dependent on its allies in the region for bases and some share of the defense burden. This country has defense agreements with several Pacific nations *(see p. 115)*. Admiral Crowe explained that the "nature and character of the Soviet challenge is such that the United States cannot protect Pacific sea lanes alone." [21]

The administration has concentrated its appeal on Japan, where it maintains several strategic military facilities. Under a "peace constitution" imposed by the United States after World War II, Japan is allowed only enough military capability to assure its own defense. Widespread pacifist sentiment in Japan has made this restriction acceptable to the country, which turned its energies to non-military industrial growth. In May 1981, at U.S. urging, Prime Minister Senko Suzuki committed his country to extending its defense arrangements to include sea

---

[18] Stansfield Turner and George Thibault, "Preparing for the Unexpected: The Need for New Military Strategy," *Foreign Affairs,* fall 1982.
[19] Interview published in *Armed Forces Journal International,* May 1985, p. 108. Crowe held the Pacific command from 1983 until 1985, when he became chairman of the Joint Chiefs of Staff.
[20] Center for Defense Information, "The Soviet Navy: Still Second Best," *The Defense Monitor,* No. 7, 1985, p. 1. The center is a non-partisan organization directed by retired U.S. military officers.
[21] Cited in *Armed Forces Journal International,* September 1985, p. 104.

lines of communication as far as 1,000 miles from shore. Yasuhiro Nakasone, his successor and the current prime minister, promised to transform his country into an "unsinkable aircraft carrier" able to protect the Sea of Japan.

This did not relieve U.S. pressure on Japan to increase its share of the regional defense burden. As the strongest economic power in the region, Japan has been heavily criticized for refusing to spend more than 1 percent of its gross national product for defense. In contrast, the United States, which suffers a growing trade deficit with Japan, spends 6 percent on defense. According to a five-year defense plan enacted last fall in response to U.S. criticism, Japan will gradually raise its defense-spending limit. Nakasone has also agreed to consider participating in Reagan's most ambitious defense plan to date, the multibillion-dollar Strategic Defense Initiative, or "Star Wars." Britain and West Germany alone have accepted Reagan's appeal to participate in the research to develop a vast space- and land-based anti-nuclear defense system.

The United States asks relatively little of South Korea, its other ally in Northeast Asia, beyond defending the border with North Korea. South Korea is undergoing an economic boom that may soon place it in a position to participate also in SDI research. On his recent trip to South Korea, Weinberger said the United States would also help the country develop its defense industry.

This country has bilateral defense agreements with two members of the Association of Southeast Asian Nations (ASEAN), the Philippines and Thailand.[22] While it was created in 1967 as an economic agreement, ASEAN attained greater political cohesion after the fall of South Vietnam and has assumed growing importance in the region's security because of Soviet naval facilities at Cam Ranh Bay.

From bases in the Philippines, U.S. naval and air forces are well positioned to follow Soviet movements from Vietnam through the Strait of Malacca and other sea lanes leading from the South China Sea into the Indian Ocean. Thailand, which U.S. forces used extensively in support of their effort in the Vietnam War, now faces the threat of Vietnamese troops occupying Cambodia across Thailand's eastern border. To help Thailand deter the threat of invasion by Vietnamese forces, the Reagan administration has proposed setting up a munitions stockpile in the country. In addition, among the world's "freedom fighters" worthy of U.S. support, it has included Cambodian rebels who are fighting to expel the Vietnamese from their country.

---

[22] Other members are Brunei, Indonesia, Malaysia and Singapore.

U.S. Pacific Command

U.S. forces in the western Pacific and the Indian Ocean are under the commander-in-chief, Pacific (CINCPAC), currently Adm. Ronald J. Hays, whose headquarters are at Honolulu. The Pacific command includes the Seventh Fleet, 12th Air Force and Army units, principally in Japan and South Korea. Some 40,000 soldiers, including two combat divisions, are in South Korea and 46,000 in Japan.

The Seventh Fleet comprises 34 warships, including two aircraft carrier battle groups. The fleet, with its own air arm and units from the 12th Air Force, protects sea and air routes in the South China Sea and the Pacific Ocean. From bases in Japan and the Philippines, these forces are in position to cut off shipping between Russia and Vietnam, and protect Southeast Asian sea lanes on which Japan and South Korea depend for oil supplies and U.S. military support. From Clark Air Base in the Philippines, the Air Force can airlift troops to the Persian Gulf.

Australia, New Zealand and the United States, allies in World War II, joined in a common defense pact, the ANZUS Security Treaty, in 1952. Although anti-nuclear movements have long been active in both island nations, it was not until February 1985 that this sentiment affected the treaty itself. New Zealand's newly elected Labor Party government of Prime Minister David Lange barred a routine port visit by a U.S. Navy destroyer. The United States, following longstanding practice, was unwilling to declare, as Lange required, that the ship was neither nuclear-powered nor nuclear-armed. No U.S. naval vessels have docked in New Zealand since. Last August both Lange and Australian Prime Minister Robert Hawke persuaded the 13-nation[23] South Pacific Forum to declare its territories a nuclear-free zone, although neither has suggested dissolving ANZUS. Hawke assured Reagan of Australia's intention to keep its part of the pact during a visit to Washington April 17.

China also blocked a scheduled U.S. Navy port call in Shanghai last summer. While China is not a U.S. ally, the Reagan administration has done more than its predecessors to foster military cooperation with the country — action that is in line with the Reagan perception than a strong China will deter Soviet aggression in East Asia. Despite recent signs of improving trade relations between Peking and Moscow, China has appeared eager to avoid allying itself too closely with either the United States or the Soviet Union.

China still considers the Soviet Union a threat to its security. Peking has declared that relations between the two countries

---

[23] Australia, the Cook Islands, Fiji, Kiribati, Nauru, New Zealand, Niue, Papua New Guinea, Solomon Islands, Tonga, Tuvalu, Vanuatu and Western Samoa.

will not become normal until the Soviets reduce its troop strength on their border, withdraw from Afghanistan and stop supporting the Vietnamese occupation of Cambodia. In contrast, China recently agreed to buy $500 million worth of aviation electronics from the United States. The military sale, which becomes final unless Congress blocks it before May 7, would be the largest to China since diplomatic relations were restored in 1972. While fostering military cooperation with China, the administration continues to sell arms to Taiwan, in accordance with a law passed in 1979 that requires the United States to provide the island with "sufficient" weaponry for its self-defense.

Debating the Options

While appealing to its allies to increase their share of the region's defense, the Reagan administration, like its postwar predecessors, places heavy emphasis on the need for a strong U.S. military presence in the Pacific theater. The concern over the fate of the bases in the Philippines is indicative of that priority. Clark Air Base, home base for a tactical airlift wing and a tactical fighter wing, is an important communications center and the logistics center for all U.S. air forces in the western Pacific. It has a greater capacity than bases in Japan and South Korea, the only other tactical air facilities in the region, to airlift personnel and equipment to the Indian Ocean and Persian Gulf. Clark also has an important training facility.

Subic Bay Naval Base, which also includes a ship-repair facility, a communications center, and a naval air station at Cubi Point, can hold carrier battle groups and amphibious ready groups in its large natural harbor. The naval complement to Clark, Subic serves as the logistics hub for both aircraft and ship operations of the Seventh Fleet.

But the main advantage of the Philippine bases is their location near the sea lines of communication connecting Northeast and Southeast Asia, and the Pacific and Indian oceans. "There is no substitute for them no matter where we go," Navy Secretary Lehman said at congressional hearings on the bases.[24] Thanks to Clark, "our air superiority is round-the-clock," he said, explaining that U.S. aircraft can provide continuous air surveillance of the choke points to the South China Sea 700 miles away. The only other way to maintain this control, he said, would be to keep an aircraft carrier in the area.

[24] Lehman testified April 10, 1986, before the Senate Armed Services Subcommittees on Sea Power and Force Projection and on Military Construction.

Richard Holbrooke, assistant secretary of state for East Asian and Pacific affairs during the Carter administration, is optimistic about the future of the bases. Having recently returned from the Philippines where he consulted with President Aquino and other government officials, he concluded that "Aquino and her government will honor the agreement in the short term and it is my guess that we will be asked to stay on. But it will cost us much more." Holbrooke told the Senate panel he shares the view expressed by many military strategists that dependency on any one basing arrangement is dangerous and that failure to create alternatives would constitute an "irresponsible and myopic policy."

Alternatives to the Philippine bases have been under study for some time, even before Marcos fell. The fiscal 1986 military construction appropriations bill required the Defense Department to present its recommendations on base options by March 1, 1986. Although the report remains classified, other studies describe the capabilities of the other locations that might be used. One such study was recently published by the Congressional Research Service of the Library of Congress.[25] The report, by Alva M. Bowen, a retired Navy captain, considered three options. One was redeployment to existing U.S. bases in Japan (Yokosuka naval base), Guam and Hawaii. He concluded that to do so would jeopardize America's ability to control the South China Sea, Indian Ocean and Persian Gulf. He estimated that one or two additional battle groups would be needed to assure adequate rotation among ships and crews whose cruises would necessarily be longer because of distant home bases.

The same drawback applies to the second option, redeployment to Micronesia. This option would entail the enlargement of existing naval and air bases on Guam and construction of new facilities on Saipan, Tinian and Palau. While Micronesian bases are less distant from strategic operating areas east of the Philippines than Japan or Hawaii are, they would not solve the problem of distance from the South China Sea. In addition, the constitution of Palau, which has granted the United States rights for military facilities as part of a "compact of free association," outlaws the presence of nuclear weapons on its territory.[26]

The third option, redeployment to another base on the South China Sea, might be feasible if a naval and air facility were also

---

[25] Alva M. Bowen, "Philippine Bases: U.S. Redeployment Options," *Congressional Research Service*, Feb. 20, 1986. See also *Congressional Quarterly Weekly Report*, Feb. 22, 1986, pp. 454-455.

[26] Palau was one of the former Japanese colonies in the Pacific which after 1947 were administered by the United States under a trusteeship arranged by the United Nations. In 1976 the Northern Marianas became an American commonwealth, the same status as was earlier accorded Guam and Samoa. Other groups of islands became "freely associated states" in the early 1980s, receiving limited autonomy. See "Changing Status of Micronesia," *E.R.R.*, 1975 Vol. I, pp. 403-422.

built in Micronesia to assure a line of communication. However, any new basing arrangement in the South China Sea would pose difficult political problems. Taiwan could offer both naval and air facilities, but their use would almost certainly incur China's wrath, and possibly rupture diplomatic relations with Washington. The ASEAN countries are unlikely to offer bases. They have been reluctant to form a close military association with the United States even though Russian-supported Vietnam is a neighbor. Even in Thailand, which has been perhaps the least resistant of the ASEAN nations to military cooperation with the United States, Weinberger's recent visit drew public protests against the stockpiling of U.S. weapons and the possibility of the United States establishing a base in the country.

"No one of these three broad approaches by itself would do," Bowen said in an interview. "A bit of all three might." He added that all would entail considerable expense, in terms of both time and money. "It would take $4 [billion] to $5 billion, plus enough time to build five carrier battle groups and seven or eight years to relocate the bases."

Local Responses to American Presence

Any of the redeployment options discussed in the study would require an airlift facility in Australia, and perhaps a naval base in Western Australia. Other analysts, including Richard Holbrooke, place great emphasis on Western Australia as a key alternative to the Philippines. Even if the Philippine government renews the basing agreement, he told Congress, "we should still look into the possibility of homeporting a carrier task force in Western Australia." An Australian base "would not increase tensions with the Soviet Union but would at the same time improve our position, since it is five days closer [than Subic and Clark] to the Indian Ocean and the Persian Gulf." While acknowledging the potential for Australian opposition to a new base, he challenged the Navy's view that these problems may be unsurmountable. "The people of Perth," he said, "would welcome it."

It is the political aspect of any foreign basing arrangement that most concerns critics of forward deployment. In the view of Lee Feinstein of the Center for Defense Information, "there is strong anti-U.S.-base — not anti-U.S. — sentiment wherever we have bases, and the Philippines are no exception." He believes the security aspect of the Philippine bases has been overstated and that more attention should be given to their political significance. "Whether or not the presence of U.S. bases on Philippine soil really affects their self-determination, they are terrifically aggravating to the Philippine people," he said.

One way to reduce local resentment of overseas bases, suggested former Foreign Service officer Robert Pringle, is to contract out some of the maintenance work instead of merely hiring local workers. In this way, he said, the surrounding community would have a greater stake in the bases' survival and the host country would become a more equal partner in regional defense.[27] Labor unrest directed against U.S. military facilities, such as the strikes that closed off Subic and Clark in March, might be less likely to occur under these conditions.

'Lesson' of Philippine Upheaval in Korea

While few analysts would suggest a complete withdrawal of U.S. forces from overseas, some question the priority given to maintaining the security of the western Pacific. The Reagan administration, long criticized by opponents for its ideological preference for "authoritarian" (rightist) regimes over "totalitarian" (communist) ones, has garnered praise from liberals and conservatives alike for its handling of the recent transfer of power in the Philippines. Holbrooke, for example, pointed to the "continued bipartisan support for the administration's policy toward the Philippines" as "essential" to the survival of democracy in the country. And he applauded the "masterful leadership of [Secretary of State] George Shultz" in helping the Filipinos carry out a bloodless revolution.

Some observers predict the Philippines may have marked the beginning of a gradual trend toward democratization among U.S. allies in East Asia, where the Confucian tradition has buttressed the permanence of authoritarian rulers in nominally democratic systems of government. No sooner had Marcos fled Manila than the opponents of South Korean President Chun Doo Hwan stepped up their campaign to change the constitution to permit direct presidential elections by 1988, when Chun is to step down. Opposition leaders have launched a petition drive to end the current system of indirect elections, which they say allows the ruling party to pick the president. Holbrooke predicted that the next two years will be "the most important in South Korea's history" since the opposition's campaign and Chun's reaction to it will determine whether full democracy will be attained. Since Marcos' ouster Chun has allowed the petition drive to proceed and relaxed his policy of brutally quelling street demonstrations.

---

[27] See Pringle's book, *Indonesia and the Philippines: American Interests in Island Southeast Asia* (1980).

Recommended Reading List

Books

The Almanac of Seapower 1984, Navy League of the United States, 1984.

Collins, John M., *U.S.-Soviet Military Balance 1980-1985*, Pergamon-Brassey's International Defense Publishers, 1985.

Murray, Douglas J., and Paul R. Viotti, *The Defense Policies of Nations: A Comparative Study*, 1982.

Pringle, Robert, *Indonesia and the Philippines: American Interests in Island Southeast Asia*, Columbia University Press, 1980.

Articles

Bacho, Peter, "Hearts and Minds in the Philippines," *SAIS Review* (publication of Johns Hopkins University School for Advanced International Studies), winter-spring 1986.

Betts, Richard K., "Southeast Asia and U.S. Global Strategy: Continuing Interests and Shifting Priorities," *Orbis,* summer 1985.

Brand, Robert A., "Australia, New Zealand, and ANZUS," *Atlantic Community Quarterly,* winter 1984-85.

"Focus: China '86," *Far Eastern Economic Review,* March 20, 1986.

Holbrooke, Richard, "East Asia: The Next Challenge," *Foreign Affairs,* spring 1986.

Nakasone, Yasuhiro, "Japan's Choice: A Strategy for World Peace and Prosperity," *Atlantic Community Quarterly,* fall 1984.

Tonelson, Alan, "The Real National Interest," *Foreign Policy,* winter 1985.

Weinberger, Caspar W., "U.S. Defense Strategy," *Foreign Affairs,* spring 1986.

Reports and Studies

Center for Defense Information, "The Soviet Navy: Still Second Best," The Defense Monitor, 1985.

Congressional Budget Office, "Future Budget Requirements for the 600-Ship Navy," September 1985.

Congressional Research Service, "Philippine Bases: U.S. Redeployment Options," Alva M. Bowen, Feb. 20, 1986.

Far Eastern Economic Review, "Asia 1985 Yearbook," Dec. 1, 1984.

Heritage Foundation, "The U.S. and the Philippines: A Five Point Strategy," Asian Studies Center Backgrounder No. 41, Feb. 25, 1986.

International Institute for Strategic Studies, "The Military Balance 1984-1985," 1984.

Organization of the Joint Chiefs of Staff, "United States Military Posture FY 1987."

U.S. Defense Department, "Soviet Military Power 1986," March 1986.

Graphics: Illustration p. 109 and map p. 113, John B. Auldridge; map p. 119, Patrick Murphy; photo p. 120, Sue Klemens.

Decision on
NICARAGUA

by

Richard C. Schroeder

**Feb. 28
1 9 8 6**

Editor's Update: In the final days of its 1986 session, Congress gave final approval to President Reagan's request for $100 million to aid the contras, plus $300 million in economic aid for Central American countries other than Nicaragua. The funding's backers persuaded their fellow lawmakers to give their approval despite an incident in the Nicaraguan civil war that is expected to result in extensive congressional hearings. On Oct. 5, Nicaraguan forces shot down a C-123 cargo plane carrying weapons and other supplies to the contras. The only surviving crew member, Eugene Hasenfus of Marinetta, Wis., was captured and placed on trial in Managua, the Nicaraguan capital, on the charge of violating "the maintenance of order and public security." Documents captured on the plane and the captured crewman's statements indicated CIA involvement in the supply operation. Reagan administration officials denied direct U.S. government participation. They said the operation was supported instead by individual Americans.

DECISION ON NICARAGUA

T he Reagan administration appears to be intensifying its war of nerves against the Sandinista government of Nicaragua. The Sandinistas' open defiance of the United States and their increasingly close ties to the Soviet Union and Cuba have made them an irritant to President Reagan since he has been in office, and the object of ill-concealed U.S. harassment for most of that time. But the administration's request, sent to Congress on Feb. 25, for $100 million in fresh funding for the anti-Sandinista "contra" guerrillas — including military assistance previously barred by Congress — represents a significant escalation of U.S. pressure on Nicaragua, one that many observers believe could presage direct U.S. military involvement in Central American conflicts.

It has been clear for some time that the administration is deeply committed to the support of a paramilitary campaign against the Nicaraguan government, which Reagan considers to be Marxist and a willing tool of the Soviet Union. Two and a half years ago, Richard H. Uhlman, a professor of international relations at Princeton University, wrote: "The Reagan administration is at war with Nicaragua. Like other wars the United States fought since 1945, it is an undeclared war. No U.S. serviceman has yet fired a shot, but American-made bullets from American-made guns are killing Nicaraguans, and the President of the United States has made the demise of the present Nicaraguan government an all-but-explicit aim of his foreign policy." [1]

Despite Uhlman's perception of Reagan's policy, the administration's goals in Nicaragua have never really been clear. Initially, White House officials denied that any U.S. funds were being given to Nicaraguan counterrevolutionaries. Jeane J. Kirkpatrick, then the U.S. representative to the United Nations, said in early 1983 that it was a "myth" that the United States had anything to do with the fighting in Nicaragua. An official State Department spokesman said the Nicaraguan civil war was an "internal problem" resulting from a "spontaneous uprising" that was "diverse, nationalist and independent." Confronted with extensive media coverage of large amounts of U.S.-

---

[1] Richard H. Uhlman, "At War with Nicaragua," *Foreign Affairs*, fall 1983, pp. 39-58.

made equipment and supplies in the hands of the contras, administration officials said U.S. aid was being used to cut off the flow of arms from the Sandinistas to Marxist rebels in El Salvador.[2]

More recently, administration officials have asserted that the continuing U.S. pressure on Nicaragua is aimed at forcing the Sandinista government to come to an "accommodation" that would wean Nicaragua away from Soviet and Cuban tutelage and establish a system of pluralistic democracy. In a speech last November, Harry W. Schlaudeman, the president's special envoy for Central America, said: "We seek an end to Nicaraguan support for guerrilla groups.... We want Nicaragua to sever its military and security ties to Cuba and the Soviet bloc.... We seek reduction of Nicaragua's military strength to levels that would restore equilibrium in the area.... We seek fulfillment

of the original Sandinista promises to support democratic pluralism.... Finally, we seek a diplomatic solution that is verifiable and enforceable...."[3]

But there is doubt whether even that formulation represents a consensus of views within the Reagan administration. Roy Gutman, a defense and foreign affairs correspondent for *Newsday,* has written: "Sharp divisions exist in the administration over whether pressures are meant to lead to overthrow or accommodation. Nearly every top political appointee seems to favor overthrow.... Those who want pressure to lead to accommodation are said to include members of the Joint Chiefs of Staff and a great many professional diplomats as well as military and intelligence analysts. A third possibility is a U.S.-led invasion. Or Reagan could simply walk away from the situation, as he did in Lebanon."[4]

Whatever the real goal in Nicaragua, there is increasing concern that current policy may lead to U.S. involvement

---

[2] "Open Secret," *The Vision Letter,* April 15, 1983, pp. 3-4. *The Vision Letter* is an English-language fortnightly political and economic report on Latin America published by *Visión,* a Latin American news magazine. The author of this report is the magazine's Washington bureau chief.
[3] Speech delivered to the Town Hall of California, Los Angeles, Nov. 26, 1985.
[4] Roy Gutman, "America's Diplomatic Charade," *Foreign Policy,* fall 1984, pp. 3-23.

in a shooting war in Nicaragua. Joseph Contreras of *Newsweek* wrote recently from Managua, the capital: " . . . [I]f the Reagan administration's objective is to get rid of the Sandinistas, as many Western diplomats in Managua and officials in Washington now contend, it could mean one of two things. Either the contras would have to deliver better results by next winter, or the administration might finally have to face the question of whether it is willing to risk its credibility — and the lives of American soldiers — in trying to do the job itself." [5]

Invoking the Reagan Doctrine in Nicaragua

Providing U.S. assistance for the Nicaraguan contras is consistent with the principles of the so-called Reagan Doctrine, which seeks to legitimize U.S. support of guerrilla insurgencies. The decision to apply the Reagan Doctrine in specific situations seems to hinge on whether a government under siege by rebel forces is in league with or receives assistance from the Soviet bloc. Using this bench mark, the administration has condemned the anti-government operations practiced by guerrillas in such countries as El Salvador, Colombia and Peru and at the same time has encouraged and supported rebels in Nicaragua, Afghanistan and Cambodia, and appears ready to extend assistance to Jonas Savimbi, the leader of the National Union for the Total Independence of Angola (UNITA), which has been battling Angola's Marxist government for years.[6]

The White House has never officially enunciated a policy of supporting anti-communist guerrilla movements, but application of the principle nonetheless has set off bitter debate in Washington. The lines of dispute do not follow the usual pattern of liberals vs. conservatives. In fact, observed *U.S. News & World Report:* "There are divisions even within the administration. Secretary of State George Shultz, hawkish on behalf of rebels in Afghanistan and Nicaragua, is opposed to aid for those in Angola. . . . [Defense Secretary Caspar W.] Weinberger insists that the U.S. support anti-Communist forces but cautions against anything that might lead to military involvement. CIA chief William Casey and Patrick Buchanan, the leading conservative in the White House, have fewer reservations about covert action." [7]

Not only has the administration's support for the contras divided Washington, it is also a source of bitter contention between the United States and otherwise friendly governments in Latin America. Congress has alternately cut off and re-

---

[5] Joseph Contreras, "Arms and the Contras," *Newsweek,* Feb. 10, 1986, p. 53. He is *Newsweek's* Mexico City bureau chief.

[6] See "Angola and the Reagan Doctrine," p. 149.

[7] "Now It's U.S. Backing Rebels," *U.S. News & World Report,* Jan. 27, 1986, pp. 27-29.

newed aid to the contras since covert U.S. assistance began
in 1981. Military support was ended in 1984, following the
disclosure that the Central Intelligence Agency had mined
Nicaraguan harbors.[8] Reagan led a successful campaign to
provide a $27 million "non-lethal" and "humanitarian" aid
package for the contras in June 1985, but that money will run
out March 31.

Questions About Effectiveness of the Contras

Opposition in the United States to a renewal of aid to the
contras arises from congressional misgivings about the origin
and composition of the rebel forces and about their ability to
make significant inroads against the growing power of the Nicaraguan army.

Contras — a shortened form of the Spanish word
"contrarevolucionarios," or counterrevolutionaries — came into
being in the latter part of 1981 when the U.S. National Security
Council approved setting up CIA-directed paramilitary and
political operations against the Cuban presence in Nicaragua
and, by implication, against the Cubans' Sandinista hosts.
President Reagan authorized the plan on Nov. 16, 1981, alloting
$19 million for the dual purpose of cutting off the arms supply
to Salvadoran rebels from Nicaragua and of encouraging internal opposition to the Sandinista regime. Congressional
committees were told the plan was to train a 500-man rebel
force inside Honduras with the help of Argentina.

As U.S. intelligence operatives moved to implement the program, they quickly found that the only viable opponents who
would cooperate with them were supporters of former Nicaraguan dictator Anastasio Somoza, who had been ousted by the
Sandinistas in 1979. Among the Somocistas were many former
members of the Nicaraguan National Guard, which had served
as the Somoza family's principal tool for repression for more
than four decades. An anti-Somocista and anti-Sandinista
group, based in Costa Rica and led by Eden Pastora, a former
Sandinista commander and hero of the fight against the Somoza
government, refused to participate in any operation that involved former National Guardsmen.

Despite the Somocista taint of the guerrilla force it had
assembled, the Reagan administration pressed forward with its
plan to foment rebellion in the Nicaraguan provinces along the
Honduran border. It hoped, vainly, to keep its activities hidden

---

[8] In early 1984, CIA personnel, operating from a mother ship just outside Nicaragua's
territorial waters, planted mines in Nicaraguan harbors and also carried out bombing raids
on oil tanks. Nicaragua filed a suit in the International Court of Justice asking condemnation of the action, but the United States notified the court that it would not recognize its
jurisdiction. Nonetheless, the mining and bombing was ended in the face of strong protests
from Congress and Western European governments.

President Reagan meets with contra leaders (from left) Alfonso Robelo, Arturo Cruz and Adolfo Calero at the White House, April 4, 1985.

from public view. A perfunctory attempt was made to cleanse the contras of the worst elements of the National Guard, but many of the field commanders of the Nicaraguan Democratic Force (FDN), the principal contra body, are still former Guard personnel. The Guard connection has given credence to charges of atrocities committed by the contras. U.S. officials and contra leaders have denied many of the atrocity charges, and defenders of the rebel forces say that more crimes are committed routinely by the Sandinistas than by their opponents.[9]

A second sticking point for members of Congress is how much of an effective opposition to the Sandinistas the contras really are. Last year was a bad one. According to reporting from the scene, the contras' front along Nicaragua's southern border all but collapsed, and internal squabbling among rebel Miskito Indian chiefs brought fighting on the Atlantic Coast virtually to a halt. "By last fall," Joseph Contreras wrote, "the largest rebel army, the Nicaraguan Democratic Force (FDN), had substantially wound down its operations and seen most of its 15,000 guerrillas pushed back near the Honduran border or into Honduran territory."

The contras have also been handicapped by a shortage of basic supplies which must move through Honduras to reach

---

[9] The best description of the presence of former Guardsmen in the contras is found in a new book, *With the Contras: A Reporter in the Wilds of Nicaragua,* by Christopher Dickey, a *Washington Post* reporter. A comprehensive study of alleged contra atrocities was compiled by Reed Brody, a New York lawyer, who published affidavits from 145 Nicaraguans and Americans who said they witnessed or were victims of contra abuses in 28 separate incidents. Ismael Reyes, a former head of the Nicaraguan Red Cross, published a lengthy report on Sandinista crimes in the Nov. 11, 1983, edition of *Diario Los Americas,* a Spanish-language daily edited in Miami.

their forces in the field. The Honduran government has blocked the aid since last October in an effort to extract concessions from the United States. Honduras' new president, José Azcona Hoyo, campaigned on a platform opposing the presence of the contra forces in Honduras. Since his inauguration, Jan. 27, Azcona has softened that stand somewhat. Azcona's aides say he still plans to move the contras across the border into Nicaragua, but that he will do it gradually to avoid a U.S. confrontation.

President Reagan's request for more aid for the contras will evidently face tough sledding in Congress. Rep. Dave McCurdy (D-Okla.), who sponsored the legislation that gave $27 million to the contras last July, recently pronounced himself opposed to further contra assistance. "The contras have not become a unified and credible democratic alternative to the Sandinistas," McCurdy wrote in *The New York Times.* "They have no political identity in Nicaragua and no meaningful contact with the internal opposition. Nor are the contras an effective fighting force. They are the largest guerrilla movement in recent Latin American history — larger than the Sandinistas were when they seized power — but their 15,000 troops are badly trained, uneducated youths, serving under fragmented leadership."

McCurdy said congressional approval of more money for the contras "hinges on the president's ability to persuade moderate members of the House that he stands by his pledge, made in an open letter to me in June, that his administration 'is determined to pursue political, not military, solutions in Central America.' Both Congress and the public must be convinced that the president has exhausted all diplomatic possibilities for a regionally based political solution." [10]

Renewal of Contadora Mediation Attempts

The new Reagan initiative on Nicaragua comes at a time when various factions in Latin America are beginning to come together over efforts to seek genuine "regionally based political solutions" to the Nicaraguan situation. The Contadora Group — Colombia, Mexico, Panama and Venezuela — which has been trying to mediate Central American strife for the past three years, is showing new signs of life after seeming to collapse in December. In January, the group issued the "Declaration of Caraballeda," named for the Venezuelan resort where it was signed, calling for negotiations between the United States and Nicaragua and the creation of a Central American parliament. The declaration was quickly endorsed by the five Central American countries. [11]

---

[10] McCurdy's article was published in *The New York Times,* Feb. 5, 1986.
[11] Costa Rica, Guatemala, Honduras, Nicaragua and El Salvador; Panama and Belize, though geographically on the Central American Isthmus, are considered apart politically from the other five countries.

Decision on Nicaragua

The Contadora Group, named for the Panamanian island where the foreign ministers of the four nations first met in January 1983, was formed to try to defuse the rising tensions in Central America and to break the diplomatic deadlock between the United States and Nicaragua. By the following September, the group had produced a 21-point "Document of Objectives" which was signed by all five Central American countries. The objectives included democratization, national reconciliation and respect for human rights, and they called for an end to external subversion, cuts in foreign military advisers, controls on troops and arms levels, and greater regional economic cooperation.[12]

The next month, Nicaragua proposed draft treaties that would have prohibited the export of subversion, including Nicaraguan aid to leftist rebels in El Salvador and U.S. assistance for the contras. The same month, Nicaraguan Interior Minister Tomás Borge said that Nicaragua was willing to ask Cuba to withdraw its military advisers as part of a regional agreement. The United States turned down the Nicaraguan offers in June 1984.

The Contadora Group has continued to seek diplomatic solutions since then, but its task has been complicated by rising intransigence on the part of both Nicaragua and the United States. The United States had indicated its willingness to engage in direct negotiations with Nicaragua, but has said a precondition to such talks would be a dialogue between the Sandinistas and the contras, a suggestion Nicaragua has rejected. Last May the United States imposed an embargo on trade with Nicaragua. The Sandinistas have likewise hardened their stance, cracking down on internal dissent, harassing the Catholic Church, tightening censorship and, late last year, imposing a state of emergency under which civil rights have been suspended.

Contadora put together another regional treaty proposal last autumn under which all five Central American countries would have to reduce their arms, evict foreign military advisers, halt support for guerrilla movements in neighboring countries and guarantee democratic pluralism at home. A Nov. 21 deadline for signing the treaty passed without action and in December Contadora suspended its mediation efforts for six months. Under the pressure of the so-called Support Group for Contadora — composed of Argentina, Brazil, Peru and Uruguay — Contadora resumed its efforts in January. The next step in the negotiating process is a meeting of Central American presidents set for an unspecified date in the spring.

[12] See Tom J. Farer, "Contadora: The Hidden Agenda," *Foreign Policy*, summer 1983, pp. 59-72, and Susan Kaufman, "Demystifying Contadora," *Foreign Affairs*, fall 1985, pp. 74-95.

Roots of Current Antagonism

Nicaragua is the largest (57,143 sq. mi.) and least densely populated (pop. 2.9 million) of the five Central American nations. A veritable backwater in Spanish colonial days,[13] Nicaragua — together with Guatemala, El Salvador, Honduras and Costa Rica — threw off Spanish rule in 1821 and for a brief period was part of the Mexican Empire under Augustín Iturbide. With the dissolution of the empire in 1823, Nicaragua became one of the five units of the United Provinces of Central America. The Central American union broke apart in 1838. From that point on Nicaragua was nominally, if not always effectively, independent.

The early days of the Nicaraguan republic were marked by a fierce political struggle between two cities and two political parties: the Liberals of León, the old colonial capital, and the Conservatives of Granada, the country's commercial center. Pervasive foreign interference, a fact of Nicaraguan life, has persisted to modern times. The principal outside influence came from the British, who had established outposts on Nicaragua's Caribbean coast during Spanish colonial rule, and from the United States, initially in the person of Commodore Cornelius Vanderbilt, who held a concession for a transport service from the Caribbean along the San Juan River and Lake Nicaragua and then overland to the Pacific — the quickest and cheapest way to travel from the U.S. East Coast to California.

The rivalry between Nicaragua's Liberals and Conservatives spawned a bizarre episode in the mid-1850s that has colored U.S.-Nicaraguan relations ever since. Central America at that time was the target of bands of "filibusters," [14] bands of private adventurers from New York, Baltimore and New Orleans who rented themselves out to different political factions for military action against opponents. In 1855, the American filibuster William Walker contracted with the Nicaraguan Liberals to aid them in a civil war with the Conservatives. Walker landed with a force of 58 men and, astonishingly, handily defeated the Conservatives. His ambition did not end with that mission, however. Walker proclaimed himself commander in chief of the Nicaraguan army and in 1856 had himself "elected" president of Nicaragua, managing to gain diplomatic recognition from the United States.

[13] See *Nicaragua: The Land of Sandino* (1981) by Thomas W. Walker, and *Central America: A Nation Divided* (1976) by Ralph Lee Woodward Jr. Walker is an associate professor of political science at Ohio University; Woodward is chairman of the history department at Tulane University.

[14] The word filibuster (Spanish *"Filibustero"*) is thought to derive from one of two Dutch words: *vrij buit* ("free booty") or *vlieboot* ("flyboat"), a small, swift craft used by sea raiders.

The turn of events alarmed the Liberals and strengthened the Conservative cause. Walker also incurred the hostility of Commodore Vanderbilt by trying to take over Vanderbilt's transit company. Vanderbilt bankrolled the Nicaraguan Conservatives who, aided by Conservative troops from other countries, renewed their offensive against the American intruder. With the tide turning against him in 1857, Walker agreed to a truce and prudently left the country under the protection of an American naval officer. Walker made two more attempts to lead expeditions into Central America and on his second try landed in Honduras where he was captured by a squad of British marines, handed over to the Hondurans, and shot to death.

Although his filibustering was a failure, Walker's intervention left its mark on Central America. It thoroughly discredited Liberal movements throughout the isthmus and in Nicaragua the Liberals were frozen out of power for the next three decades. Moreover, the spectacle of Walker and Vanderbilt, two Americans, struggling for mastery of a supposedly independent Nicaragua aroused bitter antagonisms which later action by the United States would intensify.

American Intervention Since 19th Century

Following the Walker episode, Nicaragua settled into a period of relative tranquility known as the Thirty Years. A Liberal revolt in 1893 brought José Santos Zelaya to the presidency, which he held for the next 16 years. Santos Zelaya was a dictator who ruled Nicaragua with an iron hand, but his regime brought relative prosperity and a significant degree of modernization to the Nicaraguan economy. Santos Zelaya was also a firm believer in Central American integration, managing even to establish a brief union (1896-98), called the *Republica Mayor* (Greater Republic), between Nicaragua, El Salvador and Honduras. His great mistake, however, was antagonizing the United States.

The Spanish-American War (1898) had given the United States a colonial domain, and a new taste for exercising influence outside its borders, especially in its own hemisphere. Consciously or unconsciously, Santos Zelaya's integrationist zeal clashed with the new international spirit in the United States. The Nicaraguan leader also irritated Washington by refusing to grant the United States canal-building rights that would have included U.S. sovereignty over a slice of Nicaraguan territory. Instead, the United States maneuvered the independence of Panama from Colombia and secured the same canal-building concession it had sought from Nicaragua. As recounted by Professor Thomas W. Walker:

> ... Washington eventually let it be known that it would look kindly on a Conservative overthrow of Zelaya. In 1909, when the

revolt finally took place in Bluefields, Zelaya's forces made the tactical mistake of executing two confessed U.S. mercenaries. The United States used this incident an an excuse to sever diplomatic relations and to send troops to Bluefields to ensure against the defeat of the Conservatives. Though he held on for a few more months, Zelaya was ultimately forced to accept the inevitable, to resign, and to spend the rest of his life in exile.[15]

Engineering the overthrow of a hostile Central American president was in keeping with the terms of the Roosevelt Corollary to the Monroe Doctrine. As enunciated by President Theodore Roosevelt in 1904, the Corollary held that the United States might, under certain circumstances, exercise an "international police power" in the Western Hemisphere. "Of course that view completely reversed the meaning of the original Doctrine [of 1823]," comments historian Walter LaFeber." [President] Monroe and [Secretary of State John Quincy] Adams had originally intended it to protect Latin American revolutions from outside (that is, European) interference." [16] In succeeding years, the Roosevelt Corollary would be invoked in Nicaragua time and again.

U.S. Occupation; Sandino and Guerrilla War

When Santos Zelaya resigned, the United States refused to accept another Liberal government and the Conservatives returned to power. In 1912 U.S. Marines were once again sent into Nicaragua to help quell a rebellion by the Liberal leader Benjamin Zeledon. With the Marines fighting side by side with the Conservatives, Zeledon was captured and killed. This time the Marines were not withdrawn, but stayed on until 1925, under the guise of protecting U.S. lives and property. Although small in number — only about 100 Marines were stationed in Nicaragua during this period — and called a "Legation Guard" by the United States, they assured that real political power was centered in the U.S. diplomatic mission in Managua.

Shortly after the Marines pulled out in 1925, the Liberals rebelled again. So the Marines returned in 1926, this time staying until 1933. In 1927, President Coolidge sent Henry L. Stimson, the future secretary of state, to Nicaragua to work out a compromise settlement between the Liberals and Conservatives. In the ensuing election of 1928, the Liberals regained the presidency, but the United States continued to make political and economic decisions. It was during the second Marine occupation that the United States organized, trained and armed

---

[15] Walker, *op. cit.*, p. 18.
[16] Walter LaFeber, *Inevitable Revolutions: The United States in Central America* (1983), p. 38. LaFeber is a professor of history at Cornell University.

a new Nicaraguan military force, the National Guard, to control the endless bickering between the Liberals and Conservatives. By the time the United States made its final withdrawal from Nicaragua in January 1933, the Guard had come under the command of an ambitious, English-speaking politician, Anastasio Somozo García. He and his sons were to rule Nicaragua for more than four decades.

The 1927 agreement between the Liberals and Conservatives did not end insurgency in Nicaragua. Resistance to the United States and to the National Guard was led by a charismatic and tactically brilliant field commander, Augusto César Sandino. When frontal assaults proved futile and costly, Sandino turned to harassment and hit-and-run forays. He cultivated the support of peasants in the rural areas for supplies, information about government troop movements and occasionally emergency manpower in military encounters.

The National Guard and U.S. Marines responded with aerial bombardment of "hostile" towns and forced resettlement of entire peasant villages — measures that built more support for the rebel cause. Despite the rapid buildup of U.S. forces in Nicaragua — some 5,000 Marines were thrown against Sandino's men in 1930 and 1931 — Sandino was still "as great a threat ... as he had been at any previous point in his career" when the Marines finally left Nicaragua.[17]

To the United States, Sandino was a "bandit," or worse still, a "communist." To many Nicaraguans, however, he was a nationalist hero who led the struggle against foreign occupation. To National Guard Commander Anastasio Somoza, Sandino was a threat to Somoza's plans for long-term domination of Nicaraguan politics. After the Marines departed, Sandino signed a preliminary peace agreement with the Liberal government. But early in 1934, when Sandino arrived in Managua to negotiate a final truce, he was treacherously ambushed and assassinated, almost certainly on the orders of Somoza.

Somoza Era and the Sandinista Revolution

By 1936, Somoza had consolidated his control not only of the National Guard but of the Liberal Party as well. In that year, Somoza ran for the presidency and was elected without opposition, assuming office on Jan. 1, 1937. For the next 42 years, the Somoza family ruled Nicaragua as its own private *finca* (ranch). In the brief periods when Somoza or one of his sons did not hold the presidency, a Somoza commanded the National Guard and a pliable surrogate did his bidding in the national palace.

[17] Richard Milett, *The Guardians of the Dynasty: A History of the U.S.-Created Guardia Nacional de Nicaragua and the Somoza Family* (1977), p. 32.

141

In 1956, the elder Somoza was assassinated and immediately succeeded in the presidency by the head of the National Assembly, his older son, Luis. In 1963 a Somoza-family factotum, René Schick, was installed as president and died in office in 1966. Schick's successor was the commander of the National Guard, Anastasio Somoza Debayle, the younger son of the late dictator. With the exception of a brief time in 1972, when Nicaragua was governed by a Somoza-controlled junta, the younger Somoza held the presidency until forced out by an insurrection on July 17, 1979.

The long period of Somoza rule was based on absolute control of the National Guard and the Liberal party, and close ties to the United States.[18] The Nicaraguan economy grew steadily under the Somozas, with agriculture leading the way until the mid-1960s when industrial activity assumed greater importance. But as the Nicaraguan economy expanded, so, too, did the wealth of the Somoza family. They became the country's largest landowners and major investors in industries. When the revolutionary Sandinista government seized power in 1979, it took over Somoza family holdings worth half a billion dollars, including 20 percent of the country's arable land and 154 commercial and industrial establishments. Observers point out that this was only what the family left behind; perhaps as much wealth was shipped out of Nicaragua to the United States and Europe before the Somoza regime fell.

The instrument of destruction of the Somoza dynasty was the Frente Sandinista de Liberacion Nacional (FSLN), the Sandinist Front for National Liberation, named for the old guerrilla fighter. The Front was founded in 1962 but became a serious challenge to the government only in the 1970s. Popular discontent with the Somoza government began to surface in the wake of a devastating earthquake in 1972. The Somoza family seized on the disaster to siphon off millions of dollars of disaster relief funds.

By the mid-1970s, the Sandinistas were waging open guerrilla warfare in several parts of Nicaragua, and the government responded by committing atrocities which only built further support for the guerrilla cause. Pedro Joaquin Chamorro, editor of the newspaper *La Prensa*, and a staunch opponent of the Somoza government, was assassinated in early 1978. President Somoza was widely believed to be responsible for the death, although he denied complicity. The murder consolidated opposition to the regime, not just among the poor and the peasantry

---

[18] Both Somoza sons were educated in the United States. Luis attended Louisiana State University, the University of California and the University of Maryland. Anastasio was a graduate of the U.S. Military Academy, in 1948.

but among the influential middle class and the business community. An unprecedented general strike swept the nation that Jan. 24, and by early March it was apparent that the Somoza regime was in serious trouble for the first time.[19] In June of the following year, the Sandinistas launched their "final offensive," and on July 19, 1979, the president and the other members of the family still in Nicaragua fled the country.

Persistent Foreign Influence

I n the waning days of the Somoza regime, the United States began distancing itself from the dictatorship. After Jimmy Carter became president in January 1977, Washington began to pressure Somoza to improve his human rights performance and to check the brutality of the National Guard.[20] As the end drew closer, the United States reduced its embassy staff in Managua and recalled its military attachés to Washington. At the Organization of American States (OAS), the U.S. delegation pressed for the creation of an Inter-American peacekeeping force to intervene in the Nicaraguan civil war. When that proposal was rejected, the Carter administration began direct talks with the FSLN and finally arranged for Somoza's departure to Miami.[21]

The initial relations between the United States and the Sandinista revolutionary government were good, although not particularly close. The Sandinistas assured U.S. envoys that the new government was not hostile, but would pursue an independent course, both domestically and in its foreign affairs. Recognizing that the revolution had shattered the Nicaraguan economy,[22] the United States sent a substantial amount of disaster relief immediately after the Sandinista takeover, and allowed several million dollars' worth of aid already approved for Somoza to go to the Sandinistas. Congress appropriated $75 million in emergency funds for Nicaragua, and earmarked 60 percent for the private sector. In addition, U.S. representatives in international financial institutions such as the Inter-American Development Bank and the World Bank either supported or did not try to block some $200 million in multilateral funding for the new government.

[19] See, for example, "Nicaragua: Are These the Last Days?" *The Latin American Index*, March 1-15, 1978, p. 4.

[20] See "Human Rights Policy," *E.R.R.*, 1979 Vol. I, pp. 361-380.

[21] He often traveled outside the United States and was assassinated by unknown persons in Asuncion, Paraguay, Sept. 17, 1980. Luis died of natural causes in Nicaragua in 1967. Surviving members of the Somoza family live in Miami and New York. They have extensive real estate and corporate holdings in the United States and abroad.

[22] The war left 50,000 dead, 100,000 injured, 40,000 orphaned, one-fifth of the population homeless and one-third of the work force unemployed.

Even at this stage, however, there was a split within the U.S. government on the real nature of the Sandinistas. There was, on the one hand, a view — more prevalent in Congress than elsewhere — that the Sandinistas were nationalists and social reformers who could be influenced to steer a moderate, albeit socialist, course and remain on good terms with the United States. The CIA, the Defense Department and the National Security Council, on the other hand, felt that the Sandinista core was hard-line Marxist and that it was only a matter of time until Nicaragua was "lost" to Cuba and the Soviet Union.

The latter view prevailed after Reagan became president. A year after taking office, he declared: "A new kind of colonialism stalks the world today and threatens our independence. The dark future is foreshadowed by the poverty and repression of Castro's Cuba, the tightening grip of the totalitarian left in Grenada and Nicaragua, and the expansion of Soviet-backed, Cuban-managed support for violent revolution in Central America." [23]

Washington quickly cut off Nicaraguan aid and initiated the covert insurgency program. U.S. representatives in multinational lending institutions began opposing loans to Nicaragua and the Nicaraguan sugar quota in the U.S. market fell virtually to zero. American imports of beef and other important Nicaraguan products plummeted even before the United States declared an all-out trade embargo last spring.

The Sandinistas seemed eager to prove that the blackest predictions about their intentions were correct. They seized every opportunity to attack the United States in international forums, welcomed thousands of Cuban "advisers" to Nicaragua, established close political and economic relations with the Soviet Union, supplied arms to Marxist guerrillas in El Salvador and Guatemala, and rapidly converted Nicaragua into a tightly controlled socialist — if not communist — state. The rift between Managua and Washington is now so great that most experts believe that there can be no reconciliation until there is a change of government in one — or both — of the capitals.

Russian and Cuban Presence in Nicaragua

Along with the United States, the foreign countries most embroiled in Nicaraguan controversy are the Soviet Union and Cuba. Both seek to consolidate Sandinista rule at home and to encourage Nicaragua's covert, but active, support for Marxist guerrilla movements in other Central American nations.

---

[23] Remarks Reagan delivered at the Organization of American States when he proposed his Caribbean Basin Initiative (CBI), a 12-year duty-free program for the countries of Central America and the Caribbean. See "Caribbean Basin Policy," *E.R.R.*, 1984 Vol. I, pp. 21-40.

Ortega's Rise to Power

After Samoza's overthrow, Nicaragua was initially governed by a five-member junta that included two non-Sandinistas. The two resigned in May 1980 in protest of the Sandinistas' increasingly  leftist stance and were replaced by two middle-of-the road Nicaraguans. Junta member Daniel Ortega Saavadra, a Sandinista field commander during the civil war, began to emerge as the dominant political figure. In March 1981, he was named coordinator of the junta, whose size was reduced to three members.

On Nov. 4, 1984, Ortega was chosen president in an election in which 80 percent of the voters participated but which the United States charged was fraudulent. In the election, the Sandinistas also handily won control of a newly created 90-seat National Assembly. Despite the appearance of a democratic government, real power lies with the Sandinistas' nine-member National Directorate, of which Ortega and eight other Sandinista commanders are members. The United States continues to maintain diplomatic relations with Nicaragua.

According to U.S. government documents, Soviet and Cuban assistance has enabled Nicaragua to build "the largest, most powerful armed forces in the history of Central America." [24]

A lightly armed Sandinista guerrilla force of about 5,000 men in 1979 has now grown to an active-duty force of 62,000 men; an additional 57,000 are in the reserves and militia. Much of the growth has been accomplished through conscription, the State Department said. But even this level of strength falls short of the Sandinista goal of raising a 200,000-man militia to "defend the revolution." That goal was set in February 1981, months before Reagan gave the go-ahead to the creation of the contras.

The Soviets have supplied the Sandinista army with advanced weaponry unmatched elsewhere in Central America, including tanks, howitzers, rockets, anti-aircraft guns and deadly Mi-24/HIND-D Soviet attack helicopters. According to U.S. officials, the total value of Soviet arms shipments to Nicaragua approached $500 million at the beginning of 1985. [25] The Sandinistas have reportedly asked the Soviets for MiG-22 jet

---

[24] "The Soviet-Cuban Connection in Central America and the Caribbean," Departments of State and Defense, March 1983, p. 21. Also see State Department Special Report 132, "Revolution Beyond Our Borders," September 1985.
[25] "The Sandinista Military Build-up," Departments of State and Defense, May 1985.

fighter planes and the United States has threatened retaliation if such aircraft are ever sent to Nicaragua. A second point of concern for U.S. strategic planners is the construction of a new military air base at Punta Huete northeast of Managua. The base will have a 10,000-foot runway, the longest military runway in Central America, capable of handling any Soviet aircraft.

Cuba's involvement in Nicaragua dates from the arrival of the first Cuban military advisers, on July 19, 1979, the very day the Sandinistas took over. Since then, as many as 9,000 advisers, technicians and teachers from Cuba have been stationed concurrently in Nicaragua. Current estimates put the number at 7,500; 3,000 are listed as military or security personnel. It might seem that Nicaragua — like Cuba in the 1960s — traded its dependence on the United States for an equal dependence on the Soviet Union. There is a significant difference, however. Soviet economic assistance to Nicaragua has so far been negligible, and Nicaraguan trade with Soviet-bloc countries, while on the rise, is not yet sufficient to compensate for the losses suffered as a result of the U.S. trade embargo. If the United States retains any leverage in Nicaraguan affairs, it may in the long run prove to be economic rather than military.

New European Interest in Central America

If the Russians and Cubans would leave Nicaragua and terminate their support for opposition guerrillas in El Salvador, the Reagan administration has said, the region could be restored to a more tranquil existence. But the United States, the Soviet Union and Cuba are not the only foreign powers in Central America. In recent years, the European Community (EC) has expanded its presence in the region, and in significant ways, has voiced its disagreements with U.S. policy there. It has refused to participate in the U.S. trade embargo, and last November in Luxembourg, the EC signed a cooperation agreement with the Central American countries that will substantially increase the European aid they receive and give them important trade concessions.

Moreover two parties issued a communiqué declaring that "economic imbalances and social injustice" are "in large measure at the root of political instability" in Central America and calling for the elimination of the "foreign military presence" there. It appealed to "all countries with links and interests in the region" to help create favorable conditions for the success of the Contadora peace initiative. European community officials included Nicaragua in the aid blueprint, despite objections from Washington. The Reagan administration has officially welcomed the European show of support for Central American

GI's in Honduras

The U.S. military presence in Honduras has been growing since the United States began aiding the contras in 1981. Joint U.S.-Honduran military maneuvers have been held with increasing frequency and of ever-larger size. Facilities, which the U.S. government says are temporary, have been built to accommodate these maneuvers and the cadre of American personnel. The Reagan administration has told Congress it plans to spend $50 million on base construction in Honduras during the next five years.

development, but there is also an undercurrent of concern about the potential new challenge to U.S. influence in the region.

Changing Political Currents in the Region

Other challenges to the U.S. attempt to ostracize Nicaragua are likely to come from Central America itself. A democratic tide is running strongly in the region. Three new presidents have been chosen in peaceful elections in recent months and all seem inclined to seek regional solutions to Central American problems.

Costa Rica, the oldest and most stable of Latin American democracies, elected the youngest president in the nation's history on Feb. 2, 44-year-old Oscar Arias Sanchez. The new president, due to take office May 8, is a strong supporter of the Contadora process and of negotiations with other Central American countries, including Nicaragua. In Honduras, a remarkable transition of power occurred in January. José Azcona Hoyo, 59, became the first elected civilian leader to succeed another elected civilian as president in more than half a century. During the campaign, Azcona opposed the continued presence of contra bases in Honduras, but he is expected to proceed slowly and cautiously.

The most outspoken of the new Central American leaders is Guatemala's president, Marco Vinicio Cerezo Arevalo, who assumed office on Jan. 14. Cerezo, 43, is only the second civilian president of Guatemala in three decades, and is the first in that time who does not owe his office to military support. Cerezo has said that Guatemala will seek economic but not military aid from the United States, and would not yield to U.S. pressure to isolate Nicaragua. At Cerezo's urging, the other four Central American nations have endorsed the recent Contadora initiatives, which call on the United States to cut off its support for the contras. The changing political currents in Central America suggests that the nations of the region may be ready to challenge the legitimacy of foreign pressures that have dominated their societies and governments for so many years.

Recommended Reading List

Books

Cabezas, Omar, *Fire From the Mountains: The Making of a Sandinista,* Crown, 1985.

Christian, Shirley, *Nicaragua: Revolution in the Family,* Random House, 1985.

Dickey, Christopher, *With the Contras: A Reporter in the Wilds of Nicaragua,* Simon & Schuster, 1985.

LaFeber, Walter, *Inevitable Revolutions: The United States in Central America,* W. W. Norton, 1983.

Leiken, Robert S., ed., *Central America: Anatomy of a Conflict,* Pergamon Press, 1984.

Walker, Thomas W., *Nicaragua: The Land of Sandino,* Westview Press, 1981.

Woodward, Ralph Lee Jr., *Central America: A Nation Divided,* Oxford University Press, 1976.

Articles

"Central America and the Caribbean," *Current History* (8 articles), March 1985.

Contreras, Joseph, "Arms and the Contras," *Newsweek,* Feb. 10, 1986.

Farer, Tom J., "Contadora: The Hidden Agenda," *Foreign Policy,* summer 1985.

Gutman, Roy, "Nicaragua: America's Diplomatic Charade," *Foreign Policy,* fall 1984.

Leiken, Robert S. "The Battle for Nicaragua," *The New York Review,* March 13, 1986.

Millet, Richard L. "Nicaragua's Frustrated Revolution," *Current History,* January 1986.

Nicaraguan Perspectives, selected issues.

Ullman, Richard H., "At War with Nicaragua," *Foreign Affairs,* fall 1983.

Reports and Studies

Editorial Research Reports: "Caribbean Basin Policy," 1984 Vol. 1, p. 23; "Latin American Challenges," 1981 Vol. 1, p. 271; "Human Rights Policy," 1979 Vol. 1, p. 363; "Central America and the U.S.A." 1978 Vol. 1, p. 323.

Gaspar, Edmund, "United States-Latin America: A Special Relationship?" AEI-Hoover Policy Studies, 1978.

U.S. Department of State: "Revolution Beyond Our Borders: Sandinista Intervention in Central America," Special Report No. 132, September 1985; "The Sandinistas and Middle Eastern Radicals," August 1985.

U.S. Departments of State and Defense: "The Sandinista Military Buildup," May 1985; "The Soviet-Cuban Connection in Central America and the Caribbean," March 1985.

Wiarda, Howard J., ed., "Rift and Revolution: The Central American Imbroglio," American Enterprise Institute Studies in Foreign Policy, 1984.

Graphics: Photo p. 129, Christopher Dickey/The Washington Post; map p. 132, Robert Redding; photo p. 135, Pete Souza; photo p. 145, Nancy McGirr/UPI.

ANGOLA
AND THE
REAGAN DOCTRINE

by Mary H. Cooper

Jan. 17
1 9 8 6

Editor's Update: Jonas Savimbi, head of UNITA, visited the United States in January 1986 to appeal for military aid to help in his 11-year-old fight to topple the Marxist government of Angolan President José Eduardo dos Santos. Shortly after Savimbi made his appeal, the Reagan administration informed Congress that it planned to provide UNITA with up to $15 million in covert aid this year.

Congressional opponents of the move argued that U.S. involvement in the Angolan conflict warranted consultation with Congress, not merely formal notification of the decision to provide aid. They also said that support of Savimbi, an ally of South Africa, would diminish the effectiveness of U.S. economic sanctions against the white-minority government of South Africa and harm American interests in other African nations.

ANGOLA AND
THE REAGAN DOCTRINE

ONE OF THE FIRST issues Congress is likely to address after it convenes Jan. 21 concerns the southern African nation of Angola. While American attention has focused on growing unrest in nearby South Africa, backers of the Reagan administration's policy of supporting anti-communist insurgents around the world are trying to add Angolan rebel leader Jonas Savimbi and his forces to the list of "freedom fighters" worthy of U.S. aid.

Like the "contras" fighting to overthrow the Sandinista government of Nicaragua, Savimbi's forces, known as UNITA, are seeking to topple an avowedly Marxist government that enjoys the support of the Soviet Union and its allies. And like the U.S. support of the Nicaraguan rebels, the question of aid to Savimbi promises to generate considerable controversy hinging as much on domestic political considerations as on the national security.

The United States has not given aid to UNITA — the National Union for the Total Independence of Angola — for nearly 10 years. After a bungled attempt by the Central Intelligence Agency to prevent leftist forces from taking over the former Portuguese colony in 1975, Congress passed the Clark Amendment, named for its chief sponsor, former Sen. Dick Clark, D-Iowa. The measure prohibited the United States from providing aid to any of the factions fighting in the Angolan civil war. Since Congress repealed the aid ban last July, there have been repeated calls to restore funding for UNITA.

Reports that Savimbi's military position is weakening have lent new urgency to the calls for aid. Even with the help of Cuban troops present in Angola for the last 10 years,[1] the government has not been able to dislodge Savimbi; his forces control much of the southern and eastern regions of the country *(see map, p. 152)*. But according to Savimbi, the latest government offensive, which began last summer, has been joined by Soviet military personnel operating advanced weaponry. In an apparent attempt to cut off UNITA from outside assistance, the government forces captured the town of Cazombo near Angola's borders with Zaire and Zambia. They were stopped outside

---

[1] Estimates on Cuban troop levels in Angola vary. The International Institute for Strategic Studies in London estimates there are about 19,000, the State Department puts the number at 35,000, and Savimbi says there are 45,000.

Mavinga, deep within UNITA-held territory and only 120 miles from Jamba, Savimbi's capital in the southeastern corner of the country. Savimbi is asking for military assistance before the end of the rainy season in April or May, when the government offensive is expected to resume.

The proposals to renew aid to UNITA are but the most recent initiative on behalf of what the administration calls "freedom fighters" seeking to overthrow Soviet-backed governments. According to this policy, known as the Reagan Doctrine, U.S. intervention in favor of anti-Soviet insurgents can effectively contain or even roll back Soviet expansion in the Third World. During his first term in office, Reagan had little congressional support for his doctrine, but since 1984, Congress has agreed to funnel aid to rebel forces in Cambodia, Afghanistan and — most notably — Nicaragua *(see box, p. 166)*.

Issue Intertwined With Namibia Conflict

The Angola situation must be considered in the context of the whole region of southern Africa *(see map, p. 155)*. To protest last summer's repeal of the Clark Amendment, Angolan President

José Eduardo dos Santos walked out of negotiations with South Africa and the United States over the withdrawal of South African forces from Namibia, also known as South West Africa. Since 1916 South Africa has controlled the 330,000-square mile territory separating Angola and South Africa. Its forces occupy the territory in defiance of a United Nations resolution,[2] and South Africa refuses to remove them until the Cuban forces leave Angola, saying the Cuban presence threatens South Africa's national security.

Following Angola's temporary withdrawal from the Namibia negotiations, support gathered among conservative lawmakers on Capitol Hill to provide overt aid to Savimbi and UNITA. At the same time, administration officials began to press for the renewal of covert CIA military aid to UNITA, the same type of

---

[2] U.N. Resolution 435, passed in July 1978, calls for a cease-fire, withdrawal of South African troops from Namibia and the presence in Namibia of a U.N. force until elections are held to form a government. For background, see "South Africa's 'Total Strategy,'" *E.R.R.*, 1983, Vol. II, pp. 665-666.

aid provided in 1975. "We all believe that a covert operation would be more useful to us and have more chance of success right now than the overt proposal that has been made in the

Congress," President Reagan stated flatly last November. While such aid would hardly be secret after this public acknowledgement of support, the administration has continued to express its preference for "covert" funding.

Resumption last November of the Namibia negotiations, in which the United States has played the role of mediator for the past three years, has added a new element to the aid issue. Secretary of State George P. Shultz said in a Nov. 24 television interview that the administration was seeking "a negotiated solution to the problems of Angola as well as the problem of Namibia, linked as it is to the difficulties in southern Africa generally and in South Africa."

José Eduardo dos Santos

Assistant Secretary of State Chester A. Crocker met Nov. 27 and 28 in Lusaka, Zambia, with Angolan and South African negotiators but achieved "no tangible progress," according to Jerry Gallucci, State Department desk officer for Angola.[3] Crocker and dos Santos met again Jan. 8-9 in the Angolan capital of Luanda. Gallucci said he expected the Angolans to respond to U.S. proposals calling for the withdrawal of Cubans from Angola together with South Africa's withdrawal from Namibia. In placing the ball in Angola's court, the administration sent a clear warning to the Angolan government that its continued refusal to send the Cubans home would make covert aid to UNITA a near certainty. "On the basis of this meeting," Gallucci continued, "conclusions will be drawn back here in Washington about the usefulness of the negotiating track."

Chester A. Crocker

Regional Effect of South African Unrest

The question of renewing U.S. aid to UNITA must also be considered in light of the ongoing struggle in South Africa, the

---

[3] All persons quoted in this report were interviewed by the author unless otherwise noted.

dominant economic and military power in the region. Violence stemming from the ruling white minority government's policy of apartheid has claimed the lives of more than 1,000 people in that country since September 1984, when a new constitution granting limited political rights to mixed-race and Asian inhabitants, but not to blacks, went into effect. Despite almost worldwide condemnation, the Nationalist government of President Pieter W. Botha continues to deny political rights to the black majority and its main political party, the African National Congress (ANC), which has been outlawed since the early 1960s. Refusing to denounce violence as a means of gaining power in South Africa, the ANC has claimed responsibility for a series of mine explosions that recently have spread the violence from the black townships to the white community.

As the Botha government and the Afrikaner population it represents continue to resist the eventuality of black rule in South Africa, growing numbers of white, mostly English-speaking South Africans see negotiation with the ANC as the only key to avoid all-out war between the nation's 4.3 million whites and 18.6 million blacks.[4] They say accommodation with the ANC is especially urgent because the party's older leadership appears to be ceding power to younger militants, who are considered responsible for the recent shift of attacks away from military installations to civilian targets.

South Africa has stepped up its military campaign against Zimbabwe, Mozambique, Lesotho and other neighboring countries it accuses of harboring ANC guerrillas. Its critics say South Africa's regional policy is really a campaign to destabilize neighboring black governments and thus prevent them from helping opponents of the region's only remaining white government.

Zimbabwe's Prime Minister Robert Mugabe has repeatedly denied that the ANC maintains a military presence in his country. Nonetheless, after five land mines killed South African whites near the border between the two countries in December, South Africa warned that it would send troops into Zimbabwe in "hot pursuit" of ANC guerrillas. The ANC, headquartered in exile in Lusaka, Zambia, acknowledged responsibility for planting the mines, but said it had been done from within South Africa. The rising border tension marks a sudden downturn in relations between the two countries, which had expanded economic cooperation and trade in the years since Zimbabwe — formerly Rhodesia — came under black rule in 1980.

---

[4] According to the New Africa Yearbook, 1984-85, South Africa's population of 26.1 million also includes 2.4 million "Coloureds" or people of mixed race, and 800,000 "Asians," mostly Indians.

Lesotho, a small, landlocked nation completely surrounded by South Africa, has been the target of South African raids, most recently, witnesses reported, Dec. 20, when nine people were killed in the capital of Maseru. Like Zimbabwe, the Lesotho government denies it harbors ANC militants and has lodged a complaint against South Africa with the U.N. Security Council. Earlier this month South Africa imposed restrictions on Lesotho nationals seeking to cross the border into South Africa, where many work as miners. According to villagers in Swaziland, another small black enclave located along the South African-Mozambican border, South African forces invaded their territory in late December. Pretoria denied the charge. Botswana, which lies to South Africa's north, was the target of a raid last June.

Mozambique, South Africa's neighbor to the northeast, was a frequent target of South African raids until March 16, 1984, when the two nations signed a non-aggression pact, known as the Nkomati Accord after the border town where it was signed. South Africa agreed that it would no longer attack what Pretoria said were ANC bases or support forces rebelling against the Marxist government that has ruled Mozambique since it gained independence from Portugal in 1975.[5] Under the accord, Mozambique was to expel any ANC militants, while South Africa was to discontinue any aid to the insurgents. Since then, however, South Africa has admitted to breaking the agreement in pursuit of ANC militants.

South Africa also signed a U.S.-mediated cease-fire agreement with Angola in February 1984, but an impasse was reached over the withdrawal of Cuban troops from Angola. South Africa demanded they leave before it would set a date for Namibian independence and the removal of its own forces from the territory. Angola demanded South Africa first end its aid to Savimbi and UNITA.

Pieter W. Botha

Some 2,000 South African troops have been stationed in Namibia and at times have occupied parts of Angola itself ever since the Angolan civil war broke out in 1975. Ostensibly aimed at defending the territory from the South West African People's Organization — SWAPO — seeking independence of Namibia from South African occupation, the South African military has also supported Savimbi's UNITA forces in their quest to overthrow the Angolan government. South Africa formally withdrew from Angolan territory last April, but has since then staged at least three raids into the country, one last May against the oil fields of Cabinda province, the northernmost tip of Angola some 650 miles from the Namibian border. The most recent raid occurred in late December, and the dos Santos government has charged that South African forces are still deep inside Angola.

Both the Lusaka Declaration and the Nkomati Accord represent South Africa's main peace initiatives in southern Africa, which it seeks to transform into a "constellation" of states with Pretoria at its head. South Africa promised to call off its military incursions and to offer economic aid to the region's black governments in an effort to defuse international concern with its domestic policies and end the country's increasing isolation. But South Africa's peace initiative, disparagingly dubbed "Pax Pretoriana" by its critics, appears further and further from success as the Botha government steps up repression at home and its reprisal attacks in neighboring nations.[6]

---

[5] The Mozambican National Resistance, or RENAMO, seeks to overthrow the governing party, known as FRELIMO, or the Liberation Front of Mozambique.
[6] See, for example, Kenneth W. Grundy, "Pax Pretoriana: South Africa's Regional Policy," *Current History*, April 1985, pp. 150-154.

Angola's Troubled Past

L IKE most of its neighbors, Angola has only recently emerged from centuries of exploitation by European colonialists. Angola was established as a Portuguese colony in the 15th century, but there was no permanent European presence until 1575, when Portuguese settled on the coast in what is now Luanda. Portuguese subjugation of Angola's people continued throughout its colonization. Early settlers penetrated the interior chiefly to seek mineral deposits and capture slaves. When the slave trade ended in the mid-1800s, the Portuguese launched a systematic program of military conquest to gain control of the interior and used forced labor to grow coffee, cotton, sugar and other crops.

As they moved into Angola's interior, the Portuguese built the three main railway lines that still serve the country, using them to transport crops to the coast. The Benguela railway linking the coastal port city to the eastern border also provided an essential outlet for mineral exports from Zaire and Zambia.

Portugal's treatment of Angola's people spawned widespread resentment and spurred creation of some of the nationalist groups vying for power today. The MPLA (Popular Movement for the Liberation of Angola), founded under Agostinho Neto in 1956, and the Union of the Populations of North Angola, founded in 1957 by Holden Roberto, who later incorporated it into the FNLA (National Front for the Liberation of Angola), were responsible for anti-colonial uprisings in February and March 1961. After the Portuguese crushed these uprisings the groups remained active as guerrilla forces and were eventually joined by Savimbi's forces.

Superpower Intervention in Civil Conflict

The overthrow of Portugal's government in 1974 marked the end of colonial occupation but not the end of foreign intervention in Angola. When the government headed by Marcello Caetano was deposed on April 25, 1974, his successor declared that all of Portugal's colonies would be granted independence.[7] Under an agreement signed Jan. 15, 1975, in Alvor, Portugal, the three main Angolan liberation movements were included in a transition government and elections were scheduled for October of that year to determine who would head the first indepen-

[7] Angola, Mozambique, Cape Verde, São Tomé and Guinea-Bissau in Africa; East Timor and Macao in East Asia. Only Macao is still a Portuguese-administered territory.

dent Angolan government. Independence day, when the Portuguese would turn the country over to the elected government, was set for Nov. 11. However, the three nationalist groups could not overcome traditional rivalries. Civil war broke out shortly after the Alvor agreement was signed, and outside powers quickly intervened on behalf of one or more of the three factions.

The MPLA — still headed by Neto — was a European-oriented, Marxist-Leninist group that placed the goal of national liberation above traditional loyalties to the Mbundu tribe of central and western Angola where the MPLA originated. The servants and semiskilled labor in Luanda were chiefly Mbundu; some of them, including Neto, managed to receive advanced educations, often in Europe, where they came into contact with Marxism. "Marxist philosophy alone seemed to offer an alternative to Portuguese oppression; in addition to moral support, Marxism gave them organizational skills to develop a revolutionary movement," wrote John Stockwell, former chief of the CIA's Angola Task Force, explaining the allure of Marxism for all the contending factions in Angola. "Capitalism, as espoused by the United States, firmly supported the Portuguese. Catholicism supported the Portuguese. American Protestant missionaries were at odds with the Portuguese, but in the end taught passive submission." [8] The MPLA received early support from Cuba, some Western European governments and Algeria.

Roberto's FNLA based its power largely on tribal allegiances among the Bakongo in the north. Roberto, related to the U.S.-backed president of neighboring Zaire, relied heavily on Zairean military support and was the first to receive U.S. covert aid. The most heavily armed of the three groups, the FNLA also received assistance from China, India and Romania, as well as the northern African states of Algeria, Morocco and Tunisia.

Savimbi broke away from the FNLA to form UNITA. Born in 1934 to a prominent family of the Ovimbundu tribe, Savimbi was educated at Protestant mission schools and went to universities in Portugal and Switzerland. He returned to Angola and participated with the FNLA in the 1961 uprising. In 1963 he reportedly split with the FNLA over tribal questions and began organizing UNITA among the Ovimbundu people who inhabited the central region of the country. Savimbi initially went to Egypt and later China, where he was given small amounts of supplies and provided guerrilla training for several of his followers. "With small numbers of men and limited means Savimbi became a festering thorn to the Portuguese in central Angola

---

[8] John Stockwell, *In Search of Enemies: A CIA Story* (1978), p. 65.

Angola At a Glance

Population: 7.7 million.
Area: 498,400 square miles.
Geography: Mostly plateau, thick vegetation in north.
Ethnicity: Ovimbundu, 38%; Mbundu, 23%; Bakongo, 13%;
 Mestico, or mixed, 2%; European, 1%.
Per Capita Income: $591 (in 1980).
Cash Crops: Coffee, sisal, corn, cotton, sugar, manioc, tobacco.
Industries: Oil, diamond mining, fish processing, brewing, to-
 bacco and sugar processing, textiles.

and a living legend among the Ovimbundu people," Stockwell wrote.[9]

Shortly after the Alvor accord was reached, the Ford administration authorized the CIA to provide arms to both Savimbi and Roberto so that they could hold off the MPLA until the October elections. In a critical incident in March, Roberto's forces killed some 50 unarmed MPLA activists. "The fate of Angola was then sealed in blood," Stockwell wrote. "The issue could only be decided through violence."[10] It was also during March that the Soviet Union resumed its military assistance to the MPLA, which it had cut off two years before. Separately, Neto also requested and in early summer received Cuba's first contingent of 230 military advisers.

Stockwell was one of the few Americans to have encountered Savimbi in the field. According to his account, Savimbi was known only as "a tough radical" who "had been supported by the North Koreans and the Chinese."[11] At the time of the CIA involvement in 1975, Stockwell wrote, U.S. intelligence knew little of the man: "Our alliance with him was based solely on his opposition to the MPLA."[12] Stockwell, who headed up the covert operation, gave his superiors his assessment after a trip to Angola that summer: "We had two viable options in Angola. We could give the FNLA and UNITA enough support to win — by going in quickly with tactical air support and advisors we could take to Luanda and put the MPLA out of business before the Soviets could react. Otherwise, if we weren't willing to do that, we would further U.S. interests by staying out of the conflict. The middle ground, feeling our way along with small amounts of aid, would only escalate the war and get the United States far out on a fragile limb. It would help neither the Angolan people nor us. To the contrary, it would jeopardize the United States' position in southern Africa."[13]

---

[9] *Ibid.*, p. 147.
[10] *Ibid.*, p. 68.
[11] *Ibid.*, p. 52.
[12] *Ibid.*, p. 64.
[13] *Ibid.*, p. 158.

Stockwell's advice was not taken. By July the MPLA had repelled both the FNLA and UNITA. The turning point in the war came in October, when South African troops joined UNITA and FNLA forces in a thrust on Luanda. They were decisively routed, thanks to additional Cuban troops and Soviet arms on the side of the MPLA. Meanwhile, China had abruptly withdrawn its support for UNITA and the FNLA when they turned to South Africa for additional aid. China's desire to counter Soviet expansion in the region apparently was outweighed by its reluctance to be associated in any way with the apartheid regime in South Africa.[14]

With Luanda secured, the MPLA declared the People's Republic of Angola in November, while the FNLA and UNITA set up rival governments to the south in Huambo. The FNLA soon dissolved, however, leaving Savimbi's group the only viable opposition force.

That same month the Ford administration asked Congress for an additional $28 million in covert CIA funding for the Angola effort. News of the request leaked to the press, and critics quickly complained that the United States was about to get involved in what could turn out to be another Vietnam. With that humiliating defeat still fresh in mind, Congress banned all further American covert assistance for Angola, despite Secretary of State Henry A. Kissinger's exhortation that such a ban would show the world that the United States "is willing to emasculate itself in the face of massive, unprecedented Soviet and Cuban intervention," placing in doubt its credibility as a protector of "global stability." [15]

Continued Soviet, U.S. Interest in Region

There is evidence that Kissinger, anxious to prevent Moscow from taking advantage of détente to expand its influence in the Third World, overestimated the extent of Soviet influence in Angola. Not only did the MPLA establish ties with Cuba independently of its backing from the Soviet Union and long before its victory, but Neto successfully repelled a 1977 coup attempt by a rival faction that advocated closer ties with Moscow.

"Since then," wrote Soviet analyst Raymond Garthoff, "Angolan policy has been based on a general political alignment with the Soviet Union and reliance on the continued presence of Cuban troops to prevent major external attack, but has also

[14] See Raymond L. Garthoff, *Détente and Confrontation* (1985), chapter entitled "Competition in the Third World: Angola, 1975-76."
[15] Cited in Garthoff, *op. cit.*, p. 525. The Clark Amendment was passed by the Senate Dec. 19, 1975, and by the House on Jan. 27, 1976. Rather than see his veto overridden, Ford signed the ban into law Feb. 9.

Trade, But No Diplomatic Relations

Angola is the only African country with which the United States does not maintain diplomatic relations. Yet it is also the United States' fourth largest trading partner in Africa. According to Commerce Department figures, U.S. exports to Angola almost doubled in value, from $66 million to $121 million from the first three quarters of 1984 to the same period in 1985. U.S. exports include aircraft, construction machinery and oil field equipment.

Over the same period U.S. imports from Angola fell only slightly, from $811 million to $778 million, and the United States remained Angola's biggest trading partner last year. "Of these imports, 98 to 99 percent are petroleum from various sources in Angola," explained Simon Bensimon, Angola desk officer at the Commerce Department. Much of the imported oil comes from the Cabinda offshore oil fields operated since October 1968 by the Gulf Oil Co. According to figures provided by the company, the Cabinda fields alone produce 170,000 barrels a day, most of which is shipped to the United States.

Since the abrupt departure of the Portuguese in 1975 and the disruption caused by the civil war, oil has replaced minerals and agricultural products as Angola's chief export and may be the only export commodity saving the country from economic collapse. Food shortages have been common over the past decade, and Angola is one of six sub-Saharan countries considered by the U.N. Food and Agriculture Organization to be in danger of famine again this year.

included encouragement for diplomatic and trade ties with the West." [16] The United States alone among the Western powers does not recognize the MPLA government; even China, which had worked so hard to prevent the MPLA from coming to power, maintains diplomatic relations with Luanda *(see box, above)*.

The Soviet Union signed friendship treaties with both Angola (October 1976) and Mozambique (March 1977), the other former Portuguese colony in southern African. The Soviets have helped transport additional Cuban troops to Angola, helped train SWAPO guerrillas fighting the South Africans in Namibia and supported Joshua Nkomo in his bid for power in Zimbabwe. But in all these cases Soviet aid has failed to enlarge Moscow's foothold in the region. In Zimbabwe, Nkomo rival Robert Mugabe became prime minister and distanced his country from the Soviet Union.[17] The nominally Marxist government of Mozambique, disappointed by Moscow's reluctance to match its military support with economic aid, has turned increasingly to

---

[16] *Ibid.*, p. 519.
[17] Mugabe recently visited Moscow for the first time since he was elected in 1980 and reportedly requested increased military and economic assistance.

the West for badly needed economic assistance and trade.[18] The Nkomati Accord between South Africa and Mozambique was a further blow to Soviet influence in the region. Some analysts say that Moscow's reluctance to give more direct assistance to regimes it supports in southern Africa is an indication of the region's low priority among the Kremlin's foreign policy objectives.[19]

U.S. strategic interests in the region remain the shipping lanes used by tankers carrying Middle Eastern oil around the Cape of Good Hope as well as minerals used in weapons production which the United States can obtain only from southern Africa. But Washington's policy toward the region has wavered considerably in recent decades. The Nixon and Ford administrations viewed southern Africa largely in terms of East-West competition and formulated a regional policy based on the erroneous assumption that white regimes were destined to remain in power and that black liberation movements only served the interests of the Soviet Union. At the time, Portugal still ruled Angola and Mozambique, and Rhodesia was still in the hands of the white-minority government of Ian Smith. This policy — dubbed "tar baby" by critics — was abandoned only after the failed CIA intervention in Angola and congressional passage of the Clark Amendment.

Jimmy Carter saw southern Africa in terms of human rights denied the black majorities in several countries. But in denouncing apartheid, Carter alienated the South African government just as he was trying to play a prominent role in negotiating independence for Namibia.

The Reagan administration has once again placed southern Africa in the context of East-West competition. Soon after coming to office in 1981, Reagan and Assistant Secretary Crocker declared that the United States would replace Carter's "confrontational" stance with a policy of "constructive engagement" with South Africa. This new approach was premised on the theory that the South African government could more effectively be induced to institute domestic reform by persuasion than by condemnation and economic sanctions. A corollary of the new policy was renewed diplomatic support for the "freedom fighters" in Angola, by now limited to Savimbi and UNITA.

But with growing international condemnation of South Africa's domestic and regional policies, "constructive engagement" has proved less effective than its authors had predicted. Rea-

---

[18] President Samora Moises Machel met with Reagan in Washington Sept. 19, 1985.

[19] See, for example, Sam C. Nolutshungu, "Soviet Involvement in Southern Africa," *Annals of the American Academy of Political and Social Science*, September 1985, pp. 138-146.

gan's imposition of limited sanctions on Pretoria last September under congressional pressure has not brought the region closer to peace. Violence is escalating in South Africa, and U.S. efforts to obtain the withdrawal of Cubans from Angola and South Africans from Namibia are given little chance of success.[20]

Reagan Doctrine Debate

THE DEBATE over aid to UNITA almost always turns on the debater's assessment of Savimbi's true ideological and political identity. To conservative backers of the Reagan administration's drive to restore aid to UNITA, Jonas Savimbi is unquestionably a "freedom fighter" worthy of American assistance. To critics of that aid, he is an opportunist, willing to temporarily shed his Marxist ideology in order to obtain South African and U.S. support in what is simply a power struggle with the MPLA.

To gain congressional support for his cause, Savimbi is reportedly planning to visit the United States in late January at the behest of conservative organizations and politicians.[21] He has also addressed his critics in an article published by the conservative Heritage Foundation. While defending his use of "principles of guerrilla warfare" learned from the late Mao Tse-tung, Savimbi pointedly distanced his political program from the Marxist model. "We fight for an independent Angola, free of all foreign troops," he wrote. "We believe that peasants, not the state, should own farmland. We favor democratic elections, freedom of religion, and respect for tribal customs and languages." He went on to equate Angola with Munich, where the Western powers tried to appease Hitler and avoid war with Germany: "Hesitation, the refusal to aid UNITA in its fight against the Cubans and Soviets, will be taken as a signal by all the countries in the region that the United States has abandoned them to the Soviets as the West abandoned Czechoslovakia and Eastern Europe to Hitler in 1938." [22]

After years of civil strife in Angola, said William Pascoe, policy analyst for Third World affairs at the Heritage Foundation, "it's time [for the United States] to put up or shut up."

---

[20] For an analysis of recent U.S. policies, see Thomas J. Noer, *Cold War and Black Liberation* (1985), and Sanford J. Ungar and Peter Vale, "South Africa: Why Constructive Engagement Failed," *Foreign Affairs*, winter 1985/86, pp. 234-258.

[21] Savimbi is scheduled to appear at the American Conservative Union's three-day "Conservative Political Action Conference" that begins Jan. 30.

[22] Jonas Savimbi, "The War Against Soviet Colonialism," *Policy Review*, winter 1985-86, pp. 19, 24.

Although "he's not as free-market as [Sen.] Jesse Helms, [R-N.C.]" commented Pascoe, Savimbi's stated belief in Western ideals contributes strongly to his legitimacy in U.S. eyes. UNITA, Pascoe said, is "a much more democratic organization than the MPLA."

Jonas Savimbi

Like the Reagan administration, Pascoe clearly set "freedom fighters" apart from other insurgents on the basis of ideology. "We support Savimbi because ... he's fighting a Soviet- and Cuban-backed regime," he said. "But this is not the main attribute alone, because we don't support aid to Eritrean insurgents who are fighting a similar regime [in Ethiopia] but are Marxists themselves."

Other supporters say aid to UNITA would have a positive effect on Soviet behavior elsewhere. "It would send a signal to those fighting Soviet-supported regimes that Washington is not indifferent to their plight," wrote Dimitri Simes of the Carnegie Endowment for International Peace. "Most important, by upgrading the costs of Moscow's expansionism the assistance to Savimbi would contribute to a more moderate Soviet foreign policy. Such a policy is a precondition for a better US-USSR relationship." [23]

Interference in Power Struggle Opposed

Other analysts predict a far different outcome. According to Robert Rotberg, an expert on southern Africa and professor of political science and history at the Massachusetts Institute of Technology, U.S. aid to UNITA would stiffen the MPLA's resolve to maintain Cuban troops for protection. He also ridiculed the "freedom fighter" image of Savimbi, whom he calls "one of the greatest socialist thinkers in the region and a greater Marxist thinker than those now heading the Angolan government." As for Savimbi's continued reliance on South African troops, Rotberg said, "he's just using South Africa." In his view, American conservatives are wrong to ascribe lofty principles to the Angolan civil war: "UNITA's antagonism to the Angolan government is based less on principles of authoritarianism vs.

[23] Writing in *The Christian Science Monitor*, Dec. 12, 1985.

anti-authoritarianism, or socialism vs. non-socialism, than on power: They have it, we want it."

While liberals in and out of Congress oppose aid to Savimbi on political grounds, some U.S. corporations have more pragmatic reasons for doing so. While asserting that the company maintains "strict neutrality" wherever it operates in the world, Gulf Oil has issued a statement in which it calls the dos Santos government "pragmatic, realistic and fair in dealing with Gulf" which, it goes on to say, has encountered "no problem of an ideological nature" in the country. According to Gulf, which operates a large oil concession in Angola's Cabinda province, Angola now offers several benefits to the West as a non-OPEC supplier of superior grade petroleum that can be transported to the United States less expensively and more securely than Middle Eastern crude.

Despite its expressed neutrality, it has been reported in the national press that Gulf and its parent company, Chevron Corp., are lobbying Congress to vote down aid to Savimbi.[24] Pascoe says Gulf's actions and statement are self-serving: "Communist governments in the Third World offer advantages to U.S.-based corporations because they are never overthrown and thus offer a stabler business environment" than authoritarian dictatorships or democratically elected governments. In any case, Gulf's interests offer a peculiar twist to the Angola controversy. On at least one occasion, Cuban troops have protected American lives and property in the Cabinda oil concession from attack by UNITA — the very forces the administration supports — and its South African allies.

It is Savimbi's South African connection that most galls leaders of the American campaign against apartheid. "Savimbi is indeed an opportunist," said Glenn McKeown, legislative assistant for TransAfrica, a lobby group active in the effort to isolate the Botha government. Any form of U.S. aid to UNITA, he said, "would be tantamount to giving aid to South Africa and help it further destabilize the region." This view is shared by Desmond Tutu, the Anglican bishop of Johannesburg who received the Nobel Peace Prize in 1984. "If the South African government did not believe — and believe rightly — that it would almost always be protected from the consequences of its intransigence and quite vicious actions, it wouldn't go on doing what it's doing," he said in a recent interview. "Look at the audacity that they have of constantly making incursions into Angola, knowing full well that they will get the full backing of the United States, because the Reagan administration has the same interests as South Africa has. They want to back UNITA, because they are

---

[24] See, for example, *Business Week*, Dec. 16, 1985, p. 45.

U.S. Aid to Other Insurgents

The United States is openly supporting anti-communist rebels fighting to overthrow Soviet-backed governments in three other conflicts around the world. The latest to benefit from the Reagan Doctrine are non-communist Cambodian insurgents who, along with a communist group, have been seeking to expel the Soviet-supported Vietnamese forces that have occupied the country since 1979. Congress in December appropriated up to $5 million in economic and military aid to the two non-communist rebel groups.* The administration recently announced it would provide $3.5 million in non-lethal aid.

Since Soviet troops intervened in Afghanistan Dec. 27, 1979, to help its ally quell an anti-communist rebellion, the "mujahideen" insurgents in that country have enjoyed the administration's moral support as well as covert military assistance. Congress in 1985 also appropriated $15 million in humanitarian aid for "the Afghan people."

While U.N.-sponsored negotiations on a settlement that would include the withdrawal of more than 100,000 Soviet troops and independence for Afghanistan under international guarantees are reportedly near completion, a timetable for the Soviet withdrawal remains to be defined. That issue will be addressed when talks resume in late February or early March.

The main benefactors of the Reagan Doctrine to date have been insurgents in Nicaragua, where the administration supports so-called "contras" in their fight to oust the leftist Sandinista government. After it was disclosed that the CIA had laid mines in the Central American country's harbors in 1983 and 1984, Congress cut off all military assistance to the anti-government forces in October 1984. But following a heated debate, Congress approved $27 million in "humanitarian," or non-lethal, supplies to the contras last June.

In December Reagan announced he would seek "more effective help" to counter what the administration calls growing Soviet and Cuban military support of the Sandinistas. The administration is expected to once again seek military aid for the contras when the current aid program runs out March 31.

In a speech in London Dec. 10, Secretary of State George P. Shultz attempted to counter criticism that aid to insurgents would undermine negotiations aimed at obtaining political solutions, saying that "diplomacy is unlikely to work unless there is effective resistance." He added that the proper form of aid depended upon local circumstances: "Sometimes we should give military and economic assistance to neighboring states that are threatened; sometimes we should extend moral or humanitarian or other kinds of support to those resisting. Sometimes help may be better given without open acknowledgement; covert action has been part of the arsenal of states since time immemorial, providing a means of influence short of outright confrontation."

*For background, see "Cambodia: A Nation in Turmoil," E.R.R. 1985 Vol. I, p. 253.

opposed to what they believe is a Marxist government, and any Marxist government must bite the dust, and you can use any method to accomplish that." [25]

Political Considerations Color Aid Debate

Congressional perceptions of the situation in Angola are colored by domestic considerations. This is an election year, and members of Congress hastened to identify their positions on the UNITA issue before returning to their home districts at the end of 1985. Any vote on aid to Savimbi is likely to be close in the Democrat-controlled House. In late November 101 House members, mostly liberal Democrats, sent Reagan a letter warning against renewing aid. "U.S. involvement in this conflict, whether direct or indirect, covert or overt, would damage our relations with governments throughout Africa and undermine fundamental U.S. policy objectives in southern Africa," they wrote. Another letter, signed by more than 100 lawmakers, mostly conservative Republicans, was sent at the same time supporting renewed aid.

Influential support for UNITA aid has come from unexpected quarters. In addition to pro-Savimbi proposals by conservatives, including Rep. Jack F. Kemp, R-N.Y, a 1988 presidential hopeful, Rep. Mark D. Siljander, R-Mich., and Sen. Malcolm Wallop, R-Wyo., Rep. Claude Pepper, D-Fla., introduced a bill to authorize "humanitarian" assistance to UNITA. Pepper, who has focused most of his attention on Social Security and other issues concerning the elderly, is up for re-election in a Miami district that includes a large population of strongly anti-communist Cubans who have pressed Pepper to support aid to drive Castro's troops out of Angola.

To Rotberg of MIT, such domestic considerations are out of place in formulating foreign policy. "That Claude Pepper should sponsor this legislation on the basis of his Cuban constituents is ludicrous," he said. In Rotberg's view the whole question of aid to Savimbi is "the right's counterissue to the successful campaign against apartheid in South Africa." He predicts conservatives will use the issue as "a kind of lightening rod to test correct sentiments in Congress."

The growing controversy over aid to UNITA could be neutralized if the United States succeeds in obtaining an agreement from Angola and South Africa on Namibia. But few observers see a positive outcome of this crucial ingredient of the administration's "constructive engagement" in southern Africa. During a recent MPLA party congress, President dos Santos vowed to keep Cuban troops in Angola as long as South Africa threat-

---

[25] Quoted in *The Washington Post*, Dec. 1, 1985.

ened its borders. And despite the international outcry and growing domestic unrest, South Africa shows no sign of weakening
on apartheid or Namibia. "They can keep their troops in Namibia with their left hand," Rotberg concluded.

Recommended Reading List

Books

Coker, Christopher, *NATO, the Warsaw Pact and Africa,* St. Martin's,
    1985.
Garthoff, Raymond L., *Détente and Confrontation: American-Soviet
    Relations from Nixon to Reagan,* Brookings Institution, 1985.
Marcum, John, *The Angolan Revolution,* MIT Press, 1969 (Vol. I) and
    1978 (Vol. II).
Noer, Thomas J., *Cold War and Black Liberation: The United States
    and White Rule in Africa, 1948-1968,* University of Missouri
    Press, 1985.
Rotberg, Robert I., Henry S. Bienen, Robert Legvold and Gavin G.
    Maasdorp, *South Africa and Its Neighbors,* Lexington Books,
    1985.
Stockwell, John, *In Search of Enemies: A CIA Story,* W. W. Norton &
    Co., 1978.

Articles

Clement, Peter, "Moscow and Southern Africa," *Problems of Commu-
    nism,* March-April 1985.
Crocker, Chester A., "South Africa: Strategy for Change," *Foreign
    Affairs,* winter 1980/81.
Grundy, Kenneth W., "Pax Pretoriana: South Africa's Regional Pol-
    icy," *Current History,* April 1985.
Novicki, Margaret A., "Against All Odds," *Africa Report,* January-
    February 1985.
Savimbi, Jonas, "The War Against Soviet Colonialism," *Policy Review,*
    winter 1986.

Reports and Studies

Congressional Research Service, Library of Congress, "The Soviet
    Union in the Third World, 1980-85: An Imperial Burden or Politi-
    cal Asset?" Sept. 23, 1985.
Editorial Research Reports; "South Africa's 'Total Strategy,'" 1983
    Vol. II, p. 653.
"New African Yearbook 1984-85," IC Magazines Ltd.

Graphics: Maps, Robert Redding.

DEALING
WITH
LIBYA

by

Elena Berger

Mar. 14
1 9 8 6

DEALING WITH LIBYA

A merican efforts to restrain Libyan terrorist activities have so far shown little success. The diplomatic offensive to win European support for economic sanctions was unsuccessful *(see p. 186)*. Lines of policy are confused. Secretary of State George P. Shultz advocates military retaliation when necessary. Defense Secretary Caspar W. Weinberger urges a more cautious approach, and Vice President George Bush admits "there isn't any simple answer" on an appropriate response to terrorism.[1] What President Reagan has been unable to achieve in Libya through sanctions and threats, however, may now be accomplished by the collapse of world oil prices.

The prospect invites tentative optimism in Washington. The State Department's chief of counter terrorism, Robert B. Oakley, told a Senate subcommittee recently that Libya might soon be forced to concentrate its declining oil revenues on domestic needs, leaving less to devote to stirring unrest abroad.[2]

However, foreign-affairs analysts disagree on the likely effect of Libya's economic decline. Professor Lisa Anderson of Harvard's Center for Middle Eastern Studies thinks that the drop in oil prices will cause domestic political problems only after a longer period of austerity, but notes that there is already a tendency by Libyans to equate declining living standards with the revolutionary excesses of Col. Muammar el-Qaddafi. William B. Quandt, a senior analyst of Middle Eastern affairs at The Brookings Institution, says the state of the economy is of marginal importance: "Efforts to remove Qaddafi took place even when the economy was strong. What is important is paying the military and keeping the security apparatus intact." [3]

There is agreement that Libya's economic position is deteriorating. The country prospered under Qaddafi in the 1970s, but since 1981 oil revenues have been shrinking. From $22 billion in 1980 they dropped to an estimated $10 billion in 1984, and about $8 billion-$9 billion in 1985 *(see p. 175)*. The forecast for

---

[1] News conference remark March 6, 1986, upon releasing a report on the government's policy on combating terrorism. Bush was chairman of a Cabinet-level task force that produced the report.

[2] Testimony by Robert B. Oakley before the Senate Judiciary Subcommittee on Security and Terrorism, Feb. 19, 1986. Oakley holds the rank of ambassador and head the Office for Counter Terrorism and Emergency Planning.

[3] Telephone interview with Anderson Feb. 4, 1986, and with Quandt Feb. 20, 1986.

1986 is lower still. Per capita income, which rose dramatically in the 1970s, has declined steadily in the 1980s.

Reports from Libya say consumer goods are becoming scarcer, and that there is much grumbling about empty shelves at state supermarkets. Qaddafi's revolution accustomed Libyans to a comfortable standard of living which is now being withdrawn. Instead, their leader tells them that the present austerity is necessary to teach them to work harder and depend on themselves.

If the public's complaints are not a threat to Qaddafi's rule, then discontent within the military probably is. Several attempts to assassinate him have taken place in recent years. On May 8, 1984, 12 men tried to break into his barracks to kill him. Two attempted coups were reported last spring. Rumors of another coup attempt circulated in September. The mysterious death of Col. Hassan Ishkal in late November sparked a new round of speculation about discontent in the army. Ishkal, a powerful figure in the regime, died in a car accident, according to official reports. However the foreign press carried accounts of rumors in Tripoli that Ishkal had been shot after he challenged Qaddafi over the diminishing role of the army in national affairs.

Western sources say that although the military is affected by the government's austerity program, the causes of discontent go much deeper: that the army feels its professionalism has been challenged by Qaddafi's moves to set up a people's militia and by his assignment of revolutionary guards to almost all barracks. His provocative policies toward neighboring Egypt, Tunisia and Chad are also said to be unpopular.

The revolutionary guards, who are estimated to number only 1,000-2,000, have grown in influence since the May 1984 coup attempt, and operate as watchdogs over the country's 73,000 regular troops. Many of the guards come from Qaddafi's own tribe in Libya's Sirte region, which has stirred longstanding tribal animosities. Qaddafi's humble origins in Sirte helped to shape his revolution, and the area still provides him with a power base.

Qaddafi's Coming to Power; His Vision

Qaddafi seized power in 1969 from an unstable postwar regime established under the auspices of the United Nations in 1951. Libya had been under Italian rule until British armies captured the territory in the famous desert battles of World War II. Britain established a military administration in the two coastal provinces of Tripolitania and Cyrenaica, while France administered the inland province of Fezzan.

Libya At a Glance

Population: 3.8 million (1985 est.)

Area: 679,536 square miles

Geography: Mainly desert; less than 2% of population of the country receives sufficient rainfall for settled farming; most of the population lives in coastal areas.

Capitals: Tripoli, Benghazi

Religion: 97 percent Moslem

Official Language: Arabic

Main Export: Petroleum

Gross National Product: $25.1 billion; $7,500 per capita (1983)

When Libya was granted independence at the end of 1951 the three provinces were so different in character that they seemed like separate countries. The constitution established a prominent Cyrenaican leader, Idris, as king. The new nation was miserably poor, but major oil discoveries were made in 1959 and brought unexpected benefits to the country. A privileged elite favored by the royal court amassed wealth and influence.[4]

Qaddafi's background made him hostile to the corruption that flourished at the highest levels of Libyan society. He was born into a poor, semi-nomadic family living in the Sirtic desert. As a youth he was strongly influenced by the Arab socialism of Egypt's Gamal Abdel Nasser, whose beliefs were spread by radio broadcasts from Egypt and by Egyptians working in Libya. Qaddafi became a fervent Arab nationalist, opposed to the monarchy and its pro-Western policies.

Even as a teenaged schoolboy, Qaddafi was a political activist. By the time he was expelled from school at Sebha for organizing a demonstration in support of the Palestinian cause, he had formed the core group of his future Revolution Command Council. Later, at another school in Misurata and at the national military academy in Benghazi, Qaddafi continued to recruit and inspire fellow activists, organizing opposition to the monarchy. By the time he graduated from the military academy in 1965 the framework for his Free Officer movement was in place. On Sept. 1, 1969, when Quaddafi was 27, the Free Officers mounted a successful coup d'état.

Qaddafi sees himself as the architect of a unique system of government, the founder of a Third World alternative to

---

[4] See John Wright's *Libya: A Modern History* (1982), chapters 4 and 5.

capitalism and communism, which he calls the Third Universal Theory. All this he explains in *The Green Book,* published in three parts in 1976, 1978 and 1979. In the first part, he condemns representative government, majority rule, political parties, and the class system. The people can be given direct participation in government, however, through people's committees and popular congresses. At the end of the section, with an ambiguity which is typical of his thinking, he adds that in reality the strongest elements of society will always rule.

In the second part of *The Green Book* Qaddafi describes his version of Arab socialism. It provides for a limited degree of private ownership, together with direct state intervention in the economy, and participation of the people through committees in all types of economic institutions and enterprises. Each person may own a house and car, and have sufficient income to support a comfortable way of life. All other forms of ownership are condemned, as is the concept of profit. "Partners, not wage earners," is one of Qaddafi's favorite slogans. Partners in an economic enterprise share in its earnings, and are no longer wage slaves.[5]

When Qaddafi first came to power he placed a strong emphasis on the Islamic character of the state. Later, as he clashed with local religious leaders over political matters, he began to stress the Koran as the sole source of religious authority: "The Koran is in the Arabic language and we can comprehend it ourselves without the need for an iman [religious leader] to interpret it for us." [6]

His stress on a personal interpretation of the Koran undermines traditional Moslem religious organization and is highly controversial.[7] It led him to separate religion from politics in *The Green Book,* presenting his Third Universal Theory as a secular political order not exclusively related to Islam, and applicable worldwide. He leaves no doubt that he considers himself a devout Moslem, convinced that his political theory is based on the Koran and therefore particularly valid for the Moslem world.

Fine-Tuning the Revolution He Wrought

Although Qaddafi's political concepts often seem vague or simplistic, he has established a working model for them in

---

[5] For a discussion of *The Green Book,* see Wright, pp. 189-198; John K. Cooley, *Libyan Sandstorm* (1982), chapter 7; and Harold D. Nelson, ed., *Libya, A Country Study* (1979), pp. 206-208.

[6] Speech on Feb. 19, 1978, quoted by Marius K. Deeb and Mary Jane Deeb in *Libya Since the Revolution: Aspects of Social and Political Development* (1982), p. 101.

[7] In addition to offending Libya's orthodox Sunni Moslem leaders, Qaddafi has very poor relations with Shiite Moslem leaders in Lebanon because of the mysterious disappearance of Iman Mousa Sadr on a visit to Libya in 1978. For a time the affair was an obstacle to Libya's relations with revolutionary Iran, which follows the Shiite form of Islam.

```
                        ┌─────────── Libya's Oil ───────────┐

                        Production          Price           Export
                        (barrels in     (per barrel,       Earnings
        Year            millions)          Jan. 1         (in billions)
                                          FOB Libya)

        1973              794             $  2.87            $  3.5
        1974              555               11.98               7.8
        1975              540               11.10               6.4
        1976              706               12.21               8.7
        1977              753               13.74              10.4
        1978              724               13.80               9.9

        1979              764               14.52              16.0
        1980              652               34.50              22.0
        1981              416               40.78              14.7
        1982              420               36.50              13.7
        1983              403               35.15              12.7
        1984              397               30.15              10.1
        1985              361*              30.15*              8.5*

        * estimate

        Sources: Department of Energy, International Monetary Fund.
```

Libya. As part of a cultural revolution in 1973 he began to establish "people's committees" all over the country to run government departments, schools, factories, and other institutions and enterprises. The committees soon numbered more than 2,000. In 1975 he created a network of 187 basic popular congresses to send members to a 970-member General Popular Congress (GPC) in Tripoli. Each of the basic congresses served 3,000 to 4,000 adults and was subdivided into five or six local units to facilitate debate on prepared agendas.

The GPC met for the first time in January 1976, and became the country's ruling body in March 1977 at a special session attended by Fidel Castro of Cuba. The session was held at Sebha because that was where Qaddafi began his political activities. The Revolution Command Council, which had ruled since 1969 and was now reduced from 12 to 5 members, was reconstituted as the General Secretariat of the GPC, headed by Qaddafi. The Council of Ministers was replaced by a General Popular Committee, which functioned as a Cabinet. To mark the changes in the form of government and the arrival of direct rule by the people, the name of the state was changed to Socialist People's Libyan Arab *Jamahiriyah* (state of the masses). Qaddafi considered the inauguration of the new system an event comparable to the French Revolution.[8]

_____
[8] Reported by Wright, pp. 190-193.

Qaddafi continued to refine his new system, adding layers of authority and confusion to it. In 1978 workers' committees were created to run many industrial enterprises. In the same year a network of revolutionary committees was established to "guide" the basic popular congresses. Early in 1979 Qaddafi gave up his position in the General Secretariat to devote himself to revolutionary action, which he explained was different from the daily exercise of power.

He has held no position in government since then and is not officially head of state, although he is treated as such. In practice he operates as the source of all political power and as head of the armed forces. His picture is everywhere and his cult of personality overwhelming. From an early stage of the revolution Qaddafi seems to have found the day-to-day business of government a dull chore. Since 1972 many of his administrative duties have been taken over by his trusted second-in-command, Abdel Sallam Jalloud, a member of the group he organized in school at Sebha. Qaddafi prefers to remain free to deal with matters which really interest him. These include foreign policy and the spread of his revolution abroad.

Oil's Role in His Expansion of Power

As he laid the political foundations of revolution, Qaddafi benefited from a remarkable expansion of oil revenues between 1970 and 1981. During that period the posted price of Libyan crude rose from $2.23 to $40.78 per barrel, and annual export revenues expanded from $2.4 billion to $22.0 billion. In the view of many analysts, Libya played a crucial role in world oil affairs during the early 1970s by taking the lead in forcing prices upward and breaking the control of the major international companies.

Libya's revolutionary leaders skillfully pressured the 23 oil companies operating in the country to accept their terms, using selective nationalization as a weapon. By 1974 the government had taken over about 60 percent of the country's oil production. Although this percentage went still higher, the foreign companies were not squeezed out entirely. Libya recognized that it needed their experience in exploration, development, production and sales.

Following the outbreak of war between Egypt and Israel in October 1973, Libya became a leader of the Arab oil embargo against the United States and raised the price of its oil steeply. This move generated revenues of $8 billion in 1974, more than three times those of 1970. Oil income fell back in 1975, but the upward movement soon resumed. After another slight drop in 1978, prices soared briefly above $40 a barrel and produced a peak revenue of $22 billion for 1980.

This oil wealth was an incredible windfall for a country where the population numbered less than two million at the start of the 1970s and barely three million at its end. Oil gave Qaddafi the opportunity to pursue his revolution in style. There was enough money for generous social welfare programs, for industrial and agricultural development, for arms purchases and for an ambitious foreign policy. Libyans enjoyed a sharply higher standard of living as the government invested in housing, medical care and education. The state subsidized the cost of staple items to keep prices under control, and began to take over retail trade in 1979. Before independence in 1951, per capita income was about $40; by 1970 it had risen to $2,168, and by 1979 $9,827.[9]

Thanks to oil revenues, the government was able to pursue a $6 billion development plan in 1973-75, and a $30.5 billion plan in 1976-80. The goals of the second plan were to promote agriculture and provide Libya with an industrial base which would lessen its dependence on oil. Housing, roads, ports, airports, power plants and small factories were built, but the government also invested heavily in oil refineries, petrochemical complexes, and a steel mill. Foreign economists thought the terms on which heavy industry was established were fundamentally unsound.

Libya has now embarked on its most ambitious development project of all. It is building enormous pipelines to carry water from underground reservoirs in the desert to the coastal plains, where water resources are being depleted much faster than they can be replaced. A South Korean industrial group began the first phase of construction in 1983 at a cost of $3.3 billion. A contract for the second phase, expected to cost $2 billion, is to be awarded soon. The total project, including related agricultural development, is expected to amount to $25 billion.

Libya had to import managers, technicians, and laborers for its massive undertakings. Many of the semiskilled and unskilled workers came from Egypt and Tunisia, traditional sources of labor. Contracts went to companies from North America, Western and Eastern Europe, the Middle East and Asia, all of whom sent in skilled personnel. The number of officially recorded foreign workers in the country rose to 223,000 in 1975; the actual number presumably was far higher, for many workers went unregistered. The total is estimated to have peaked at 567,000 in 1983. After that a decline set in, although it is not known how many remain today.

The effect of declining oil revenues has been tempered somewhat because the country had amassed foreign exchange re-

[9] By 1983, it had fallen back to $7,500.

serves. However, these reserves dwindled from $13 billion at the end of 1980 to $3.3 billion at the end of 1984, and according to press reports, dipped to $2.6 billion late last year. Libya is only now starting to face the full consequences of the downward trend in international oil prices.

Pursuit of Revolution

L ibya has used oil earnings to buy vast amounts of military equipment. France, an early supplier, had delivered 110 Mirage jet fighters by 1974. Then, the Soviet Union became the major supplier, providing battle tanks, MiG warplanes, Tupolev-22 bombers, and various types of surface-to-air missiles. The value of these purchases was estimated at over $20 billion by 1983.[10]

Libya's armed forces cannot use all of the arms that have been acquired. The London-based International Institute for Strategic Studies reports that as many as 1,400 tanks and 450 combat aircraft are in storage. Foreign help is needed to support operational equipment. Soviet, Syrian, Palestinian, Pakistani and North Korean pilots are reported to fly Libyan planes.[11] Russians, East Germans and Cubans provide technical support, training and advice on security matters. The number of Soviet military personnel in Libya is uncertain. Estimates range from 3,500 to 8,000.

Qaddafi's ties to Moscow raise questions as to whether he is willing to serve as a Soviet surrogate in the Middle East and Africa. He undoubtedly enjoys friendly relations with the Russians, but many Western experts see the relationship as one of opportunism on both sides. The Soviet Union has been willing to overlook Qaddafi's distaste for communism, praising instead his non-aligned stance and anti-imperialism. For his part, Qaddafi has been uncharacteristically quiet about the Soviet occupation of Afghanistan. There is concern that America's aggressive posture and his growing economic difficulties may lead him into a closer association with Moscow. The arms sales have been a valuable source of hard currency for Russia, and although Qaddafi may have less to spend in the future, Libya is still a supplier of petroleum to the Eastern-bloc countries.

---

[10] Lisa Anderson, "Qadhdhafi and the Kremlin," *Problems of Communism*, September-October 1985, p. 29. The Libyan leader's name is rendered in to English under various spellings because the sounds of many letters in the Arabic alphabet have no exact equivalent in the English language.

[11] The International Institute for Strategic Studies, *The Military Balance 1985-86*, p. 80.

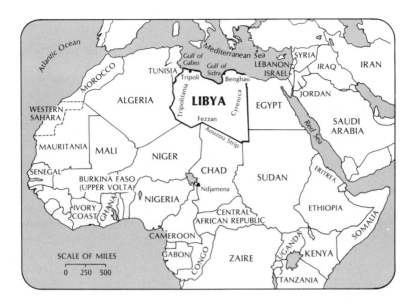

Elusive, Quixotic Quest for Arab Unity

When Libya started to accumulate arms they were destined for the support of Egypt in its struggle with Israel. Qaddafi's most cherished goals were Arab unity and a unified campaign to free the Palestinian homeland from Israel's control. Over the years his idealism has encountered many disappointments. Other Arab leaders refused to cooperate with his plans. Mergers failed, alliances shifted. Far from becoming a significant figure in Middle Eastern politics Qaddafi often seemed isolated, outside the mainstream of events. His revolution made little impact in the area that mattered to him most.

In 1971 Qaddafi persuaded Egypt and Syria to join Libya in forming the Federation of Arab Republics. Then, dissatisfied with this loose tie, he started to pressure President Anwar el-Sadat of Egypt for full political union. Sadat resisted, and in October 1973 Egypt and Syria attacked Israel without giving Libya a major role in the war. All prospects of union fell apart. After the cease-fire, Qaddafi became a bitter opponent of Sadat. Relations deteriorated steadily, to the point where fighting flared on the Egyptian-Libyan border in July 1977. Sadat's peace mission to Jerusalem that November provoked Qaddafi to organize an opposition group — the Front for Resistance and Confrontation, composed of Libya, Syria, Algeria, South Yemen and the Palestine Liberation Organization (PLO).

The Camp David accords, signed by Egypt and Israel in September 1978 at President Jimmy Carter's urging, inflamed Qaddafi's radical tendencies.[12] Even the PLO was not, in his

---

[12] For background on the accords, see "Middle East Transition," *E.R.R.*, 1978 Vol. II, pp. 881-904.

view, sufficiently committed to the struggle against Israel. His inclination to back the most extreme Palestinian groups led to a break with PLO leader Yasir Arafat at the start of 1980. Subsequently Israel's invasion of Lebanon and its expulsion of Arafat's followers from Beirut confirmed Qaddafi in his belief that the future of the Palestinian movement lay with radical factions.

In September 1980 Qaddafi signed an agreement to unite Libya with Syria, and reportedly agreed to pay for arms Syria had purchased from the Soviet Union. In the same month war broke out between Iran and Iraq. Both Libya and Syria backed Iran's revolutionary regime. Qaddafi announced that Islamic solidarity with Iran — a non-Arab country — justified opposing an Arab power. As a result, he became progressively more isolated in the Arab world, particularly after he signed a strategic alliance with Iran in June 1984. Meanwhile, the projected union with Syria came to nothing.

As in the Middle East, Qaddafi's activities in North Africa have not aided the cause of unity. Neighboring Tunisia, like Egypt, is fearful of Libyan intervention. A short-lived plan for the union of Libya and Tunisia in 1974 was followed by years of friction, especially after petroleum was discovered offshore in disputed territorial waters in the Gulf of Gabes. In 1980 Libya backed a guerrilla raid on the southern Tunisian town of Gafsa in an attempt to foment rebellion, leading Tunisia to break relations. As Libya's economy deteriorated in 1985 Qaddafi sanctioned mass expulsions of Tunisian and Egyptian workers, hoping to cause labor problems in their homelands.

During the long war between Morocco and Algerian-backed Polisario Front rebels for control of Western Sahara, a former Spanish colony, Libya supported Algeria. Morocco's King Hassan, an absolute monarch backed by the United States, was a regular target for Qaddafi's invective. In a surprising move apparently initiated by the king, Libya and Morocco signed a pact of union in August 1984. Hassan realized that he could end Qaddafi's aid to the Polisario guerrillas by catering to the Libyan leader's unfulfilled interest in Arab unity.

The alliance is not a close one, enabling Morocco to continue its association with the United States, and to back Iraq in the Persian Gulf war. Meanwhile Libya's relations with Algeria have become strained, and the Polisario Front is deprived of an important source of support. Qaddafi has found an unlikely partner in his faltering drive for unity in the Arab world.

Africa has provided Libya with a tempting field for intervention through diplomacy, subversion and military maneuvers.

Qaddafi has eagerly tried to influence African states in favor of the Arab cause and to promote the Moslem faith. He also has tried to destabilize pro-Western governments and spread his own revolutionary beliefs. For all these efforts, he has achieved little success and incurred bitter opposition; this hostility undermined his bid in 1982 to become president of the Organization of African Unity.

Libya's Ventures Southward Into Africa

One of Qaddafi's most striking African alliances was with Idi Amin, the murderous dictator of Uganda who happened to be a Moslem and a supporter of the Palestinian cause. Libya marked the start of the alliance by airlifting some 400 soldiers to help Amin fight off an invasion from Tanzania in 1972. Seven years later Qaddafi tried to save the tottering regime from another Tanzanian invasion, this time airlifting 2,000 to 3,000 troops to Entebbe, the Ugandan capital.

The effort failed and Amin fled to Tripoli, leaving behind turmoil and a death toll as high, by some estimates, as 500,000. Nor did Qaddafi's military support for another dictator, Emperor Bokassa of the Central African Republic, prevent his fall later the same year. Recently Libya's interest in Uganda revived. The new ruler, Yoweri Museveni, has admitted that his guerrilla forces received arms and other aid form Qaddafi.

Libya, meanwhile, became involved in Chad and set itself on a collision course with France, which retained an active interest in its former African colony. In 1973 Libya began to occupy the Aouzou Strip along the border with Chad, a region reputedly rich in deposits of phosphate, uranium and iron ore. Three years later Libya issued new maps showing revised southern boundaries taking in 52,000 square miles of territory from Chad, Algeria and Niger.

Then Qaddafi began to intervene in a complicated, long-standing civil war in Chad, sending more than 6,000 troops into the country. They occupied the capital, Ndjamena, in November 1980 and installed the new president, Goukouni Oueddei, who signed an agreement uniting Chad with Libya. Oueddei later ordered the Libyan troops to leave, but after he lost power the following year he was forced to ask for Quaddafi's support again. Libya's return to Chad was contested by French troops. In 1984 France and Libya agreed to withdraw their forces, but Libya failed to comply, maintaining its troops at the 16th parallel and effectively occupying northern Chad. That September the Chadian government alleged that Libya was behind a plot to assassinate President Hissene Habré.

181

This February Libyan and rebel forces moved south from the 16th parallel in a new offensive, and France countered by sending a small air strike force to Ndjamena. About 5,000 Libyan troops are reported to be in Chad. The country's civil war continues, offering Libya further opportunity for expansion in the region, and Qaddafi seems to be determined to take it.

Senegal and Gambia broke off relations with Libya in 1980, claiming that Qaddafi was training forces to use against them. Mali and Niger have made similar allegations. Government officials in Nigeria reportedly worry that he will stir up trouble in the Moslem north. Before he was deposed in 1985 President Gaafar Mohammad Nimeiry of the Sudan, a close ally of Egypt, feared a Libyan-inspired assassination attempt; President Mobutu Sesse Seko of Zaire, who sent troops into Chad to oppose Libya in 1983, also fears a Libyan-backed conspiracy.

Only lately has Qaddafi's government broken out of its isolation in Africa. The regimes in Ghana and Burkina Faso (formerly Upper Volta) are friendly, as is the regime which replaced Nimeiry in the Sudan last April. After Nimeiry's downfall, Libya sent representatives into the Sudan to establish revolutionary committees and influence political developments there. In Burkina Faso, Capt. Thomas Sankara, chairman of the National Revolutionary Council, announced the establishment of a "jamahiriyah" system at the end of 1985.

Exporting Terrorism

L ibyan-sponsored trouble extends far beyond the Middle East and Africa. The State Department said in a recent report that "Qadhafi's use of political, economic and military resources in support of anti-Western activities worldwide may be surpassed only by the Soviet Union, its East European allies, and possibly North Korea or Cuba." [13] In retaliation for American hostility, Qaddafi has several times threatened to export terrorism to the United States.

Libya acquired its present reputation soon after Qaddafi seized power. By 1972 there was already speculation abroad that he was aiding various guerrilla and dissident groups, ranging from the Palestinians to opposition factions in Morocco, Tunisia and Chad, to the Eritrean Liberation Front and even the

---

[13] Department of State, "Libya Under Qadhafi: A Pattern of Aggression," January 1986, p. 1.

Stress in U.S.-Libyan Relations

June 1970. U.S. evacuates Wheelus Air Base in Libya.

October 1973. War between Egypt and Israel; Libya places an embargo on oil sales to the U.S.

November 1977. Sadat's visit to Israel; Libya at forefront of Arab opposition to American-sponsored peace accords (signed 1978) between Egypt and Israel.

December 1979. Mob in Tripoli burns U.S. Embassy in show of support for occupation of U.S. Embassy in Iran.

May 1981. U.S. closes Libyan People's Bureau (Embassy) in Washington.

August 1981. U.S. Navy fighters shoot down two Libyan SU-22s over the Gulf of Sidra.

November 1981. U.S. charges that Libya plans to send "hit teams" to attack President Reagan and other prominent Americans.

March 1982. U.S. bans oil imports from Libya.

May 1985. Plot to assassinate Libyan dissidents living in the U.S. uncovered.

November 1985. *The Washington Post* reports that the U.S. government has authorized covert action against Qaddafi.

January 1986. Reagan imposes economic sanctions against Libya, following terrorist attacks at Rome and Vienna airports; U.S. Navy conducts maneuvers offshore.

underground Irish Republican Army. He gave a clear indication of his sympathies when he offered sanctuary to three surviving Black September guerrillas who participated in the killing of 11 Israeli athletes at the 1972 Olympic Games in Munich. The five Palestinian terrorists killed there were buried with honors in Libya.

Claire Sterling, in her 1981 book *The Terror Network,* depicts Qaddafi as part of an international network of sponsors and agents of terrorism. Sterling wrote that Libyan money, arms and training have been offered in various combinations as far afield as southern Thailand, Mindanao in the Philippines, and New Caledonia in the South Pacific. She said large training camps for guerrilla activities were set up in Libya with Russian, East German and Cuban instructors.

In 1976-77, U.S. investigators began to probe links between Qaddafi and Edwin P. Wilson, a former agent for the U.S. Central Intelligence Agency (CIA). Wilson and his associates were organizing arms shipments and providing other assistance for undercover activities. He eventually fled to Libya but was later tricked into going to the Dominican Republic. There he was turned over to authorities in the United States, where he was tried and convicted in 1982-83 trials of illegal shipments of arms and explosives, and of attempting to murder two federal prosecutors. He drew long prison sentences.

Qaddafi developed connections with some of the most significant figures in international terrorism, inviting speculation as to how far he was involved in their activities. There is evidence that in the 1970s he cultivated the Soviet-trained Venezuelan terrorist "Carlos" (Ilich Ramirez Sanchez) and bankrolled some of his operations.[14] In the past two years Libya has provided growing support for the radical Palestinian group headed by Abu Nidal (Sabri al-Banna). This organization tried to undermine Jordanian interests in 1985 to disrupt Yasir Arafat's talks with King Hussein over participation in Jordan's peace initiative.

The same group may have been responsible for the November 1985 hijacking of an Egyptair jetliner to Malta, which ended with Egyptian commandos storming the plane. Sixty persons died in the incident. Abu Nidal has also been accused of carrying out the attacks at the Rome and Vienna airports last Dec. 27, killing 18 people and wounding 80. Three of the attackers in Vienna used Tunisian passports, which investigators said were obtained through sources in Libya. Qaddafi has denied that Palestinian groups have terrorist training camps in his country or that he had any connection with the airport raids. U.S. officials vigorously contest his denials.

Stalking Libyan Dissidents Living Abroad

Qaddafi's name is closely associated with international terrorism, but much of Libyan terrorist activity is only incidentally international in character. Many opponents of the revolution have gone into exile, and the regime stalks them overseas, exporting its domestic quarrels across national boundaries in remarkably casual fashion.

Exiled foes are numerous and varied in their backgrounds. Some of the opposition is tribally based, reflecting the lack of unity in the country which was clearly visible before 1969. Some have connections with the royalist elite which was displaced by the revolution. Others are members of the middle classes who lost property under Qaddafi.

Prominent political figures, especially those who have taken refuge in Egypt, have been the object of kidnapping or assassination attempts. In 1976 agents tried to capture two exiled members of the Revolution Command Council, one of whom had plotted a coup the previous year. In November 1984, Egypt arrested members of a team hired to kill a former Libyan

---

[14] See Haley, *op. cit.*, pp. 40-41; and Cooley, *op. cit.*, pp. 170-172.

American Business in Libya

America's trade with Libya was worth only $336 million in 1984 — the latest year for which official figures are available — but American companies have important interests there. Five American oil companies operate in Libya: Occidental Petroleum, Conoco, Marathon Oil, Amerada Hess, and a unit of W. R. Grace Co. In normal circumstances they are responsible for one-quarter to one-third of the country's total oil production. Many smaller U.S. companies service the oil industry through engineering, drilling or equipment supply contracts. Two companies, Brown & Root Inc. of Houston and Price Bros. Co. of Dayton, Ohio, have significant roles in Libya's huge water project.

The sanctions imposed by the U.S. government Jan. 7 required all American companies to cease doing business with Libya after Feb. 1. But the five oil companies were given special licenses to continue operations there while they try to arrange an orderly disposition of their assets, which the Reagan administration estimates to be worth at least $1 billion. Their profits are estimated at $100 million-$200 million per year.

Some other U.S. businesses have also applied for special licenses. Many American companies have been handling operations in Libya through European subsidiaries, using European employees, and they are likely to try to continue on that basis.

The government banned travel to Libya on Dec. 10, 1981, and the number of Americans working there fell considerably. Some Americans ignored the ban, however, and Libyan authorities helped them to evade it. On Dec. 13, 1984, the government again asked its citizens to leave. When President Reagan ordered all citizens to leave by Feb. 1, 1,000-1,500 Americans were still in Libya.

prime minister, Abdul Hamid Bakkush. In an elaborate hoax, Egyptian authorities sent evidence of the killing to Qaddafi and allowed him to announce that it had been carried out, before they revealed that Bakkush was still alive and the plotters were in detention. Last November another assassination attempt on Bakkush was uncovered.

The recent State Department report on Libya chronicles Libyan terrorism between 1980 and 1985.[15] It lists operations directed against many individual Libyans in a number of countries, including a wave of attacks in 1980 in which 11 exiles were killed in Greece, Italy, West Germany and Britain. In another outbreak in 1984-85, 10 exiles died and a former Libyan ambassador was badly wounded. These attacks took place in Egypt, Cyprus, Greece, Italy, Austria and West Germany.

---

[15] State Department, pp. 5-8.

Libyan people's bureaus (as embassies are called) are depicted as centers for illegal operations. The United States closed down the Washington bureau in 1981 because its activities included involvement in an assassination attempt on a Libyan student the previous year. In 1984 a British policewoman was killed outside the London bureau when shots were fired from the building at anti-Qaddafi demonstrators.

In 1983 Qaddafi detained eight West Germans to force the government in Bonn to release a Libyan convicted of killing one of his exiled opponents. In 1984 he arrested British citizens in order to exert pressure on the British government during the crisis over the London bureau. Foreign embassies in Tripoli have been deprived of police protection during periods of tension. The U.S. Embassy was sacked in 1979.[16] The French and Tunisian embassies were attacked by mobs in 1980, and the Jordanian Embassy was burned in 1984.

Reagan's Response; Succession Question

After the terrorist attacks at the Rome and Vienna airports, President Reagan declared there was "irrefutable evidence" of Qaddafi's involvement. At the same White House news conference on Jan. 7, he announced the imposition of economic sanctions against Libya, blocking trade between the two countries and placing controls on Libyan government property in the United States. The president ordered all American citizens to leave Libya immediately.

The effect of these sanctions has been small. Reagan had already banned the import of Libyan crude oil in 1982. Western European nations could not be persuaded to impose sanctions too. The contrast between Reagan's hostile response and the low-key European attitude led some commentators to suggest that the United States overreacts to Qaddafi's provocations, giving him the publicity on which he thrives and enabling him to rally nationalist sentiment when public opinion might otherwise be focused on food shortages.

Others view Qaddafi as a menace to Western security, the "Daddy Warbucks of international terrorism" [17] who fully merits a fierce response. Holding this view of him, American officials no doubt speculate about the benefits of his removal. If he is displaced, however, there is no certainty that a regime favorable to the United States would emerge. Some observers think a pro-Soviet government is a possibility. Another radical

---

[16] The United States broke diplomatic relations with Libya May 8, 1981. The Belgian Embassy in Tripoli handles U.S. interests in Libya and the United Arab Emirates' Embassy in Washington handles Libya's affairs in the United States.

[17] So characterized by Claire Sterling, "Quaddafi Spells Chaos," *The New Republic*, March 7, 1981, p. 16.

Europe's Business Links

Italy, which ruled Libya from 1911, is its leading trade partner, purchasing oil worth $2.5 billion in 1984 (24 percent of Libya's total exports), and selling goods worth $1.8 billion (27 percent of Libya's total imports). In December 1976 Libya made a $415 million investment in the Fiat industrial complex, taking a 9.5 percent share in the enterprise. This stake has now risen to 13 percent. About 15,000 Italians work in Libya.

West Germany is the second most important trading partner, buying petroleum worth almost $2 billion in 1984, and selling goods worth $885 million. About 1,500 West Germans work in Libya.

Spain, which is highly dependent on Libyan natural gas, made purchases worth almost $1 billion in 1984, and sold goods worth $293 million.

France has cut back its trade with Libya as relations became strained over events in Chad. Nevertheless France bought oil worth $753 million in 1984 and sold goods worth $233 million.

Italian, West German, Spanish and French oil companies operate in Libya, Turkey, Yugoslavia, Switzerland, the Netherlands, Greece and Rumania are all substantial customers for Libyan oil. Britain cut back trade and halted arms sales after the shooting of a policewoman outside the Libyan embassy in London in 1984. Nevertheless, a moderate amount of commerce continues, and some 5,000 British citizens work in Libya.

leader could appear, with views as extreme as Qaddafi's. He has been in power long enough to indoctrinate large numbers of people, especially the country's youth, to his beliefs, and anti-American sentiments are widespread.

Professor Anderson thinks that the present machinery of government would not survive without Qaddafi himself to direct it. She considers that his removal would create a period of domestic instability marked by tribal competition and factional disputes. If Libya under Qaddafi is a cause for concern to the United States, it is liable to remain so under his eventual successors.

Recommended Reading List

Books

Cooley, John K., *Libyan Sandstorm: The Complete Account of Qaddafi's Revolution,* Holt, Rinehart and Winston, 1982.

Deeb, Marius K., and Mary Jane Deeb, *Libya Since the Revolution: Aspects of Social and Political Development,* Praeger, 1982.

Haley, P. Edward, *Qaddafi and the United States Since 1969,* Praeger, 1984.

Legum, Colin, ed., *Africa Contemporary Record,* Africana Publishing Co., annual volumes.

Nelson, Harold D., ed., *Libya, A Country Study,* Foreign Area Studies, American University, 1979.

The Middle East (6th ed.), Congressional Quarterly Inc., 1986.

Wright, John, *Libya: A Modern History,* Johns Hopkins University Press, 1982.

Articles

Anderson, Lisa, "Qadhdhafi and the Kremlin," *Problems of Communism,* September-October 1985.

Bennett, Alexander J., "Arms Transfer as an Instrument of Soviet Policy in the Middle East," *The Middle East Journal,* autumn 1985.

Birks, Stace and Clive Sinclair, "Libya: Problems of a *Rentier* State," in *North Africa: Contemporary Politics and Economic Development,* eds. Richard Lawless and Allan Findlay, Croom Helm, 1984.

Sterling, Claire, "Qaddafi Spells Chaos," *The New Republic,* March 7, 1981.

Reports

Editorial Research Reports: "Arab Disunity," 1976 Vol. II, p. 785; "Anti-Terrorism: New Priority in Foreign Policy," 1981 Vol. I, p. 229.

United States Department of State, Special Report No. 138, "Libya Under Qadhafi: A Pattern of Aggression," January 1986.

United States Department of State, Current Policy No. 744, Robert B. Oakley, "Terrorism: Overview and Developments," October 1985.

Graphics: Illustration p. 169, Robert Redding; map p. 179, Kathleen Ossenfort.

DEALING WITH TERRORISM
Opening a New Chapter

by

Mary H. Cooper

May 30
1 9 8 6

Editor's Update: A rash of incidents beginning in September 1986 dispelled hope that the U.S. raid on Libya had brought an end to terrorism. On Sept. 5 four Arab gunmen seized a Pan American World Airways jet in Karachi, Pakistan. Pakistani troops stormed the aircraft and arrested the alleged hijackers, but not before 18 passengers were killed and more than 100 wounded.

The Karachi incident appeared to have sparked a new wave of terrorist incidents in the Middle East and Europe. The next day two Arab gunmen killed 22 Jews as they worshipped in Istanbul, Turkey. The West German Red Army Faction, an urban terrorist group whose attacks have been aimed at undermining NATO, claimed responsibility for two bombings in that country.

A group of Middle Eastern terrorists — the Committee for Solidarity with Arab and Middle East Prisoners — caused turmoil in Paris with a series of attacks that month. The stated aim of the attacks was to win the release from French prison of Georges Ibrahim Abdallah, a Lebanese Maronite Christian suspected of involvement in the 1982 killing of a U.S. military attaché in Paris. Five bomb explosions in early September claimed the lives of 10 people and injured more than 270, spurring French Prime Minister Jacques Chirac to introduce strict police measures.

DEALING WITH TERRORISM

When President Reagan ordered the air strike against Libya he opened a new chapter in America's war against terrorism. This was not the first use of military retaliation for terrorist attacks: Israel has long applied a consistent policy of retaliation for attacks launched from outside its borders. But Israel has acted alone. In requesting collaboration in the Libyan strike from America's allies in the North Atlantic Treaty Organization (NATO), Reagan tried to involve several nations of Western Europe in its new counter-terrorist approach. He was rebuffed by all but Britain's Prime Minister Margaret Thatcher, who allowed the Libya-bound American F-111s to depart from British air bases. The decision caused an uproar in Europe, whose cities were filled with "Rambo Reagan" posters in the biggest and most vocal anti-American protests since the Vietnam War. At home, an indignant public accused the "Eurowimps" of appeasing Col. Maummar el-Qaddafi.

Predictions of NATO's imminent collapse under the strain proved to be premature, however. The annual economic summit of the seven leading industrial nations held in Tokyo just three weeks after the April 14 air strike produced the most far-reaching international agreement to date on how to deal with terrorism (see p. 204). As the leaders of the United States, Britain, France, Italy, West Germany, Canada and Japan narrowed their differences over counter-terrorist policy, the tenor of trans-Atlantic name-calling also died down.

But the precedent has been set for an American military retaliation against any state found to support terrorist attacks against American citizens. And as Syria becomes implicated in the Berlin disco attack that prompted the air strike against Libya, the Reagan administration is faced with a dilemma. Unlike Libya, isolated both politically and geographically even from most of the Arab world, Syria under President Hafez al-Assad has a central involvement in most of the Middle East's many conflicts. An attack on Syria, the Soviet Union's main ally in the region, would carry a far heavier risk of escalation into wider conflict.

The decision to single out Libya was not taken hastily. While Qaddafi has long been accused of supporting terrorism in the Middle East, Africa and Western Europe, these attacks had

been aimed at Libyan dissidents or at destabilizing such
neighboring countries as the Sudan, Chad and Egypt.[1] But
beginning late last year his stamp has been found on several
attacks against non-Libyan and chiefly Western targets. The
shift appears to have occurred when a terrorist group headed by
Abu Nidal, a defector from the mainline Palestinian Liberation
Organization (PLO), transferred his base of operations from
Syria to Libya.

Abu Nidal's group claimed responsibility for the Nov. 23
hijacking of an Egyptian airliner to Malta, in which an American woman and 56 other passengers were killed when Egyptian
troops stormed the plane in a rescue attempt. It also claimed
responsibility for the Dec. 27 attacks against passengers at the
Rome and Vienna airports, in which 18 persons, including five
Americans, died and more than 100 were wounded.

But it was not until the April 5 bombing at a GI hangout, La
Belle disco in West Berlin, that the administration claimed
"incontrovertible evidence" of Libyan involvement in a terrorist
attack. Announcing the air strike April 14 in a televised address
to the nation, Reagan said a message had been sent in late
March from Tripoli to the Libyan People's Bureau (embassy) in
East Berlin to attack Americans and "cause maximum and
indiscriminate casualties." Reagan hastened to add that
"thanks to close cooperation with our friends," some other
Libyan-sponsored attacks had been averted.

West German Chancellor Helmut Kohl supported the U.S.
claim, reportedly on the basis of intercepted messages between
Tripoli and Berlin. The French government also supported
Reagan's assertion that French and U.S. authorities had earlier
acted together to thwart a planned attack by Libya-sponsored
terrorists against people lined up in front the of U.S. embassy's
visa office in Paris.

Division Between U.S., European Opinion

As the evidence mounted of Libyan support for these and
other terrorist incidents in Western Europe, the Reagan administration appealed to the European nations to join in isolating
Qaddafi by applying political and economic pressure on his
regime. But European acceptance of Reagan's accusations
against Libya did not translate into support for the air strike
itself. European governments — with the exception of Britain
— criticized the retaliatory action either explicitly, in the case
of Italy and Greece, or implicitly, as did France and Spain by
denying the U.S. warplanes permission to fly through their air
space on the way the Libyan targets, thus adding 1,200 miles to
the flight.

[1] See "Dealing With Libya," p. 169.

Defense Department photo of one of the targets of the 11½ minute U.S. air strike against Tripoli and Benghazi, Libya, which began around 2 a.m. April 15 local time (7 p.m. April 14 Eastern Daylight Time). The 13 F-111 fighter bombers that flew out of Britain were joined by 12 A-6 attack planes launched from aircraft carriers in the Mediterranean.

"The American action shocked European public opinion even more than it did the governments," said a West European diplomat who spoke on condition she not be identified. "Just look what happened in Britain, where the government was nearly voted out of office for permitting the use of the bases." Speaking of her own government, which openly criticized the move, the diplomat added, "it's not that we condemned the American action, we just expressed our disagreement with your approach toward defeating terrorism."[2]

In the minds of many Americans, the air strike was long overdue and completely justified despite the loss of innocent lives and property damage caused by at least five U.S. bombs which the Pentagon later conceded had missed their military targets. A *Washington Post*-ABC News poll, taken April 24-28, indicated that 76 percent of the American public approved of the strike. The same poll also indicated that 70 percent approved of Reagan as president. That was the highest mark he has achieved except during the period he was recovering from gunshot wounds inflicted in the 1981 assassination attempt.

Polls taken in Europe, however, reflected striking differences not only with American public opinion but also between Euro-

<hr />

[2] All persons quoted in this report were interviewed by the author unless otherwise noted.

193

peans and their governments. British protests were among the most vocal, as Thatcher was accused of being Reagan's "lapdog" for allowing the bases to be used. In contrast, the French public endorsed the strike, while the government of President François Mitterrand drew U.S. criticism for not permitting the planes to fly over France. According to the BVA opinion research organization, Reagan enjoyed a higher approval rating among the French (65 percent) than either Mitterrand (52 percent) or Prime Minister Jacques Chirac (53 percent).

Despite their enthusiasm for the raid, the French showed their traditional disdain toward perceived infringements on their country's independence in foreign affairs. They supported their government's refusal to grant overflight rights to the American attack force, reasoning that France was not invited to be an equal partner in the attack but merely presented with an after-the-fact U.S. decision. French officials have since bolstered their argument by adding that Mitterrand had backed an even heavier military offensive against Libya for fear that a limited strike would only spur Qaddafi and other Arab radicals to step up their terrorist attacks.

More terrorists attacks did indeed occur, from Beirut to London, in apparent retaliation for the American action. Abu Nidal claimed responsibility for the murder of a British tourist April 27 in Jerusalem, while at least two other British subjects were killed in Beirut. They were among some 15 foreigners who have been missing and presumed to be held hostage by radical Arab groups in Lebanon since 1984. Several other attacks were foiled. Turkish authorities apprehended two Libyan embassy employes on charges of trying to blow up a U.S. military officers' club in Ankara April 18. The previous day at London's Heathrow Airport, explosives were discovered in a bag being carried on board an Israeli passenger jet by the girlfriend of a Jordanian living in Britain. He was arrested and awaits trial.

Fear of reprisals is an obvious reason why Europeans are reticent to use military means to combat terrorism. Italy is a case in point. When Italian Prime Minister Bettino Craxi said "this military action risks provoking explosive reactions of fanaticism and criminal and suicidal acts," the hundreds of terrorist attacks in his own country over the past two decades cannot have been far from his mind. Most acts of terrorism by Arab radicals have taken place in Western Europe, many of them in Italy. Qaddafi swore vengeance not only against the United States and Britain for the air strike, but all the NATO countries.[3] His one acknowledged act of reprisal — an unsuc-

---

[3] Belgium, Britain, Canada, Denmark, France, Greece, Iceland, Italy, Luxembourg, the Netherlands, Norway, Portugal, Spain, Turkey, the United States and West Germany.

cessful attempt to carry out a ship-to-land missile attack — was directed against the Italian island of Lampedusa.

More than any other European country, Italy has close relations with Libya, which lies just to the south of Sicily. Once an Italian colony (l911-43), Libya became home to a sizable community of Italians, many of whom remained after Qaddafi seized power in 1969. Until recent months, there were 17,000 Italians living and working in Libya, and its trade is important to the Italian economy. Overall, Libya ranks 16th among importers of goods from the 12-nation European Economic Community and 10th among exporters to the EEC.[4] While food makes up the bulk of Europe's sales to Libya, virtually all imports from Libya are oil; Italy gets most of its oil from Libya.

Italy and Belgium, whose foreign minister, Leo Tindemans, "regretted" the air strike as not "the best way of fighting terrorism," have additional diplomatic roles in Libya. Belgium has represented U.S. interests in Libya since Reagan closed the Washington People's Bureau in 1981. Britain formally broke relations with Tripoli after an unarmed British policewoman was killed in a London street by a gunman firing from inside the Libyan People's Bureau.

Since then, Italy has protected British interests in Libya, looking after 5,000

International Terrorist Attacks, 1985

By Region

400 — Number of Attacks

■ Attacks on U.S. citizens and property
☒ Other Attacks

Middle East, Europe, Latin America, Asia-Pacific, Africa, North America

Source: Dept. of State, preliminary figures.

British citizens working there. Diplomatic sources say 3,000 remaining Italian workers may be in danger. An Italian official explained: "There is a palpable sense of fear since Qaddafi has declared holy war on all countries that denounced Libya, including Italy. The Italian public feels that the use of military means to combat terrorism carries the risk of increasing terrorism, at least in the short term, not diminishing it."

European diplomats concede that actions taken by the Euro-

---

[4] Belgium, Britain, Denmark, France, Greece, Ireland, Italy, Luxembourg, the Netherlands, Portugal, Spain and West Germany. For background, see "Common Market in Disarray," *E.R.R.*, 1984 Vol. I, pp. 409-428.

pean Community since the air raid were, in the words of one, "to prevent further military actions by the United States, which we feel are too risky." At a meeting of foreign ministers in Luxembourg on April 21, all EEC members except Greece named Libya as a state supporter of terrorism in Europe — something the Reagan administration had been pleading in vain for them to do for months. They also decided to drastically reduce the number of Libyan embassy personnel and restrict their travel. It was further agreed that any Libyan diplomat expelled from one community nation would not be admitted into another and that all arms sales to Qaddafi's regime would be suspended.

American Reaction: Stay-at-Home Tourists

But the European measures do not appear to have impressed many Americans. Already alarmed by the growing number of U.S. victims of terrorist incidents in Western Europe in the past year *(see p. 205)*, travelers have cancelled European vacations in droves, 1.8 million out of 5.1 million who planned to go, according to State Department figures. Some sports teams have opted not to participate in competitions in Europe this summer, and movie stars and directors — including "Rambo" himself, Sylvester Stallone — decided not to attend the Cannes Film Festival in May.

The public's mood is mirrored in Congress, which is considering legislation to rebuild or reinforce U.S. embassies abroad to improve their security.[5] In Washington, huge concrete blocks have been placed at entrances to the White House, State Department and some other public buildings for added protection against terrorist attacks, and money has been requested to build a fence around the Capitol grounds. A more sinister reaction was perceived in Congress' initial rejection of an administration proposal to sell advanced weapoms to Saudi Arabia.[6] Opponents of the sale invoked the specter of the weapons — especially the shoulder-held Stinger missile — falling into the hands of Arab terrorists. Supporters of the sale said the vote was an expression of a growing anti-Arab sentiment that could undermine U.S. relations with this moderate Arab nation.

European perceptions of Americans' reactions to terrorism point up fundamental differences in approach between the two sides of the Atlantic. John Hughes, press secretary at the British Embassy in Washington, acknowledged that American tourists, especially tour groups, have cancelled trips to Britain since

---

[5] On May 14, the Senate Foreign Relations Committee approved $1.1 billion for the embassy program during the next two years; the administration had requested $4.4 billion over five years.

[6] President Reagan on May 21 vetoed a bill, passed by large majorities in both houses of Congress, that would have halted the sale. In an attempt to persuade Congress to uphold the veto, the White House said the Stinger was removed from the sale weaponry. The Senate is due to vote June 5 on whether to override the veto.

April. He expressed some surprise, saying "Our position really is that terrorism is something that we unfortunately have had to contend with for very many years, that the number of incidents that take place in the U.K. [United Kingdom] has not gone up and that our security forces are well used to dealing sufficiently with terrorist threats." He added that the "likelihood of being shot at or hurt in some way is much greater walking through most American cities than it is anywhere in the United Kingdom, including Northern Ireland." His thoughts were echoed by several other Western European diplomats.

European Experience

"People in all parts of Europe have been the subjects of terrorist attacks for many years," John Hughes said. "It is difficult to think of many Western European countries where there have not at some time been terrorist bombings or what have you. So it's something in a sense that, while not acceptable, people have accepted happens every now and then." In contrast to Europe today and some past periods in its own history, the United States is virtually free of political terrorism, even though it remains a heavily armed and relatively violent society.[7]

The European awareness of terrorism goes back to the last century, when Russian anarchists introduced the "philosophy of the bomb" to the streets of St. Petersburg where they assassinated Czar Alexander II in 1881.[8] But when Europeans speak of their greater experience in fighting terrorists, they refer to the past two decades. Although it began at the University of California at Berkeley, the student protests of the late 1960s had their biggest and most lasting impact in Europe.

Protest against U.S. involvement in the war in Vietnam, the main focus of the movement on American campuses,[9] evolved in Europe into a more general rejection of capitalism and traditional values. Student protesters declared their own governments guilty of imperialism by association with the United States and called for revolution at home and abroad. Street

---

[7] For background, see "Violence in American Life," *E.R.R.*, 1968 Vol. I, pp. 405-424, and "Political Terrorism," *E.R.R.*, 1970 Vol. I, pp. 339-360. While both reports pointed to an apparent resurgence of terrorists acts in the United States, terrorism faded during the 1970s. By 1980 an expert on terrorism, Brian M. Jenkins, could point in a Rand Corp. study, "Terrorism in the United States," to a low level of political terrorism in this country, which he attributed partly to its lack of ethnic-based separatist movements and the weakness of ideology in political life.

[8] For background on the history of terrorism, see Walter Laqueur's *Terrorism*, Little, Brown and Co., 1977.

[9] See "Campus Unrest," *E.R.R.*, 1965 Vol. I, pp. 361-380.

demonstrations and student occupations of campuses and factories were the hallmark of 1968, the launching point of the student protest movement. Acts of violence were directed primarily against property, while clashes between police and protesters mostly involved Molotov cocktails and billy clubs. Massive arrests of demonstrators overloaded the criminal justice systems of Europe.

Around 1970 the student protest movement began to fall apart in most countries of Europe, as it became apparent that the workers were unwilling to abandon the official political parties of the left — to which they had traditionally turned to protect their interests — for the promises of revolution being offered by primarily middle-class youth. As in the United States, most of the students then left the movement or decided to bring about change through other means.

In the wake of the unsuccessful student protest movement came much smaller, nominally leftist groups that turned increasingly to violence against people, formerly the trademark of neofascist organizations. During the latter half of the decade a group led by Ulrike Meinhof and Andreas Baader in West Germany and the Red Brigades in Italy began their "kneecappings," kidnappings and killings of industrialists and public figures in their

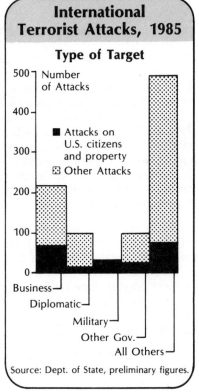

International Terrorist Attacks, 1985

Type of Target

Source: Dept. of State, preliminary figures.

countries with the stated aim of bringing down the state. Germany, between 1975 to 1980, was the scene of 411 bombing attacks; in that time 42 deaths and 310 woundings were attributed to terrorism.

In 1977, the peak of terrorist incidents in Germany, the chief federal prosecutor and a bank chairman were killed outright, and the head of the federal employers' union was kidnapped and later found dead. In Italy, Aldo Moro, a former prime minister and leader of the Christian Democratic Party, was kidnapped and killed the following year.

Other indigenous European groups took up the banner of long-standing disputes.[10] The underground Provisional Irish Republican Army (IRA) stepped up its attacks against British interests in Northern Ireland and Euzkadi Ta Askatasuna (ETA — "Basque Land and Liberty") championed the cause of Basque separatists in Spain with terrorist acts. It was during the late 1970s that many European governments formulated their counter-terrorist policies in an effort to suppress these indigenous groups. They gave the police and judiciary special powers to deal with suspected terrorists, and trained the police in new anti-terror techniques. In 1977, for example, West German government special forces freed the passengers being held hostage aboard a hijacked Lufthansa airliner in Mogadisho, Somalia. The Germans took their cue from Israel, which had acted similarly the year before in freeing hostages from an airliner held in Entebbe, Uganda.

Like other Europeans, Italians emphasize that they have been fighting terrorism for a long time. "We were very successful in defeating domestic terrorism," said one official. "And we defeated it without resorting to measures or decrees that would have limited the citizens' democratic freedoms." By the end of the 1970s the Red Brigades had been debilitated and many of its leaders were brought to justice.

Trend Toward Terrorists' Collaboration

But while calling for recognition of Italy's success in quelling domestic terrorism, the official acknowledged that "the domestic terrorism that we faced is different from international terrorism, in the sense that we were able to infiltrate it and break it from within." The 1980s, by contrast, have seen the rise of international terrorism. No longer limited to national grievances, groups that mount attacks in any one country may aim to destabilize the Western alliance or to harm U.S. prestige by attacking American citizens or property in that country.

As the frequency of transnational terrorist attacks in Europe increased, speculation mounted that the indigenous groups had not acted alone but had received support from an outside power. Given the vaguely leftist ideological pronouncements made by many of these groups, the Soviet Union was increasingly named as the chief state supporter of West European terrorism. American journalist Claire Sterling advanced this thesis in her book, *The Terror Network*. Published in 1981, the book launched a controversy in Europe that grew with the implication of Soviet ally Bulgaria in the May 1981 assassination attempt against Pope John Paul II.

---

[10] For background, see "Nationalist Movements in Western Europe," *E.R.R.*, 1969 Vol. I, pp. 287-306.

"There have always been doubts about the origin of domestic terrorism in Italy," explained the Italian official. "It probably originated in Italy and only later was infused with a foreign element, since evidence of links to German groups was found. This view was expanded upon several years ago, when then-President Sandro Pertini flatly declared that terrorism in Italy was of international origin." Prime Minister Craxi has also stated that Italian terrorists linked to the Red Brigades have found refuge in other countries, including Nicaragua, lending his support to the belief that an international terrorist network exists, at least to the extent that ideologically similar groups give one another such support as providing hiding places.

There is also talk of "Euroterrorism," the transnational collaboration among indigenous groups in Europe. According to a West German official, terrorist attacks by the Red Army Fraction, heir to the defunct Baader-Meinhof gang, are on the rise this year. "We've noticed certain contacts with the French and the Italians," he added, referring to Action Directe, a French terrorist group implicated in recent bombings in Paris, and remnants of the Red Brigades still active in Italy, as well as a more recent group, the Belgian Fighting Communist Cells. British embassy spokesman Hughes recalled several occasions on which the IRA has killed Britons in continental Europe; in fact the British ambassador to the Netherlands was assassinated there in 1979. "There was quite a lot of press speculation on the extent to which mounting that operation required local assistance," he said.

In some cases, increased cooperation among European governments is proving effective against "Euroterrorism." The IRA appears to have been weakened by an Anglo-Irish agreement signed last November that included a promise of cooperation between Britian and the Republic of Ireland in apprehending terrorists. Called the Hillsborough agreement after the Irish castle where Thatcher and Irish Prime Minister Garret Fitz-Gerald signed it, the accord has enabled the police forces of the two nations to foil several IRA bombings.

European Stage for Arab Extremists' Acts

But European measures have not succeeded in quelling terrorist attacks by Middle Eastern groups that use Europe as the stage for their attacks. "There are known and clear connections between quite a number of European and Middle Eastern groups," said Robert H. Kupperman, a senior adviser at Georgetown University's Center for Strategic and International Studies in Washington. "If a Middle Eastern group operates successfully in, say, Germany, it's got to have a logistical base, perhaps within an Arab community or the RAF [Red Army Fraction].

They may not be inseparable, but they are entwined." Initially directed against Israel, Arab terrorism surfaced in Europe at the 1972 Olympic Games in Munich, where the Palestinian group Black September claimed responsibility for the killing of 11 Israeli athletes. Since then, numerous terrorist groups in the Middle East have focused on targets in Europe.

Hughes said a connection between Libya and the IRA has been known since March 1973, when the Irish Navy intercepted an arms shipment from Libya destined for the IRA. Libyan involvement in terrorism in Britain reached a peak in 1984. After the policewoman was killed by a shot fired within the London People's Bureau, Qaddafi declared that he did not consider the IRA a terrorist army and said, "We are not ashamed to support it with all the means we have." Britain responded to the incidents by severing diplomatic relations with Libya, instituting stricter visa requirements for Libyans coming into the country and stopping sales of arms as well as government export credit guarantees for trade with Libya.

Until this year, other European governments did not name specific state sponsors of terrorism in their territories, in part because of lack of tangible evidence. An Italian official explained that while Europe became the "battleground" for Middle Eastern terrorism long before the United States was targeted for attack, "international terrorism is a thousand-headed monster because it is impossible to identify those responsible for it. Every now and then it reappears only to go underground again." Often several groups claim responsibility for a single incident, while new groups may crop up never to be heard of again. Abu Nidal's group, for example, uses different names from one attack to the next. Some groups may be nothing more than a front name for a government.

While they are not believed to be linked in any organizational sense, 22 Arab, Islamic terrorist organizations joined together last year to form the "Pan-Arab Leadership of Arab Revolutionary Forces" with the declared aim of "confronting American imperialism and Israel." While the identity of many of these groups remains unclear, they are thought to include mainly Palestinians who are opposed to the mainline PLO headed by Yasir Arafat for its "soft" position on Israel; followers of Libya's Qaddafi and Syria's Assad, also bent on trying to undermine any chances for peace between Arab nations and Israel; and radical Shiite followers of Iran's Ayatollah Ruhollah Khomeini, who are conducting a holy war against all Western influence in Moslem countries.

Middle East Connection

What holds the diverse Middle Eastern extremists groups together is their vision of the West, and the United States in particular, as their common enemy. Ironically, this vision in regard to America has arisen largely as a result of its efforts to help the various warring factions in the Middle East make peace among themselves. President Carter dedicated much of his term in office to formulating a peace treaty between Israel and Egypt, militarily the strongest of Israel's Arab opponents. The Camp David Accords, signed by Carter, Israeli Prime Minister Menachem Begin and Egyptian President Anwar el-Sadat in 1979, was hailed as the beginning of a "peace process" between Israel and each of her Arab neighbors.

But Carter's achievement in one part of the Middle East was matched by failure in another. The Shah of Iran — whom the United States had championed as a guardian of stability in that region — was overthrown in January 1979 and replaced by Khomeini and the Islamic fundamentalist fervor of his followers.[11] Islamic militants, declaring the United States the "Great Satan" bent on destroying their values, captured the American embassy in Teheran later that year and held 52 U.S. citizens hostage for 444 days, releasing them only as Carter left office.

Carter's inability to free the hostages sooner led to his political demise. Ronald Reagan came to the White House in 1981 promising to make America "stand tall again" after its humiliation in the Middle East. He vowed to punish terrorists whenever American interests or citizens were attacked. "Let terror-

---

[11] For an analysis of U.S. policy toward Iran, see Gary Sick, *All Fall Down: America's Tragic Encounter with Iran* (1986). For background on Islamic fundamentalism, see "Iran Between East and West," *E.R.R.*, 1979 Vol. I. pp. 65-84.

ists beware," he said upon taking office, "that when the rules of international behavior are violated, our policy will be one of swift and effective retribution." At the same time, Reagan tried to maintain U.S. diplomatic influence in the Middle East even after the "spirit of Camp David" was crippled by the 1981 assassination of Sadat, a message to all moderate Arab governments that accommodation with Israel would not be tolerated.

A far more ominous turn of events for Arab perceptions of U.S. intentions and for America's role in the region was the June 1982 Israeli invasion of Lebanon. Israel undertook "Operation Peace for Galilee" to drive Palestinian guerrillas from their sanctuaries in Lebanon. But the massacre of thousands of Palestinian refugees in the refugee camps of Sabra and Shatilla outside Beirut was blamed on Israel and its chief ally, the United States.[12] The United States assumed a higher profile in Lebanon when it tried to mediate a settlement of the civil war by sending a contingent of Marines as part of a multinational peacekeeping force which also included troops from Britain, France and Italy. But the effort was short-lived: on Oct. 23, 1983, a terrorist drove his truck into the Marine barracks at Beirut Airport detonating a bomb that killed 239 U.S. servicemen. Shortly thereafter, the administration withdrew its forces.

Thus various movements and governments came to view the United States as their common enemy. "For the Palestinians — seeking revenge, stripped of their sanctuary in Lebanon — America stood between them and a Palestinian state," wrote Fouad Ajami, professor of Middle Eastern studies at the Johns Hopkins School of Advanced International Studies. "For the theocrats in Iran and Shiite Lebanon, America stood for cultural defilement, and it stopped them from overrunning their rivals in the region. And for the Syrians, there America was, cutting deals that excluded them — with the Lebanese, the Palestinians and the Jordanians — and sustaining an Israeli drive to remake the politics of the fertile crescent. This amorphous world took America on the only way it could — with terror."[13]

France, which also lost soldiers of its peacekeeping unit in Beirut to terrorist attack, retaliated by attacking suspected terrorist bases in the Bekaa Valley east of the city. The United States, despite its tough rhetoric against terrorism, was unwilling to risk causing civilian casualties and did not retaliate against suspected terrorist bases, much less against Syria and Iran which were thought to have supported them.

---

[12] The Palestinians were killed by Lebanese Christian militiamen who were admitted inside the camps by occupying Israeli forces. For background, see "American Involvement in Lebanon," *E.R.R.*, 1984 Vol. I, pp. 169-188, and "Reagan's Mideast Peace Initiative," *E.R.R.*, 1982 Vol. II, pp. 829-852.
[13] Writing in *The Washington Post*, April 17, 1986.

The decision to strike back at terrorism this year came after a prolonged policy debate between the Defense and State Departments, in which the Pentagon has been portrayed as opposing military retaliation in fear of escalating the hostilities. This position gave way to calls for action by Secretary of State George P. Shultz after a series of terrorist incidents last year took the lives of 25 Americans.

Policy options presented in February by a task force on terrorism headed by Vice President George Bush included the use of military retaliation for attacks against Americans. But the report cautioned that "counter-terrorism missions are high-risk/high-gain operations which can have a severe negative impact on U.S. prestige if they fail." [14]

New Responses After the Tokyo Summit

Judging from the joint communique issued May 5 by the seven participants at the Tokyo summit, differences between the United States and its allies over counter-terrorist policy appear to have been smoothed over. The 1978 Bonn Declaration, also signed by the summit nations, addressed only hijackings, while a statement issued in London at the 1984 summit called on the seven nations to "review" their arms sales to nations that sponsor terrorism. The Tokyo statement went much further, naming Libya as a state sponsor of terrorism and committing the signatories to take specific actions against any country found to support terrorism: no arms exports to such countries, limits on the size of their diplomatic missions, stricter immigration requirements toward their citizens, improved extradition procedures and closer intelligence and police cooperation.

Reagan returned from Tokyo saying he was "more than pleased" at the outcome, even though the statement avoided all mention of two important measures for which the administration had been trying to gain European agreement, economic sanctions against state sponsors of terrorism and, failing their effectiveness, military intervention. An official in the State Department's Office for Counter-Terrorism and Emergency Planning predicted that it would be some time before the European countries succeed in coordinating their policies. "Individual countries are doing a good job in investigating incidents, but a less good job in sharing the information they get so we can discover broader patterns of terrorist organization. If there is greater multinational sharing of the information it becomes easier to stop the organization from acting and you know where the pressure points are. That's what we want the Europeans to do and we want us to be a part of it."

---

[14] "Public Report of the Vice President's Task Force on Combatting Terrorism," February 1986, p. 13.

Terrorism in Europe Involving Americans

1985

Madrid, April 12: Islamic Holy War claims responsibility for bombing at restaurant frequented by U.S. military personnel; 18 Spaniards killed, 14 Americans and 68 others wounded.

Athens to Rome, June 14: Lebanese Shiite terrorists hijack TWA plane in flight from Athens to Rome and divert it to Beirut; one American killed, the remaining hostages, including 103 Americans, released after 17 days.

Frankfurt, Aug. 8: Action Directe and Red Army Fraction claim responsibility for car bomb explosion at U.S. Rhein-Main Air Base; two Americans killed, 20 Americans and Germans wounded.

Mediterranean, Oct. 7: Four men of Palestine Liberation Front hijack the *Achille Lauro*, an Italian cruise ship, and kill one American before surrendering in Egypt. U.S. fighters force plane carrying suspected terrorists, including leader Abu Abbas, to land in Italy. Citing lack of incriminating evidence, Italian government releases Abu Abbas, who remains at large.

Athens to Cairo, Nov. 23: Abu Nidal and other groups claim responsibility for hijacking of Egyptair plane diverted to Malta; one American killed by terrorists, 56 others killed during Egyptian attempt to free hostages.

Frankfurt, Nov. 24: Abu Nidal group suspected of exploding car bomb at U.S. military facility; 35 wounded, including 33 Americans.

Rome and Vienna, Dec. 27: Abu Nidal group claims responsibility for shooting of passengers at both airports; 18 killed, including five Americans, more than 100 wounded.

1986

Rome to Athens, April 2: Bomb blows hole in TWA plane over Greece; one American killed by blast, three others fall to their death.

West Berlin, April 5: Several groups claim responsibility for bombing of disco frequented by U.S. servicemen; two killed, including one American and 204 wounded, including more than 50 Americans.

Despite the widespread support he found among the American public for the Libyan air strike, Reagan faces several challenges at home over the wider implications of counter-terrorist policy. The Senate Foreign Relations Committee is split over the ratification of a U.S.-British extradition treaty signed last June. Federal judges have turned down requests from British authorities for the custody of IRA members charged with killing British soldiers on the ground that these acts are political in nature and thus qualify their perpetrators for political asylum in the United States.

The new treaty would include such terrorist acts as hijacking and hostage-taking — previously considered political crimes — among the crimes for which a foreigner might be extradited. But a coalition of Democrats led by Sen. Joseph R. Biden Jr., D-Del., citing the importance of maintaining the U.S. tradition of granting political asylum, are trying to amend the treaty to exempt from extradition those accused of crimes against policemen and soldiers.

The British government, which alone among the European allies supported the Libyan air strike, considers the Democratic amendment — in the words of embassy spokesman Hughes — "completely unacceptable." And while the administration has given the new treaty its full support, the Senate's refusal to ratify it could, in European eyes, undermine U.S. credibility as a reliable ally in the fight against terrorism. An extradition treaty has been in effect in all Western European countries except Malta since 1977.

The question also remains about the suitable means for co-ordinating counter-terrorist policies. At the time of the Libyan air strike, the North Atlantic Treaty Organization (NATO) emerged as the principal forum for policy coordination: the United States consulted with its "Western allies" on the military action and European demonstrators called on their governments to pull out of NATO in response to the attack. European diplomats tend to downplay the role of NATO in countering terrorism and look instead toward the European Economic Community as the more suitable structure for coordinating policy on the continent. "NATO hasn't done very much coordination of anything," remarked Robert Kupperman of Georgetown University, who added that inefficiency is a drawback to all such multilateral organizations.

Expanding U.S. participation in the European counter-terrorist effort requires what the American official called "very adroit diplomacy, to allow the Europeans to feel their way and at the same time stay involved with them so that we can get the kinds of policies together that will be effective." Rather than working through NATO, the EEC or even the summit group, he said, the United States should try to coordinate counter-terrorist policies with Britain, Italy, France and West Germany — what he called the "core group" of major industrial nations most concerned with combatting terrorism. "If we have their agreement, we can begin to work on policy together."

Kupperman shares the European view that the Libyan strike poses risks. "We spent so much time debating doing it and so much time trying to convince our allies that it was in a way anti-climactic," he said. "In another sense, it gave us such a sense of well-being and catharsis that we now think it is a trivial matter" to strike back militarily at terrorists. By repeatedly vowing to strike back at state supporters of terrorism, he said, Reagan has backed himself into a corner. "I think it is silly to telegraph our punches, and I think this is what we're doing. The president is doing himself a disservice by making too many and excessive promises. It may force us to precipitously ratchet up the scale militarily and take on countries we wish we had not."

Ticklish Question of Syria's Involvement

This risk becomes greater if Syria's involvement in recent terrorist incidents in Europe is clearly established. According to British and West German investigations, Syria was behind both the Heathrow bombing attempt and the West Berlin disco bombing — which the United States attributed to Libya alone. Britain expelled three Syrian diplomats after the embassy refused to allow them to be interrogated on the Heathrow incident. However, Prime Minister Thatcher said on May 23 she could not determine that the Syrian government sponsored the terrorist acts. Israel contended that its intelligence network proved Syrian responsibility for the two incidents. Most recently, Italian authorities have reportedly informed the Central Intelligence Agency that the sole terrorist survivor of the December attack on the Rome airport has said he was trained and accompanied to Rome by Syrian agents.

Since seizing power 15 years ago, Syrian President Assad has led the "rejectionist" Arab states in their effort to undermine the peace process with Israel. He scored an important victory in February, when King Hussein of Jordan finally bowed to Arab pressure and rejected a plan presented by Reagan in September 1982 for a peace agreement between Jordan and Israel. As the chief power broker in much of the Middle East, Assad is hardly an easy target for U.S. retaliation. He reportedly brokered the release of 39 passengers aboard the TWA airliner hijacked last June, and may be able to obtain the release of at least four remaining U.S. hostages held in Lebanon, which is largely under Syrian control.

Thus the Reagan administration, while still calling Syria a terrorist nation, has refrained from blaming Syria for specific terrorist attacks. Assad has denied any involvement in the incidents. Given the evidence of Syrian complicity in the same incidents Reagan attributed to Libya, together with the overwhelming support the American public has shown for military retaliation against terrorists, the administration may be forced to act. But not, in Kupperman's view, against Syria itself. "We could accuse Libya again even if Syria is responsible."

Recommended Reading List

Books

Carter, Jimmy, *The Blood of Abraham*, Houghton Mifflin Co., 1985.
Dobson, Christopher, and Ronald Payne, *The Terrorists: Their Weapons, Leaders and Tactics*, Facts On File, 1979.
Jansen, G.H., *Militant Islam*, Harper & Row, 1979.
Kedourie, Elie, *Islam in the Modern World*, Holt, Rinehart and Winston, 1980.
Kupperman, Robert H., *Terrorism: Threat, Reality, Response*, Hoover Institution Press, 1979.
Laqueur, Walter, *Terrorism*, Little, Brown and Co., 1977.
Netanyahu, Benjamin, ed., *Terrorism: How the West Can Win*, Farrar, Straus, Giroux, 1986.
Sterling, Claire, *The Terror Network*, Berkley Books, 1982.

Articles

MacLeod, Scott, "How Assad Has Won," *The New York Review of Books*, May 8, 1986.
Newhouse, John, "A Freemasonry of Terrorism," *The New Yorker*, July 8, 1985.
O'Brien, Conor Cruise, "Thinking About Terrorism," *The Atlantic Monthly*, June 1986.
Rubin, Barry, "The Untouchable," *The New Republic*, June 2, 1986.
"Terrorism — What Should We Do?" *This World*, fall 1985.

Reports and Studies

Center for Strategic and International Studies, Georgetown University, "Combatting Terrorism: A Matter of Leverage," June 1986.
Editorial Research Reports: "Anti-Terrorism: New Priority in Foreign Policy," 1981 Vol. I, p. 229; "International Terrorism," 1977 Vol. II, p. 909.
Francis, Samuel T., "The Soviet Strategy of Terror (revised)," Heritage Foundation, June 1985.
"Public Report of the Vice President's Task Force on Combatting Terrorism," February 1986.
State Department, Bureau of Public Affairs, "International Terrorism," Selected Documents No. 24, 1986.

Graphics: Illustration, George Rebh; graphs, Kathleen Ossenfort.

INDEX

210

211